Mountain Biking North Carolina

Help Us Keep This Guide Up to Date

Every effort has been made by the author and editors to make this guide as accurate and use-ful as possible. However, many things can change after a guide is published—trails are rerouted, regulations change, techniques evolve, facilities come under new management, and so on.

We would love to hear from you concerning your experiences with this guide and how you feel it could be improved and kept up to date. While we may not be able to respond to all comments and suggestions, we'll take them to heart and we'll also make certain to share them with the author. Please send your comments and suggestions to the following address:

The Globe Pequot Press
Reader Response/Editorial Department
P.O. Box 480
Guilford, CT 06437

Or you may e-mail us at:

editorial@GlobePequot.com

Thanks for your input, and happy trails!

Mountain Biking
North Carolina

Second Edition

Timm Muth

FALCON®

GUILFORD, CONNECTICUT
HELENA, MONTANA
AN IMPRINT OF THE GLOBE PEQUOT PRESS

A FALCON GUIDE ®

Copyright © 2003 by The Globe Pequot Press
Previous edition published by Falcon Publishing in 1998.

All photos are by the author unless otherwise noted.

Library of Congress Cataloging-in-Publication Data is
available.

ISBN 0-7627-2513-3

Manufactured in the United States of America
Second Edition/First Printing

For Justin, T-Bone, Laura Lou, and Curt-o—my truest crew along the trails of life. And one day soon to join us, Pierce Montgomery, the Little Stone from the Mountain. But most of all, this is for Alli, my sweet Mud Pie—the finest, craziest gal any poor trailrat ever chanced upon. You put the spin in my wheels.

Contents

North Carolina Overview

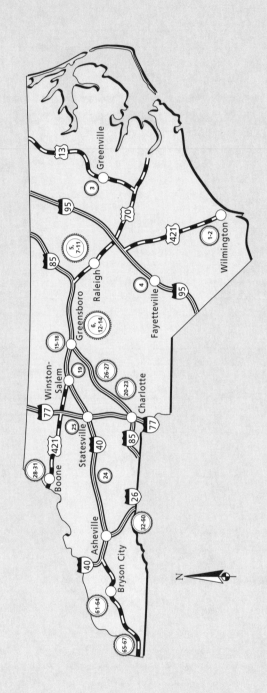

Uwharrie National Forest 97

Boone 105

Pisgah National Forest 121

Preface

As I struggled to leave the clutches of the corporate world, someone once told me, "Timm, no one's ever going to pay you to ride your bike, you know." My thanks to whoever gave me that first push.

What price do you put on nearly 2,000 miles of singletrack? That's what I received for putting this book together. A priceless sum of ecstasy, of flight, of wind in my hair, bugs in my teeth, and the taste of childhood in my soul. Rolling, flying—it's all the same. Come celebrate with me some time, and let me show you my world.

In case anyone is wondering, here's what it takes, hardware-wise, to put together a book like this:

- 5 head shocks
- 3 rear shocks
- 6 wheels
- 3 computers
- 2 GPS units
- 4 micro-recorders
- 9 tires
- countless tubes
- 2 frames
- 4 rear derailleurs
- 2 front derailleurs
- 2 sets of shifters (SRAM rules!)
- countless brake pads
- 3 sets of pedals
- 2 handlebars
- 4 bar ends
- 4 sets of shoes
- lots and lots of bearing replacements
- 2 bottom brackets
- 2 cassettes
- 4 chains
- 10 sets of cables
- 3 seats
- 2 seatposts
- several pounds of flesh, and a few pints of the red stuff
- at least 5 good, permanent scars
- about 30 visits to the chiropractor
- 2 trips to the ER
- roughly 27,000 miles on my truck
- an endless supply of fine singletrack and excitable riding buddies

Acknowledgments

This book was nothing at all like a solo effort. On every trip I had the company of one or more of my crew, someone to share the adventure with me. Their energy often made the difference between thrashing and crashing, between a cool, fun ride and a painful, heartbreaking one. It's their book, too. My thanks then to Ned, David T, Jeffrey, Daniel the Excitable Boy, Brian Beatty, and my intrepid bud Curt-o, who would ride his bike downhill in a hurricane and just call it "slick and fast." A special thanks to the Grand Ambassadors of Pisgah, Butchie and Tony Landolfi, who opened their hearts and their home to us, offered us fine singletrack and cold beer, and taught us what it really means to be young.

Thanks to all the folks who gifted me with new paths to ride and then gladly showed me the way. Some I know by name, and others were just friendly spirits along the path. Particular thanks to Jason, Claude, and David at Fontana, who took us all in and made the Village our second home.

I couldn't have ridden the first mile without a tight-running bike. For that, my humble thanks to Bob at the Clean Machine and Fred at Cycle Center. Night or day, whatever it took, these guys kept me rolling. They also taught me the fine art of un-tacoing a tire. Thanks to Scott, Art, Todd, Mark, and the rest of the crew at the Clean Machine for always believing my stories (really, I didn't even hardly crash!) and hooking me up with warranty returns, repairs, and replacements. Thanks to Chris Kuhlkin at Cannondale for a supreme hookup, and kudos to Cannondale for making one helluva tough machine. Thanks to Jason at Carolina FATZ for all our local support in Pisgah.

Thanks from riders everywhere to the landowners and managers who've allowed us to build, maintain, and enjoy bike trails all across the state. Thank you for your foresight and consideration and for sharing your forests and woodlands with us.

For this edition, a special thanks is due to Alli, for keeping me on schedule, joining me for marathon rides, dragging me out on night rides, not laughing too much when I crashed, and constantly reminding me that I'm still not too old to be having such fun. I love ya, hon!

Thanks, of course, to Globe Pequot and particularly to my editors, Liz Taylor, Shelley Wolf, Jan Cronan, and Heather Carreiro, for making this adventure a possibility.

And all the thanks in my heart to the Creator for blessing us with such a beautiful world and for granting me the chance to venture out in it.

Introduction

Between these pages lies a treasure map of singletrack gems tucked away across the Tar Heel State, from the beaches to the Smoky Mountains. Anything you could want in a mountain bike ride you can find here somewhere: roots, rocks, twisty sylvan highways, mudholes, tortuous climbs, jagged descents, breathtaking scenery, and lakes of adrenaline. We generally didn't include greenways or other commuter paths and avoided riding on roads (graveled, paved, or otherwise) when at all possible. This book is about singletrack: twisty hardpack, slaloming through trees and roots and rocks, rising through heartbreaking climbs, and descending in sometimes frightening fashion. That's what we came to ride; that's what it's all about.

Roughly half of the book is dedicated to rides near the major metro areas so that wherever you live or travel in North Carolina, you can find a cool trail nearby. Between the first edition of this book and the second, we've enjoyed many new trails that have opened across the state. In the Triangle area, stalwart bike supporters like Sig Hutchinson, Gaynor Collister, and others have added many miles of legal track to our riding pleasure through their dogged political efforts and trail-building expertise. Find your local trail advocates, and thank them for their hard work. Without them, we might as well all be riding hybrid bikes.

The remainder of the book pays homage to our own bits of singletrack heaven. Pisgah and Nantahala National Forests hold some of the most beautiful singletrack anywhere in the world. Rides out here are longer, steeper, faster, and rougher than most other places you've probably ridden. You can cruise along the buffed berms of Tsali for miles and miles. And you can get lost in the depths of Pisgah Forest for days. You can climb for hours to a hidden gap, then return on a long ridgeline run, or maybe just turn and plummet through 2,000 feet of vertical in 2 miles. It's the big leagues of riding, and you'll come back humbled. But you'll keep coming back.

Although only fully legal tracks could be used for this book, many other new trails have opened up on a less-than-official status. On most of these the property owners have given tacit permission to build trails and ride but can't promote them as true public bike trails because of the liability issues. Others are happy to let us ride in their woods until their multimillion-dollar development deal comes through and the bulldozers move in. In any case ask around at your local bike shop, or check the various Web sites for locations of some of these trails. Cherish them and ride them while you can, and continue to remind the rest of the world what a great thing free, legal trails are to all of us. And if you know of any great legal track that ought to be included in the next edition of this book, write to me at Dirt_Addiction@ yahoo.com, and I'll come check it out.

How to Ride

To retain the trails we treasure and to hold promise for new trails in the future, everyone needs to ride responsibly. Obey all trail rules (even if you don't always agree with them), help anyone who seems to need it, use the proper safety equipment, ride only when weather permits, take care of the trail, and just generally don't mess the place up.

Trail Conditions

Some trails can suffer considerable damage if ridden in wet conditions, as can the relationship with said trail's owners. Soft loamy surfaces can stay fragile for several days after a good rain. Other trails, often those on steeper hills, drain very quickly and can be ridden in just about all conditions. The simplest rule of thumb: Don't tear the trail up, and respect all trail closure signs.

Trail Maintenance

If you truly enjoy the many hours you spend riding your favorite trails, you ought to be willing to spend a little time helping to maintain or expand them. Trails seldom just grow there, and without proper maintenance, they'll eventually get worn out, overgrown, and useless. Joining the local club that maintains the trails is your best bet, or ask the park rangers or trail owners when they schedule maintenance days. You can help pay back earlier trail builders and maybe even get to add a feature or two of your own. Riding a pyramid or bridge you helped build adds a special zip to the flavor of the trail.

Note: Nothing enrages a trail builder more than finding that some bonehead has cut through a log or moved a boulder that used to be a cool trail feature. Although it's generally okay to remove loose debris from the trail, check major obstacles for chain-ring marks; if anyone else is obviously trying it, then leave that big ol' log or rock alone, and consider it a challenge for your next ride.

If you're working solo though, or just want to clean some as you ride, here are a few guidelines for tweaking the trail and avoiding some common trail problems.

- Trim back small branches that have grown out into the trail, or bend them back and tuck them behind the next tree.

- Slow-drying or perpetual mudholes can be covered with smooth branches or small logs placed across the line of the trail. This technique, often called *corduroy*, keeps you and your crew from digging the hole deeper as you ride while allowing the water to continue to drain through.

- Cut back all stubbies—saplings that someone else cut and left sticking up 6 inches out of the ground. Those trailside punji sticks can wreak havoc on your derailleur or spokes (or ribs, for that matter) when you catch a wheel on one unexpectedly.

- Stream crossings are unpredictable beasts at best. What used to be an easy in-and-out splash in the stream can turn into a wheel-sucking muckhole after a hard rain or horse troop. Laying some large, flat rocks along the bottom of your ford can help to slow the erosion and keep your journey a bit more steady.

Companions

Nothing makes a ride more enjoyable than good riding companions. Someone to laugh with, laugh at, swap stories and sketchy lines, someone to cheer your successes and haul your broken body to the hospital if need be. Riding buddies make the trip safer just by being there, which—by some thinking—frees you to push things just a little harder than you would alone. With a crew to ride with, you've always got the right tool, an extra Cliffy, and enough energy to make it to the top.

It's cool to ride with folks who can suck you up long grinders in their wake, or who can show you the one thread line of safety through a nasty rock garden. But the best buds are those who simply enjoy riding as much as you do. Try to match up with riders of similar ability levels to maximize your fun.

On a special note, it's been my great fortune to marry a crazy woman who seems to love the dirt as much as I do. There are few things more fun than watching your sweetie nab a tough pyramid or swan dive into a mudhole and come up with a smile on her face. But be aware that introducing your new significant other to the joys of mountain biking can cause some serious strain on things, particularly if you set them up *not* to have a good time. Leave them struggling a mile behind you, with a bruised shin and dragging brakes, and you'll probably be riding by yourself next time. But warm them up to it gradually, with some easier trails and lots of encouragement to start, and you just might end up with mud on your face one day, courtesy of your sweetheart.

Control

Try to maintain control of your bike at all times, because being out of control often directly precedes a major biff. Crazy, bombing descents are a blast, but crashing big—or worse, running someone down—will really dampen the entire riding experience. Unless you know the trail is clear ahead, use extra caution where sight is limited. And always, always hang on to your bike.

Trash

There's just one rule: Don't leave trash behind! If that tube or Power Bar wrapper didn't weigh too much to carry in, it certainly doesn't weigh too much to carry out. And that goes for the Clif Shots too: They're not biodegradable, you know. The worst violators of this rule seem to be racers, who can't afford the extra second to stash their trash. Come on folks: It's not only disrespectful to the earth, but it points the finger at us as surely as an empty can of Vienna sausages says "Bubba was here." Let's continue the widely accepted consensus that mountain bikers are the least intrusive users of the forest.

High tech minus batteries equals junk. DAVID TOLLERTON PHOTO

Mountain Biking Guidelines

If every mountain biker always yielded the right-of-way, stayed on the trail, avoided wet or muddy trails, never cut switchbacks, always rode in control, showed respect for other trail users, and carried out every last scrap of what was carried in (candy wrappers and bike-part debris included)—in short, if we all did the right things— we wouldn't need a list of rules governing our behavior.

The fact is, most mountain bikers are conscientious and are trying to do the right thing; however, thousands of miles of dirt trails have been closed due to the irresponsible habits of a few riders.

Here are some basic guidelines adapted from the International Mountain Bicycling Association (IMBA) Rules of the Trail. These guidelines can help prevent damage to land, water, plants, and wildlife; maintain trail access; and avoid conflicts with other backcountry visitors and trail users.

1. Only ride on trails that are open. Don't trespass on private land, and be sure to obtain any necessary permits. If you're not sure if a trail is closed or if you need a permit, don't hesitate to ask.

2. Keep your bicycle under control. Watch the condition of the trail at all times, and follow the appropriate speed regulations and recommendations.

3. Yield to others on the trail. Make your approach well known in advance, either with a friendly greeting or a bell. When approaching a corner, junction, or blind spot, expect to encounter other trail users. When passing others, show your respect by slowing to a walking pace.

4. Don't startle animals. Animals may be easily scared by sudden approaches or loud noises. For your safety—and the safety of others in the area as well as the animals themselves—give all wildlife a wide berth. When encountering horses, defer to the horseback riders' directions.

5. Zero impact. Be aware of the impact you're making on the trail beneath you. You should not ride under conditions where you will leave evidence of your passing, such as on certain soils after rain. If a ride features optional side hikes into wilderness areas, be a zero-impact hiker, too. Whether you're on bike or on foot, stick to existing trails, leave gates as you found them, and carry out everything you brought in.

6. Be prepared. Know the equipment you are using, the area where you'll be riding, and your cycling abilities and limitations. Avoid unnecessary breakdowns by keeping your equipment in good shape. When you head out, bring spare parts and supplies for weather changes. Be sure to wear appropriate safety gear, including a helmet, and learn how to be self-sufficient.

Getting Ready to Ride

Most importantly, take a good attitude. Things happen in the woods: Bikes break, riders biff, trails end, the weather turns, and people get lost. Some days you ride well, and some days you suck. It's just all part of the adventure, so relax and remember to enjoy yourself. The things listed below will help you to maintain this good attitude and will keep you riding longer.

Safety Equipment

Some riders, both novices and advanced, will stand there almost naked on the trail and tell you, "Oh, I don't need a helmet/glasses/gloves. I'm not going to fall down or get poked in the eye." This is a bigger myth than the Easter Bunny. If you ride, you will fall down. Hit a single rock wrong, and even the tamest green path can slap you down and chew on you for a while. Busting in some of the nasty stuff without a helmet could make you wish you'd been in a car wreck instead.

In short, this safety gear works, and it's a whole lot cheaper than brain surgery. Get it and wear it.

At a minimum, use the following:

- Helmet—no excuse. Get one that fits right, and wear it properly.
- Riding glasses (because eyeballs are fragile things—two per customer).
- Gloves (unless you really don't like skin on the palms of your hands).
- Arm guards (optional). Lately though, this has been my personal armor of faith.

First Aid

Crashing is usually not as bad as you think it'll be, but it's seldom a lot of fun. Just think of it as the coin we have to pay for such enjoyment. That puts it all in perspective.

Let me start by saying that I am not a doctor or other trained medical professional. I'm just a guy who's crashed a lot. If another rider gets hurt, and you don't know what to do, then *don't move* him or her! Just try to keep him warm and calm, make sure no other riders come along and run into him, and send someone for help.

To really know how to fix busted people on the trail, take the appropriate rescue courses. For the rest of us, when you crash, be calm and take your time. First, assess the injuries. If it's really serious, of course, just stop any major bleeding and get some help. But for most biffs and endos, get up out of the dirt and get yourself and your bike out of the trail (getting run over won't help your day any). Try to wash any crud out of your cuts and scrapes with water from your bottle or backpack. You can try to medicate and bandage yourself on the trail, but a little light bleeding helps to flush the wound, and it lets everyone know you're really enjoying the ride. Clean things out good when you get home, and use some Possum Grease or your favorite healing salve. Better yet, let your significant other do it, and get some sympathy in the process. Obviously, if things still look bad, go see a doctor.

Remember that everyone's comfort level and pain tolerance are different. Some riders I know will stitch up their own leg, then continue pedaling. Others are ready to bail after the first round with the dirt monkeys.

Keep checking on post-crash victims through the rest of the ride, even if they say they're okay. Sometimes shock, adrenaline, or foolish pride can mask a serious injury for a bit. Recent crash victims will often want to hang at the back of the pack to recover for a while, so be sure they don't get dropped or follow up with another crash. Here's a good rule to help determine whether you turn back or keep riding after a big bust: Is the crash victim still having a good time? If not, then call it a day and head home. But if that victim's still grinning, still hungry for adventure, then ride on, brave soul.

Tools and Spares

Some folks like to ride light with no tools or spares, then just hike back to the car and drive to the shop when things break. If you'd rather ride than push, carry and know how to use these items, and you can fix 90 percent of your breakdowns on the trail.

- spare tube
- tube patches
- tire patch (milk-jug strip, dollar bill, or bar wrapper)
- 10 mm wrench
- 4, 5, and 6 mm Allen wrench set
- air pump or cartridges
- small screwdriver
- spoke wrench
- several sizes of zip ties
- chain breaker

Food and Water

Second only to a good attitude, adequate water is probably your most essential item on a ride. Dehydration can reduce a hard-charging mountain goat into a whiney ground sloth in about twenty minutes flat. So be sure to bring more than enough water for yourself, and maybe a little extra for your partner who always runs dry. For me, a hydration pack is always better than a bottle, because the pack allows me to drink as I ride, without stopping. Okay, and it also allows me to stuff about twenty pounds of food and tools and zip ties and extra socks and a cell phone inside, just to satisfy my pack-rat nature. But however you carry it, be sure to bring plenty of water on any trip. And in hot weather, an extra bottle just to squirt over your head will help drop your temperature and bring you back to life for those last 2 miles.

You can do without extra food on short rides, but nothing will help you kick it on the end of that five-hour death ride like some power food. Trail mix, fig bars, or any of the many bars or goops, it's all good. Just take enough for that friend of yours who always forgets his.

Weather

North Carolina is a wide state, and the weather can really vary from one end to the other on any given day. But except for the mountains up near Boone, you can generally plan on riding year-round. Winter temperatures are mild with some unexpected

I hope I brought enough tubes.

short-sleeve days in the middle of February. High temperatures and humidity can be a problem in the summer, unless you like air the consistency of hot chicken soup.

Be aware that thunderstorms can crop up suddenly over the mountains. Pouring rain and a sudden thirty-degree drop in air temperature is a good recipe for hypothermia, so carry rain gear or keep moving. It's always an excellent idea to keep a dry change of clothes waiting at your vehicle, because at the end of a long, cold, wet ride, nothing feels better than some dry socks and a sweatshirt.

Terrain

The terrain gradually steepens as you travel west across North Carolina: flat in the beaches to the Sandhills, rolling hills from Raleigh through the rest of the Piedmont, then climbing into the emerald embrace of the Blue Ridge Mountains. Pisgah National Forest stretches in wide strokes from Boone down past Asheville to the Cradle of Forestry, encompassing the highest peaks east of the Mississippi. Travel farther west, and you drop into Nantahala National Forest, a temperate rain forest of lush, dark mountains. Entering these hills always feels like venturing into Mother Earth's womb. It's a welcome return to home.

The rides in this book can be divided between urban/suburban rides and mountain rides. The urban/suburban rides are those in the Sandhills and Coast area; the Triangle area; the Triad area; and the Charlotte, Statesville, and Morganton area.

Mountain rides are those in the Uhwarrie National Forest, the Boone area, the Pisgah National Forest, and the Nantahala National Forest.

How to Use This Guide

We tried to give you enough information to pick a trail that you'll really enjoy, find your way there, and ride it without getting lost.

Maps

Every effort was taken to ensure the accuracy of the maps and the directions. The maps show where to start, which direction to take, and all the main intersections and side branches. They may not show every twist and turn of the trail, but we tried to include enough landmarks to keep you on your way. Just remember that back in the big woods, old trails can get rerouted or overgrown, new trails can appear like magic, and everything takes longer than you think.

Elevation Profiles

The elevation profiles show the relative elevation gain or loss along the trail and give you an idea of what gravity has in store for you on a ride. Gravity in one direction usually means speed, adrenaline, and air potential. Gravity in the other direction usually means pain. The profiles show trail elevation (in feet) up the side and distance in miles along the bottom. Small changes in grade aren't shown, but they are usually mentioned in the write-up. Recognize that the profiles were compressed to fit on the page, so the slopes may look steeper than they feel—and then again, they may not.

The profile charts also give the technical rating for each section of trail, as well as the trail surface.

Trail Information

Ride name and number: The rides in this book are numbered roughly east to west as they appear across the state. Use these numbers to locate trails on the state map or in the ride index. Names of the trails were taken from posted signs when possible and local lore when necessary.

Overview: Directly under the ride name and number is a brief summary of the trail—thoughts of the ride, distilled to reveal its dirt-encrusted essence. It includes remembrances of climbs conquered, of technical battles both won and lost. You may also find philosophical musings on the transcendence of weightlessness, the sublime arch of a long carved berm, and the joy found astride our two-wheeled steeds.

Location: Approximate location and driving time from the nearest major metro area.

Distance: The ride's total length in miles. Out-and-backs are measured out and back.

Approximate riding time: A range of average riding times for the trail, listed from advanced riders to novices. Times include a normal complement of stops along the way, if warranted. Base your time estimates on distance and technical requirements, because 5 miles can take you three hours if it's brutal enough.

Difficulty rating: This scale of 1 to 5 gives you an idea of what it takes in terms of balance, body English, and riding skills to survive the trail and have a good time. Everyone's scale is a little different, so ride a few of the trails and see how your skills match the ratings. Note that the trails located in the mountains generally rank an order of magnitude higher in difficulty than their flatland cousins.

Tech 1: Smooth, buff track, flat or slightly rolling, with little or no technical challenges.

Tech 2: Mostly clear track, with small rocks, roots, and other obstacles that are fairly easy to avoid or roll over.

Tech 3: More serious obstacles requiring intermediate skills to clean: small boulders, breaching roots, erosion gullies, patches of loose chicken heads, 1- to 2-foot logs. Steep descents may add a point to the rating. Opportunities for a nasty biff begin to appear.

Tech 4: Continual assault of major technical moves, most of which carry a serious penalty in case of failure. Things like 3-foot water bars, large boulders and rock slabs, waist-high logs, long nasty root carpets, gaping erosion gullies, and dragon-toothed descents. Extreme steeps in either direction may add to the fray.

Tech 5: All-or-nothing moves that you either ride or talk about at the ER. May include large boulder and staircase descents; vertical drops; lethal landing zones; high bridges; sketchy, narrow track with long fall lines; and other things that can hurt you bad.

Trail surface: Types of surfaces you'll be riding across and approximate distances for each.

Highlights: In short, this is what to expect along the trail: types of obstacles, elevation changes, sites of interest, or any particular fun or sketchy spots.

Land status: Tells who owns/manages that piece of prime singletrack you're about to nab: city or county park, national forest, watershed, or private land. Also lists any entrance fee, when required.

Contacts for trails are listed in Appendix A.

Maps: Lists other maps available of the area and trails. May include U.S. Geological Survey topographic maps, USDA Forest Service maps, trailhead signs, Internet sketches, or third-party trail maps.

Finding the trailhead: How to get there and where to find the trailhead. Most directions take you in from the closest metro area or interstate.

Miles and Directions: This is a point-by-point description of the ride, with all major turns, obstacles, and other features noted and marked. Most of these notes were recorded during the ride itself, so it gives you a pretty good feel for the rhythm of the ride. Realize that different bike computers rarely measure exactly the same, so take all distances as approximate.

Map Legend

Interstate	(90)	Campground	▲
U.S. Highway	(12)	Picnic Area	⊓
State or Other Principal Road	(22) (222)	Buildings	■ or ▢
Forest Road	444	Peak/Elevation	▲ 4,507 ft
Interstate Highway		Bridge/Pass	
Paved Road		Gate	
Gravel Road		Parking Area	P
Unimproved Road		Boardwalk/Pier	
Trail (singletrack)		Railroad Track	
Start or Trailhead		Power Lines	
Trail Marker	(00)	Park Boundary	
Waterway		Map Orientation	N
Lake/Reservoir		Scale	0 ——— 1 Miles
Marsh/Swamp			

Sandhills and Coast

N orth Carolina gets awfully flat once you move east past Raleigh. Although you might grab your surfboard if you're heading in that direction, you probably wouldn't think to grab your bike as well—and you'd miss out, my friend. Here are four excellent rides, and none with more than 20 feet of elevation gain, if that. Nab UNCW or Blue Clay the next time you're heading to Wilmington and the beach. If your rounds take you anywhere near Greenville, be sure to check out the Bicycle Post Trail. And if orders condemn you to living in Fayetteville, Smith Lake will at least put a smile on your face.

1 UNCW

This trail is open to riders of all ability levels. There's no elevation gain, but hey, you're at the beach—what do you expect? The many humps are lots of fun, and the logs are big enough to require some attention and effort. There's a maze of trails in here, but the blue arrows mark the loop fairly well.

Location: University of North Carolina, Wilmington campus.
Distance: 6.4-mile loop.
Approximate riding time: 45 minutes to 1.5 hours.
Difficulty rating: Tech 1+. Smooth easy track for the most part with a number of cool, knee-high humps. Some tech 2 roots and several tech 3 logs.

Trail surface: Sand singletrack and double-track. Most of it is surprisingly hardpacked. Crossing the loose fire roads will have you sinking and flailing at times, though.
Highlights: Logs; pyramids; lots of humps; tight cruising.
Land status: University property.
Maps: USGS Wilmington.

Finding the trailhead: Take Interstate 40 East to Wilmington. As it enters town, the freeway ends and turns into College Road. Turn left at Randall Avenue into the UNCW campus. Follow this road to the dining hall parking lot. Ride your bike around the dining hall to the left until you get to the dormitory known as Madeline Suites. Look for a small wooden bridge to your left. The trail clearly begins just across the bridge.

Miles and Directions

0.0 From the bridge the trail begins as tech 1+, fairly hardpacked, sand and pine needle singletrack. Ride over a series of humps and through some tech 2 roots.

0.3 Trail drops out onto Rose Avenue (paved). Turn left, run the track on the edge of the road for 30 feet, then left again back into the singletrack.

0.4 Turn right and follow the blue arrows.

0.7 Bear right at this Y, following the blue arrows.

0.9 Cross a log pyramid, then turn left to follow the arrows.

1.0 Turn right just before a wide sandy fire road and follow the blue arrows.

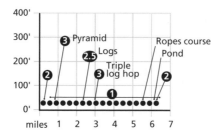

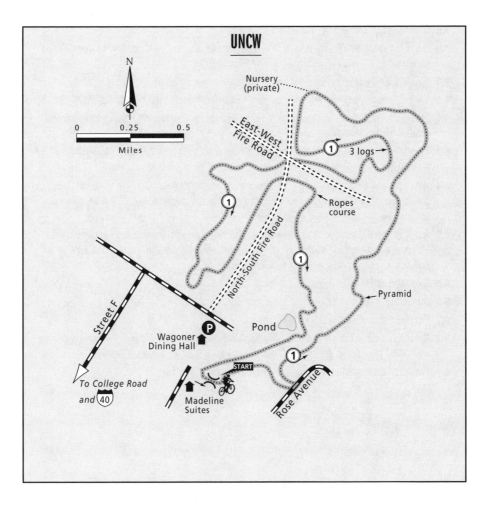

1.2 Bear right at this Y and follow the blue arrows. Trail skirts the edge of an old burnt section of woods.

1.5 Turn right at first Y, then left at second Y, following the arrows. Track dumps you into an old sandy doubletrack.

2.1 Turn left as doubletrack ends at a private nursery, which puts you on a very loose sandy road. Take the immediate left onto very obscure track; look closely for the arrows. Trail opens up again as soon as you get back into the trees.

2.2 Turn left, following arrows.

2.4 Go over two respectable log hops, then cross a deep, sandy wash.

2.5 Follow the arrows, turning left, left, right, left in close succession. It's not nearly as confusing as it sounds.

3.0 Take three solid, tech 3 log hops in a row.

3.3 Turn left just before you hit the east-west fire road, following the arrows.

3.5 Cross a small bridge of broken cinder blocks.

3.6 Cross the north-south fire road. This is a chance for you to figure out how to ride in deep sand.

3.9 Turn left and follow the blue arrows. Small, sandy berms follow.

4.2 Trail hops a respectable log, then turns around and hops it the other direction.

4.4 Turn right and follow the blue arrows. Then bear left as trail starts to parallel the paved road in front of the dining hall. More of those fun sandy humps.

5.0 Turn left just before you hit the north-south fire road, and start heading away from campus again. Lots more humps.

5.4 Turn right just before you hit the intersection of the north-south and the east-west fire roads. Cross the north-south fire road and pick up the track on the other side. Watch for the arrows.

5.5 Turn right and follow the blue arrows past the ropes course. Then take a quick left, just before a waist-high log walk (part of the ropes course). Take another left, this time at a Y. Follow the arrows and run through a fern glen.

5.9 Turn right at the T.

6.0 Turn left at the Y.

6.1 Turn right onto this hardpacked dirt road.

6.2 Come up on a small pond. Follow the bank around the left of the pond, and drop out the other side past some gravel piles. Trail ducks into a tight little forested tunnel.

6.4 Return to the trailhead, although on the other side of the bridge.

2 Blue Clay

This is an excellent little technical gem, particularly for an area that's mostly swamp, pine groves, and sand dunes in some combination. The logs and pyramids just keep coming, and the big creek crossing will give even the most foolhardy a moment's pause. This is a good test of balance, handling, and unclipping skills. The trail is well laid out, making good use of the terrain and natural obstacles. A trials area near the parking lot is continually under development and offers an even higher level of skill training. Watch for recent road construction, which may cause some rerouting of certain sections.

Location: Ten minutes west of Wilmington.
Distance: 3.2-mile loop.
Approximate riding time: 30 minutes to 1 hour.
Difficulty rating: Tech 2+ overall. Some smooth track with lots of tech 3 logs and pyramids; tons of steep, little drops and climbs; serious tech 4 log bridge. Trials area for anyone feeling really cocky.

Trail surface: 2.8 miles of sandy and hard-packed singletrack; 0.4 mile of grassy doubletrack.
Highlights: Liberally sprinkled with logs; nice roller-coaster action; trials area by entrance.
Land status: New Hanover County Park.
Maps: Flyer and map available at local bike shops.

Finding the trailhead: Take Interstate 40 East toward Wilmington. Exit onto North Carolina Highway 132 North (exit 420). Drive roughly 3.5 miles, turn right onto Blue Clay Road, then turn right onto Juvenile Center Road. Drive to the end of the pavement and park in the grassy field under power lines.

Miles and Directions

0.0 Start from grassy area at end of Juvenile Center Road. Follow power lines past trials area and pick up grassy doubletrack in middle of field.

0.1 Cross wide, muddy stream and turn right to follow singletrack into woods.

0.2 Six-foot climb as you enter woods, immediately dropping down to a choice of bridges. Follow track over the right bridge.

0.4 Two respectable log pyramids in an otherwise flat, smooth, twisty piece of track. Muddy section is a quagmire after rain.

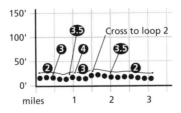

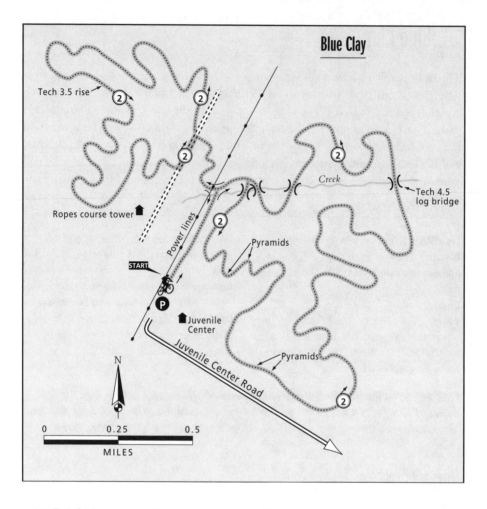

0.8 Tech 3+ log crossing with another pair of pyramids.

1.1 Stream crossing over long, single, split-log bridge. A 12-inch-wide log sits 4 feet or so above a skanky creek. It's certainly wide enough to ride, but the run-in sucks and the exit isn't much better; call it a tech 4 move to clean it all. Penalty for failure would be high on this one.

1.3 Lots of little drops and uphill lunges as you cross back and forth over little ridges. Drop from the ridge to cross one wooden bridge, then a second bridge, before finishing this loop and shooting back out to the power line clearing.

1.4 Ride back across power lines toward muddy stream crossing, but follow singletrack into opposite woods instead of turning to cross stream. Second loop starts with a pair of bridges, a short but steep tech 3 climb, and a tough uphill switchback.

1.5 Log bridge. This one is a walker pending further construction. A legion of ridable log crossings still awaits.

Crossing a dicey bridge at Blue Clay.

1.7 Turn right onto grassy doubletrack at the T. Ropes course tower is back to the left.

1.8 Turn left onto sandy singletrack. Track is a little unclear at first, but look for orange flags and know that it opens up quickly. Starts with a sweet little 2-foot drop-in; extremely fun riding with track like a sandy roller coaster. Much smoother and less twisty than first loop.

2.0 Series of tough humps leads to a sharp turn up a 3-foot, root-laced riser. Call it a tech 3+ move; I was denied both tries. Remember though: A trail that you don't master the first time out is a trail that you'll ride again.

2.2 Trail runs into clearing. Hug right side of clearing to pick up track. Track begins to cross and recross a pair of parallel ditches, yielding a dozen or more trippy little humps, dips, and sharp cutbacks in a row.

2.4 Singletrack gradually turns into a wide, sandy doubletrack, which dashes through some small pine groves. **Warning:** The mudholes are a lot deeper than you think—believe me.

2.7 Complete loop and return to intersection near tower. Turn left into woods to follow track back to the beginning.

3.0 Three big humps and a sketchy bridge for a little parting adrenaline shot just before you leave the woods. Return to the power line field and turn right across the muddy stream crossing.

3.2 Return to parking area.

3 Bicycle Post

If you want to ride a really well-laid-out trail, come check this one out. It's fast and fun, with plenty of room to stretch your legs and spin, and plenty of obstacles to keep your attention. Whoever laid this out knew what they were doing, 'cause the trail swoops and twists with just enough room through the trees to let you keep your speed up. The many pyramids and berms are all very well constructed for your increased riding pleasure. There's a good bit of everything thrown in—except for any monumental climbs, that is.

Although it can get to feel like a bit of a maze in here, it's not too tough to find your way through. We tried to follow the clearest track and the red flags whenever possible. Be aware that this trail is continually being upgraded, so expect anything at any time.

"Oh yeah, definitely, definitely a fun ride. Yeah." —Rainman

Location: Fifteen minutes west of Greenville.
Distance: 8.6-mile loop.
Approximate riding time: 1 to 1.5 hours.
Difficulty rating: Tech 2. Mostly smooth, tech 1+ cruising track. Lots of hops, dips, humps, logs, and pyramids (tech 3 to 3.5 stuff) thrown into the mix. The toughest stream crossing borders on a tech 4 move.
Trail surface: Singletrack—nothing but singletrack (well, except for two minuscule pieces of doubletrack that don't even count).

Highlights: Fast flatland cruising; logs; pyramids; stream crossings; berms; dips.
Land status: Private land, managed by the Bicycle Post for the exclusive use of mountain bikers. Membership dues are $50 for a year or $25 for three months.
Maps: USGS Greenville NW.

Finding the trailhead: Because this is a private trail and the folks at the Bicycle Post have to pay for the lease and insurance, it isn't fair to give directions here so that anyone can go and poach it. Stop by either of the Bicycle Post shops in Greenville for directions, map, and membership fees. To get to the Bicycle Post from points west, come into town on U.S. Highway 264. Turn right onto Memorial Boulevard, then left onto Arlington Boulevard. The shop is on the left side of the street, next to the Buccaneer Theater.

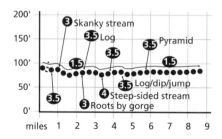

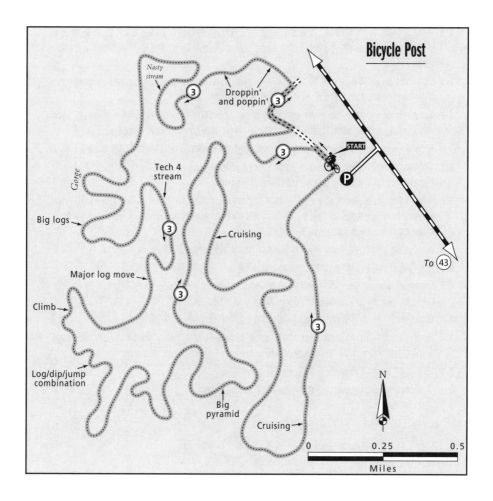

Miles and Directions

0.0 Although there is a trail entrance right next to the Bicycle Post sign, it looked to me like most riders end here. Turn right and ride up the side of the field 200 feet or so, then break left into the woods at the next entrance. Trail starts off as smooth, flat, wide-open, tech 1 singletrack.

0.2 First of many log pyramids, a respectable tech 3 number. Then turn right at the T, following the arrows. Some small logs and another pyramid to follow.

0.4 Trail pops back out of the woods, not far from where you put in. Turn left and follow the dirt doubletrack as it hugs the edge of the field.

0.5 Trail turns left to slip back into the woods and starts to parallel the hardtop road. Watch for an 8-foot rooty drop (tech 3+), then lots of droppin' and poppin' as the track dives in and out of an old roadbed. Most of the trail is still a clear, tech 1+ run.

1.2 Skanky stream crossing—a slippery and gooey tech 3 move that you don't want to watch too closely from behind.

1.3 Bear right at the Y and hop an old log that's obviously been ridden a lot. Believe it or not, shortly after you even get a bit of a zippy downhill, quick running with well-packed sandy berms.

1.9 Continue straight past the (blue-flagged) turn. Then some short drops and climbs, a little back-and-forth gully action, and a short wooden bridge.

2.3 Small gorge down to the right with that dark, unsettling look of the snake-infested, tech 3 roots along the lip threatening to toss you down into its depths if you blow it.

2.5 Tech 3+ log hop, then shortly after a dip/log/dip combination for another tech 3+ move.

3.2 Another muddy stream crossing with rooty banks on either side. Tech 3+ to tech 4, depending on the severity and depth of the slime.

3.7 Nice 4-foot drop, backed by a 20-inch log hop—another tech 3+ move. Trails start converging from all sides at this point, and it's easy to get turned around. Try to follow the clearest line, which jags right then left.

4.4 A surprise climb, with some tech 3 roots along the way. Turn right at the top.

4.5 A 6-foot drop, in and out; then a tough, tech 3+ log/dip/jump combo.

4.9 Excellent whoop-dee-doos, followed by another short but steep rooty climb. Some off-camber logs and nice dips to follow keep you hopping.

5.7 Massive, 3- to 4-foot-tall pyramid, then a pair of 18-inch logs.

6.3 Continue straight, following the main track. Excellent fast, twisty track through the trees. Curves and berms are laid perfectly to allow you to just *crank* through here.

7.5 Turn right on this branch, following the red flags.

8.6 Trail ends and pops out right by the Bicycle Post sign.

4 Smith Lake

Smith Lake is an excellent introductory trail—a good place to take friends where they'll have a good time and where they won't biff. The track is most often smooth and flawless, and if you're expecting lots of loose sand here in the Sandhills, think again. The pine needles and sand pack down like pavement between the trees, leaving smooth berms and dozens of perfect bunny-hop opportunities. The trail is broken into three loops (Green, Blue, and Black), but just about all riders will be able to negotiate the entire thing. The local bike club and trail gurus continue to add new sections to the trails, so check the bulletin board at the trailhead for any map updates.

The fee for riding is $5.00 a day or $20.00 per year, payable at the park office, which is farther down the gravel road by Smith Lake.

Location: Smith Lake Park, Fort Bragg.
Distance: 8.2 miles total, for all three loops.
Approximate riding time: 1 to 2 hours.
Difficulty rating: Tech 1 overall. Lots of jumps, both small and large, almost all perfectly smooth. A few tech 3 root drops and some nice, high log pyramids add a little spice.

Trail surface: 8.2 miles of well-packed, sandy singletrack.
Highlights: Fast, easy cruising; lots of berms and bunny hops; pyramids and bridges.
Land status: U.S. military base; recreation facility.
Maps: USGS Vander.

Finding the trailhead: From Raleigh, head south on U.S. Highway 1 to Sanford. Exit onto North Carolina Highway 87 South, toward Fayetteville. Follow NC 87 through the heart of Sanford, then south into the rural wastelands—about a half-hour drive. Pass through the town of Spring Lake, and you'll reach the edge of Fort Bragg. Turn left at the light across from the base entrance onto Murchison Road, North Carolina Highway 210 South. Follow NC 210 for 5 miles. As you pass Simmons Army Airfield, turn left at brown sign: SMITH LAKE RECREATION AREA. Pass a dirt road on the right, with a prominent bike trails sign. Continue straight to the Smith Lake Park office to pay your admission, then backtrack to the dirt road. Follow it for roughly 2 miles, and you'll see the yellow smith lake bike trails sign on the right. Parking area, map and info kiosk, and trailhead are all right there. (**Note:** The park folks are serious about paying, and the game wardens will check for your pass.) And the sign at the trailhead says no pets, so best to leave Old Blue at home.

Miles and Directions

0.0 Beginners (Green) Loop begins about 30 feet behind the trail kiosk, heading to the right. Hardpacked sandy track, smooth tech 1 with a few roots here and there. White sand makes it easy to follow the track at this point.

0.7 Cross sandy fire road. Trail picks up clearly on the other side. Smooth riding and excellent spinning throughout.

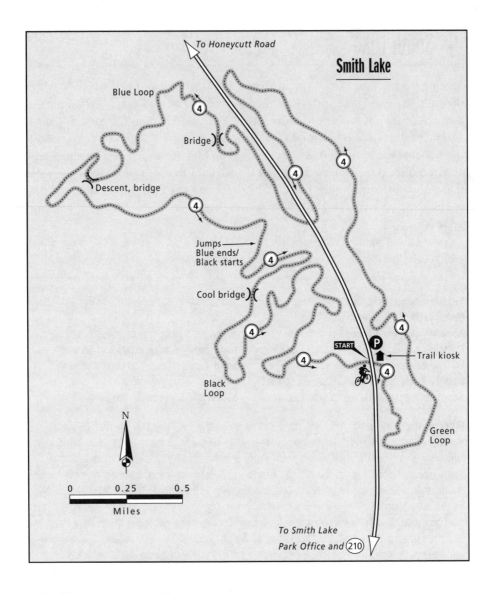

2.3 Nice bunny-hop potential.

2.5 Turn right at this branch to cross the road and continue on to the Advanced (Blue) Loop. To finish out the Beginner Loop, just keep heading straight instead, and you'll pop out at the trailhead in another half mile.

2.8 Blue Loop offers some more humps and roots, with small pyramids appearing at sudden intervals.

3.2 Cross a log pile on a bridge of landscaping timbers. Nicely made—and played.

3.8 Set of three nice 4-foot dips to pop in and out of.

4.0 First climb of the ride, and it's not much.

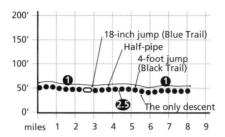

4.3 Descend and cross a bridge. New and old tracks converging make the trail a bit tough to follow at times. Look for the orange flags and the clearest track.

4.5 Trail splits right with little notice. Old overgrown track straight can fool you, so don't miss the turn. Then cross another bridge back over the same creek, this time with blue pallets.

5.0 Cross gas line clearing; trail continues straight, with the option for a ramp up and over a 3-foot log pile.

5.4 Pop over a sweet 3-foot hump and run out across a sandy fire road. Expert (Black) Loop continues on other side of road and starts off with its own 4-foot-tall hump, just ready-made for some soaring. You'll probably want to hit these aerial bookends a few times.

6.2 Several ramped pyramids, a foursome of humps, and a nice 12-inch ledge drop right in the beginning of a turn, just perfect for practicing those midair direction changes.

7.2 Respectable rooty climb, then a nice slab ramp over a 2-foot log.

7.5 Quick descent toward bottom suddenly sweeps left. Look for tape marking the turn, because it's easy to miss it and then hammer straight into a section of old rocky track and rotten bridges that you'd just as soon avoid.

7.8 Set of rooty drops, then trail cuts quickly left. Track straight is signed OFF LIMITS. Remember, this is a military base. Don't be an idiot and go wandering into a bombing range somewhere.

8.2 Exit the woods just across the road from the trailhead.

Triangle

Since the first edition came out, riders and trail advocates in the Triangle have opened up a number of new legal and semilegal trails. Beaverdam offers us the first legal singletrack in a North Carolina state park. Harris Lake has opened up 6 miles of trail so far, with more in the works, and Lake Crabtree continues to expand. New Light, Regency Park, Atlantic, High School, and other trails in the area continue to live under the shadow of the developers' bulldozer blade, and so they weren't included in the book. But they're worthwhile trails all the same, and you can find info on them at a number of local mountain bike Web sites, including www.trianglemtb.com.

5 Beaverdam

Four separate loops recently opened here, as an experiment with the first official, legal singletrack mountain bike trail allowed in a North Carolina state park. Hats off to Sig Hutchinson and the North Raleigh Mountain Bike Association for their tireless pursuit of this project and their trail-building expertise.

We've laid out here a trip around both West Loop and South Loop. Riders should explore the Inner and Outer Loops on their own. This is good use of terrain for a challenging set of trails that will only get better as they are seasoned with use. The climbs will challenge most intermediate riders, and together with the length of the South Loop, many will wonder if they've bitten off more than they can chew. With the new track in particular, it takes a lot of time and energy to move far, so anticipate a longer ride than you'd normally expect. But the view out over the lake is worth it, sharing your solitude with no one except for the ducks and the wind.

Location: Beaverdam State Recreation Area, Falls Lake.

Distance: 8.9 miles total, for both West Loop and South Loop.

Approximate riding time: 2 to 4 hours.

Difficulty rating: Tech 1 to tech 2, with occasional tougher roots, pyramids, logs, and dips.

Trail surface: 8.9 miles of singletrack—nothing else.

Highlights: Roller-coaster downhills; excellent view of lake; challenging aerobic trail.

Land status: North Carolina State Recreation Area.

Maps: USGS Falls Lake.

Finding the trailhead: From the Raleigh Interstate 440 Beltline, exit at U.S. Highway 70/North Carolina Highway 50, heading north. At the light across from Crabtree Valley Mall, turn right to follow NC 50 (Creedmoor Road). Continue on NC 50 north until you cross North Carolina Highway 98, and then cross Falls Lake. Once over the lake, take the second park entrance on the right, which is clearly signed BEAVER DAM RECREATION AREA. Follow the entrance road straight in, park in the first lot on the right, and look for the trailhead kiosk on the left side of the road.

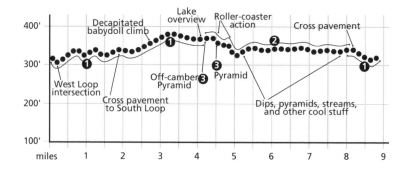

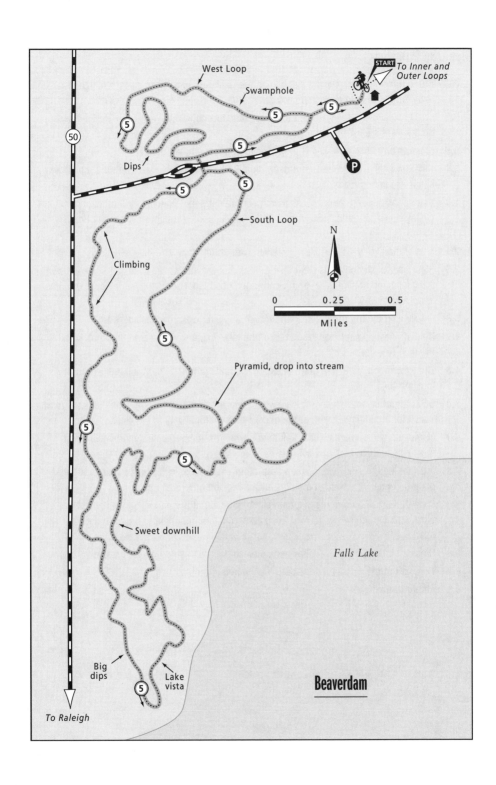

Miles and Directions

0.0   At the three-way intersection just behind the trailhead, turn left to follow the sign TO WEST LOOP. You get to start off with a cool, swoopy descent.

0.2   Cross two wooden bridges, then turn right at intersection with West Loop. Red reflectors on the trees clearly mark the way.

0.5   Major swamphole, for a first (but not the last) chance to get muddy.

1.4   Nice downhill dotted with 5-foot-deep dips. Cross a double bridge, then hit a mucky seasonal streambed full of goo.

1.8   Trail opens out onto park access road, near the entrance. Opening for South Loop is clearly signed on other side of road. Follow signs, and bear right when you hit South Loop.

2.1   First of many bridges. Trail clearly marked with orange tape and blue reflectors.

2.5   Slow gradual climb. Trail is clear tech 1 track, but the soft surface can still bog you down. Babydoll head staring down from tree branch shows that someone has a sense of humor about litter.

3.3   Finally gain the top of the ridge, and realize this ain't exactly a beginner's trail.

4.1   Beautiful resting spot along the edge of the lake. Tough work to get to this spot, so take the time to enjoy it.

4.5   Zippy roller-coaster action down into a cove. Loads of fun . . . then you realize you've got to climb back out.

5.0   Solid 2-foot pyramid, then another sweet swoopy downhill out along a long finger of land. Watch for a sudden left turn at the end, or prepare for a bath in the creek.

5.2   Numerous short, tough climbs, well-made pyramids, dips, logs, and mudholes. It just seems to keep coming and coming.

7.1   A 2-foot log crossing, with a steep drop off the back side. Tech 3 move with good face-plant potential. Afterward, more dips, pyramids, and other trail treats.

8.2   Drop through one more big dip, then climb back out at the park entrance again. Head back across road for signed West Loop entrance, and bear right to return to the trailhead.

8.4   Cross a Forest Service road. Trail continues straight, with smooth tech 1 track.

8.7   Turn right at the wooden bridge onto the connector trail.

8.9   Return to trailhead.

6 Hog Run

Hog Run has shown a remarkable trail evolution, from a spongy-treaded, too-tight, no-speed, too-short trail a few years ago to a 6-mile piece of hardpacked track dotted with pyramids, stream crossings, and extremely cool dip sections. In a few short years, this trail has become a favorite with many riders in the Triangle area. Many other park offerings (such as Frisbee golf, fishing, volleyball, and playgrounds) make this a great spot for a day trip with the whole family, with lunch waiting right after the ride.

Location: Harris Lake County Park in New Hill.
Distance: 6.1 miles total, for three interconnected loops.
Approximate riding time: 45 minutes to 1.5 hours.
Difficulty rating: Tech 1 to tech 2. Some of the dips on the back side of the Advanced Loop are seriously steep and require total commitment and good body English to avoid a faceplant or ungainly tumble to the bottom. Occasional tougher roots, pyramids, and logs.
Trail surface: 5.8 miles of singletrack; 0.3 mile of doubletrack.
Highlights: Roller-coaster playground on Advanced Loop; pyramids; views of lake.
Land status: Wake County Park.
Maps: USGS New Hill.

Finding the trailhead: From the Raleigh Interstate 440 Beltline, take U.S. Highway 1 South. About twenty minutes outside of Raleigh, take the New Hill exit. Turn left at the top of the ramp, and head south on New Hill Road back over the highway (brown sign for Harris Lake Park). Go 4 miles, past the Shearon Harris Visitors Center, then turn right into the entrance for Harris Lake County Park. Follow the entrance road through the park all the way to the end. The trailhead sign and information kiosk sit at the edge of the last parking lot.

Miles and Directions

0.0 Begin at the trailhead by the information kiosk. Bear right at the split in the trail. Smooth, tech 1 track of hardpack and pine needles.

0.5 Intersection with the Beginner Loop return leg. Turn right to continue on Intermediate Loop. To bail out here instead, head straight on old Forest Service road, then turn left about 30 feet down onto the clearly marked singletrack.

0.8 Follow trail across bridge over stream, or detour left to try to ride a flattened log: 20 feet long, 10 inches wide, ramped at each end. A very useful tech 3 maneuver to help you train for other tricky stuff.

1.0 Turn right as this track Ts into the return trail. Immediately after, hang another right as the track empties onto a gravel Forest Service road.

1.1 Turn right at the clearly signed entrance for the Intermediate Loop. You'll notice right away more tech 2 roots and more dips than the Beginner's Loop.

1.6 Pass old homesite. Even in February, the daffodils are blooming.

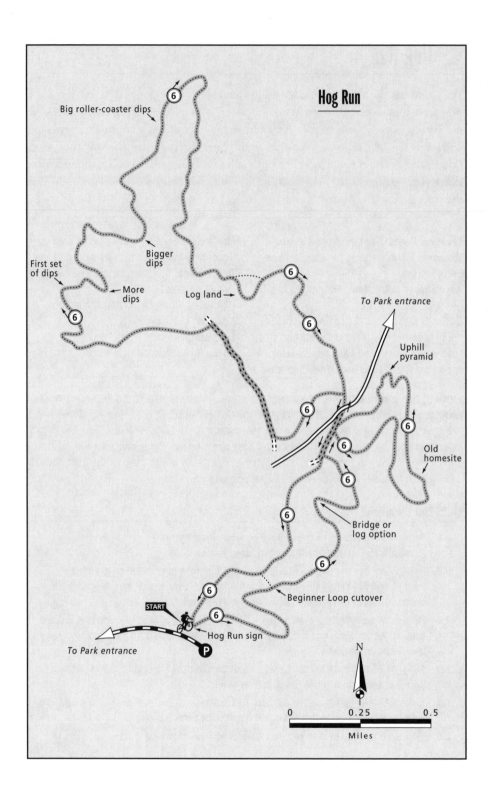

Hog Run

Big roller-coaster dips

Bigger dips

First set of dips

More dips

Log land

To Park entrance

Uphill pyramid

Old homesite

Bridge or log option

Beginner Loop cutover

START

Hog Run sign

To Park entrance

P

N

0   0.25   0.5

Miles

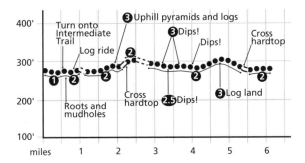

2.0 Tough tech 3 uphill pyramid, with a bypass on the right, then another one shortly after.

2.1 Return to gravel road. Turn right to head to Advanced Loop.

2.2 Cross paved road to clearly marked entrance for Advanced Loop. Bear left at immediate split in trail.

2.5 Trail merges with old forest road. Smooth, tech 1 doubletrack.

2.7 Forest road splits; bear left as road dwindles down to singletrack again.

2.8 Cross another Forest Service road. Posted sign and map show where trail continues.

3.3 First set of big dips, maybe eight in a row. Definitely learn to keep your butt back on these. Bypass trail skirts dips on uphill side.

3.5 Trail merges with old forest road. Continue straight on singletrack. Second set of dips offer a low track (3-footers) and a high track (6-footers)—take your pick.

4.0 Third set of dips, and this one's the biggest, marked with a double black diamond. Roller-coaster tracks lace back and forth, allowing you to link them up and drop and hop to your heart's content. Dips get progressively bigger and livelier as you go, with some 20-foot-deep monsters at the end. Return trail runs along the bottom by the lake edge, all the way back to the beginning. Bypass trail hovering along the top lets cautious riders watch the bold ones.

4.8 Trail splits, with right track leading down the slope over eight or nine logs of various heights, and left track heading to the stream crossing directly. Funky, steep bridge requires you to keep pedaling to avoid a stall and a plunge into the muck.

5.4 Return to beginning of Advanced Loop. Continue straight across the paved road and down the gravel road.

5.5 Pass the two Intermediate Loop entrances ridden earlier, then swing left into the woods along a high, bermed curve. As soon as you enter the woods, make an immediate right up and over a big hump. This puts you on the return track to the trailhead.

5.8 Return loop for Beginner Trail intersects from the left. Continue straight.

6.1 Return to trailhead.

7 Lake Johnson

This is an excellent in-town Raleigh ride, one that can be linked with Centennial Campus via greenways and a short bit of road riding. Ridden in either direction, you get a decent warm-up before hitting the root extravaganza waiting in the woods. Beginners have an easy bailout option if the learning curve proves too steep or painful, because the greenway is always circling just uphill of the singletrack. Intermediate riders will push the limits of their slow-speed balance and navigation skills, and even more advanced folks will be pressed by some of the dicey root moves and the big stream crossing. When in doubt at any trail branching, pick the track that runs closest to the lakeshore.

The point on the backside of the lake looks over the breeding grounds of some gorgeous geese, swans, herons, kingfishers, and a variety of ducks. And I guess to be fair, I should mention the proliferation of turtles sunning along the walkway and lakeside sections, for those of you who like your critters cold-blooded.

Location: Lake Johnson Nature Park, southwest edge of Raleigh.
Distance: 4.9-mile loop.
Approximate riding time: 30 minutes to 1 hour.
Difficulty rating: Greenway and doubletrack are tech 1; singletrack is a constant tech 3 root garden, spiked with a tech 4 climb and an optional tech 4 stream crossing.

Trail surface: 2.4 miles of singletrack; 1.3 miles of doubletrack; 1.2 miles of paved greenway.
Highlights: Excellent test of root-crossing skills; greenway provides fun option for those not fond of dirt and falling. Overlook gives nice viewpoint of lake. Lake abounds with birds, turtles, and even a few beavers.
Land status: City park.
Maps: USGS Raleigh West.

Finding the trailhead: From Interstate 440 (the Raleigh Beltline), take Western Boulevard into Raleigh. At about 3 miles turn right onto Avent Ferry Road at the light by the Mission Valley shopping center. Follow Avent Ferry for another 3 miles, then turn left into the entrance for Lake Johnson Park, just before you go over the lake.

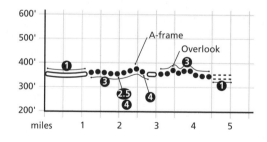

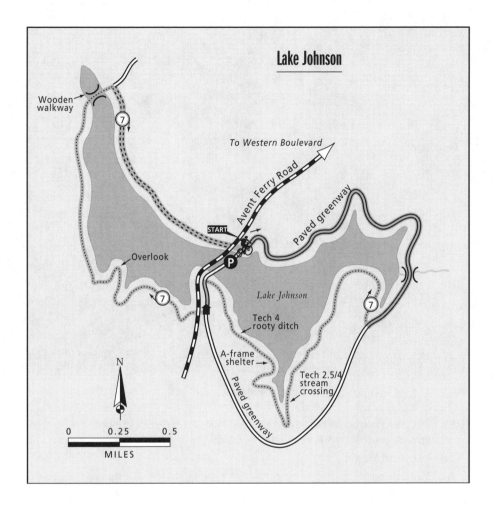

Lake Johnson

Miles and Directions

0.0 Starting from Lake Johnson parking area, follow the paved greenway path.

0.8 Greenway splits. Turn right to continue clockwise around lake.

0.9 Cross lake dam and wooden bridge over spillway. Again, bear right when greenway splits to continue around lake.

1.0 Short sections of singletrack drop off from greenway to run along the lake's edge a bit before popping back onto paved path. Okay to jump on just for the warm-up.

1.2 As paved path enters area of obvious storm damage and moves uphill a bit, watch closely for singletrack down to the right that runs along the lake's edge, showing green blazes. Hardpack track begins with immediate tech 2+ root barrage, filled with stubbies, root interlaces, and small dips. If terrain is not to your liking at this point, best bail out now, 'cause this is a good sampling of the track to follow.

Be sure to bring extra food for your hungry buddies.

1.6 Tech 3 root interlace in middle of short, steep climb. Rooty descent afterward. Constant up and down; not much flat running to be found.

1.8 Tech 3 rooty descent.

2.0 Tricky, off-camber roots as you descend to large stream. Lower stream crossing is tech 2+ with a steep entry. Crossing higher up is a tech 4 move, requiring a very tight line through a gap in the large rocks on the far side. To make this move, swing high upstream, then double back and drop into the stream at an angle to line up with the gap. Blow this move, and you're either wet or in need of a new derailleur.

2.1 Three-way fork; turn right and follow green blazes. Immediately after, hit another fork; turn left (uphill) this time and work up a steep, rooty climb.

2.3 Trail follows stream up away from lake, then curves back for an easy crossing.

2.4 A-frame shelter at top of rooty climb is a good rest spot and viewpoint. Trail crosses paved path and drops down other side. Descent is ugly, steep, rooty, and washed out—tech 3+. I've never been able to climb this section when riding the other direction. Try it if you don't believe me. Watch for rooty ditches at bottom.

2.6 Deep, root-filled, tech 4 ditch to cross. Novices and intermediates should walk this, as it's a bad faceplant zone. Swing high up if you try to ride it, or go lower if you've got trials skills.

2.7 Trail drops you back onto the paved greenway. Turn left to continue to other side of lake. Right returns you to parking area via a long, wooden walkway across the lake.

2.8 Pavement splits; turn right.

2.9 At edge of parking area, make immediate right to cross Avent Ferry Road and resume singletrack. Choice of tracks; follow either one to wooden bridge at the bottom.

3.0 Cross another short wooden bridge. Follow main track up to the left for a tough climb and a fun descent. Green blazes still evident on trees.

3.3 Track splits. Turn right and continue following track along lake's edge.

3.5 Three-way fork; continue straight to ride up to overlook. Nice view out over lake. Leaving overlook, follow track and green blazes back down to lake's edge.

3.6 Cross stream, then get ready for the toughest climb of the ride. Loose surface, laced with roots, and sprinkled with chicken heads. After this climb, the trail drops you onto a wide woodchip and hardpacked tech 1 doubletrack to catch your breath. Bear right to continue around the edge of the lake.

3.8 Tech 3 stream crossing: steep sided with loose rocks in the bottom.

4.0 Rooty descent down to long wooden walkway; tech 3 move to negotiate the roots and hop up the steps. Walkway crosses a wide swampy area; good spot for spotting various wildlife and for trying to decipher the animal tracks in the mud.

4.2 Turn right off walkway onto wide, dirt doubletrack.

4.8 Cross over Avent Ferry Road again. **Warning:** Watch for cars, as they come around the blind corner to the left very quickly.

4.9 Return to Lake Johnson parking lot.

8 Lake Crabtree

This is an excellent beginner trail, a good place to send folks just starting out, or a great lunchtime ride. It's smooth and safe with just enough roots and humps to keep it interesting. The park management and NC Fats Mountain Bike Club deserve a big round of applause for their foresight in constructing the first legal singletrack in Wake County. Be careful of heavy bike traffic and idiots without helmets on the weekends. The park also offers picnic shelters, boating, volleyball, fishing, and playgrounds for the rest of the family.

For ease of navigation, this route goes in on entrance 1, then takes mostly lefts to work its way around all three loops. Note that two additional loops were under construction at the time of this writing, so check the trailhead map for trail updates.

Location: Lake Crabtree Park, five minutes west of Raleigh.
Distance: 3.9-mile loop.
Approximate riding time: 25 minutes to 1 hour.
Difficulty rating: Tech 1+. No serious technical challenges, but not exactly a greenway either; there are enough roots to make sure you pay attention.

Trail surface: 3.9 miles of singletrack.
Highlights: Tight cruising; bridges; water bars; easy access to Black Creek Greenway and fire roads in Umstead Park.
Land status: County park.
Maps: USGS Raleigh West; park map available at office.

Finding the trailhead: From Interstate 40 near the Raleigh-Durham airport, take exit 285, Aviation Parkway, south. Turn left at the Lake Crabtree Park entrance, just 200 yards down the road. Turn right off the entrance road into a gravel parking area. The trailhead is just across the entrance road, clearly marked by a small wooden bridge, a trail conditions sign, and an information kiosk.

Miles and Directions

0.0 Start off at entrance 1 by the wooden bridge and information kiosk. Trail starts off with smooth, tech 1+ hardpacked singletrack.

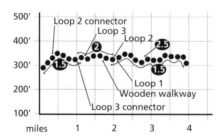

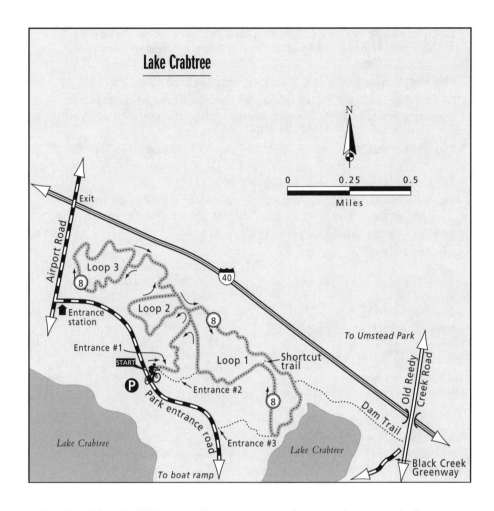

Lake Crabtree

0.1 Bear left at this Y. Either way will take you up to the loops, but the maps and mileage were made using the left branch.

0.3 Trail drops you onto the lower section of Loop 1. Turn left, go across the opening for the gas line easement, and immediately hit the intersection with Loop 2. Turn left onto Loop 2. Sign points left and right for Loop 2 and right for Loop 3.

0.8 Turn left onto the Loop 3 Connector Trail (red blazes). Sign points left for Loop 3 and right for return to Loop 1.

1.1 Turn left onto Loop 3 (yellow blazes).

1.2 Multiple switchbacks. Small bridge and some tech 2 roots.

1.7 A 20-foot-long wooden walkway.

1.8 Return to Loop 3 Connector Trail. Turn left, following the red blazes.

2.1 Intersection with Loop 2. Turn left, following the yellow blazes. After about 100 yards, turn left again at intersection with Loop 2 Connector Trail.

2.2 Cross the opening for the gas easement again, then take an immediate left onto Loop 1 with yellow blazes; clearly signed. Flat running, then fun descent over seven or eight small water bars.

2.6 Bear left to continue on Loop 1. Shortcut trail cuts off to the right.

2.7 Tall, tech 2+ root with a sharp right turn just after. Here's a spot for beginners to test themselves. Turn right at signed intersection to continue on Loop 1. Sign points left for access to Umstead Park, Black Creek Greenway, and dam.

3.0 Continue straight on Loop 1. Entrance 3 breaks off left and heads toward the boat ramps.

3.2 Continue straight on Loop 1. Shortcut trail cuts right.

3.4 Old homesite on left. Immediately after, entrance 2 is on your left by green ENTRANCE sign. Continue straight to complete the loop or bail out here; either choice is okay.

3.6 Turn left onto entrance 1 by green sign.

3.9 Return to trailhead.

9 Forest Theater

This is an excellent in-town trail running from the edge of the UNC campus to near University Mall. Multiple tracks offer options for different ability levels. The doubletrack is ridable by novices, though they might find some of the uphills a bit rocky. Various sections of singletrack offer up slick, off-camber roots, boulder-heading opportunities, and connecting bridges that will test your low-speed handling skills. Although it seems like there are a lot of turns on this route, it's just the clearest track to navigate. Pick almost any line you want, follow the stream, and you can't get lost. Take an easy ride over to the UNC Outdoor Education Center Trail for some more singletracking.

Note that this trail sees a *lot* of pedestrian use, particularly on the weekends. Drop your speed on the curves, and watch for family mobs festooned with strollers, poodles, and scampering bikers-to-be.

Location: At the edge of UNC campus, in the heart of Chapel Hill.
Distance: 4 miles out-and-back.
Approximate riding time: 30 minutes to 1 hour.
Difficulty rating: Tech 2 overall, with several tech 3 root-and-rock combinations, wicked stairs, and some tricky maneuvering from bridge to bridge. The technical challenges won't impress advanced riders, but novices will probably have their hands full.
Trail surface: 4 miles of singletrack.
Highlights: Numerous streambed crossings; tight, twisty, rooty singletrack; lots of bridges, steps, and landscaping timbers.
Land status: University property and Chapel Hill town easement.
Maps: USGS Chapel Hill.

Finding the trailhead: From the U.S. Highway 15/501 bypass in Chapel Hill, take South Raleigh Road to the first light and turn right onto Country Club Road. You'll pass the amphitheater to your right in the woods. Hang a sharp right onto Boundary Street. You can park in the small amphitheater lot on your right on weekends or continue on a little farther to a public lot.

Miles and Directions

0.0 Start at parking lot behind amphitheater stage. Follow track up around amphitheater to the left, which brings you out at the top by picnic tables and Country Club Road.

0.1 From picnic tables look for a clear, wide tech 1 doubletrack off to the left leading back down into the woods. Smooth doubletrack gains speed quickly; watch for serious jump on left side of trail, for those who want to try out their wings early in the day. After jump tread changes to hardpack with small roots and tech 2 washouts.

0.3 Follow singletrack as it branches off and drops down to the left. Short, tech 2+ rocky and rooty descent may have newbies wondering if they've bitten off more than they can chew. Turn right immediately after a short, gap-toothed bridge. Singletrack crosses doubletrack; continue straight on singletrack. Watch for short drop through rooty, tech 3 rock garden.

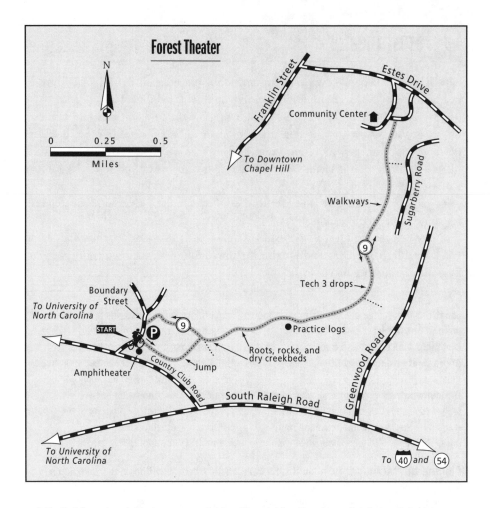

Forest Theater

0 0.25 0.5

Miles

0.7 Trail branches right, down across bridge. Cross bridge, then immediately turn left. Note that a right turn after the bridge is a dead end, but it leads over two good, knee-high logs with plenty of run-out for some fun technical practice.

0.8 Turn left onto long, wooden walkways, past SUGARBERRY ROAD/COMMUNITY CENTER PARK sign. Transitions on and off walkways can be pretty severe, with some tight turning required.

0.9 Signs: SANDY CREEK TRAIL/GREENWOOD ROAD pointing right and SUGARBERRY ROAD pointing left. Turn left, travel across another bridge, through a little tunnel, and past another sign.

1.1 Off-camber, rooty climb, followed by a drop over a long set of washed-out landscaping timber steps. Keep your weight off the front wheel here or pay the dentist bill. Shortly after, there is another series of walkways, all at ninety-degree angles. Tough slow-motion moves.

1.3 Turn right as singletrack follows stream, tech 3 roots, rocks, and drop-offs.

1.4 Turn right at sign for Sugarberry Road.

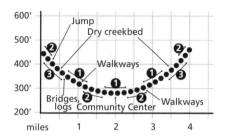

1.5 Turn left, following sign TO COMMUNITY CENTER PARK. Shortly after, trail pops out onto paved road (Shepherd's Lane) behind apartment buildings. Turn left again, follow the sidewalk a short bit, then left again over a small bridge, to head to the community center.

1.8 At the community center parking lot, turn around and head back the way you came. Follow the gravel path back around the maintenance building, cross the bridge, and turn right on the sidewalk.

2.1 Entrance to trail is signed BATTLE BRANCH TRAIL. Take an immediate left at first T.

2.9 Go straight past branching and sign for UNC campus.

3.4 Bear left across a (normally) dry creekbed for a short, tech 3 boulder-head section. Some grassy doubletrack follows, then some tech 3 root and rock combo and another streambed.

3.6 Continue straight on the doubletrack, as the original entrance singletrack cuts across your path.

3.8 Trail drops you out at the edge of Park Place Road. Turn left to follow a track beside the road, then a left again at Boundary Street.

4.0 Return to the amphitheater parking lot.

10 UNC Outdoor Education Center

If you come here expecting to cruise an easy 2.5 miles without dabbing or break-ing a sweat, you're in for some disappointment. From the humbling of the opening climb to the last hairy drop out of the woods, you'll be challenged. The back sec-tion of singletrack is a good bit friendlier with lots of easy whoop-dee-doos and drops. The final section of grassy track across the golf course ends with two big, 20- and 30-foot drops that you can roll or just sail down. **Note:** Due to recent con-struction, portions of the trail might be rerouted. Check for trail changes at the UNC Outdoor Education Center.

> "It was a humbling experience." —Daniel, the Excitable Boy

Location: Outdoor Education Center, Univer-sity of North Carolina, Chapel Hill.
Distance: 2.5-mile loop.
Approximate riding time: 30 to 45 minutes.
Difficulty rating: Tech 3+ for the chutes and ladders section; tech 2 overall for the rest.

Trail surface: 1.7 miles of singletrack; 0.8 mile of dirt and grassy doubletrack.
Highlights: Extremely steep drops and climbs; big logs; creek crossings; lots of spinning and some big air along the golf course.
Land status: University property.
Maps: USGS Chapel Hill.

Finding the trailhead: From the U.S. Highway 15/501 bypass in Chapel Hill, take South Raleigh Road to the first light and turn left onto Country Club Road. Look for a big green box by the second turn to the right. Follow the driveway down to the Outdoor Education Center and the parking area. From the parking lot, take the paved path that drops down past the tennis courts toward a ropes course area. **Caution:** Watch for a cable gate across the path at some point. As the paved path ends, bear right along the edge of the woods, around the ropes course, ignoring the first sets of arrows. Just as the path narrows, look for the entrance trail and sign (and possi-bly more blue arrows) in the woods up to the left. The trail starts and ends here.

Miles and Directions

0.0 No mercy to start. Trail begins with an imposing climb: off-camber, extremely steep, and set with a couple of massive roots. It's got to be a tech 4+ move. I never made it.

0.1 Trail doubles back and pops you suddenly over the edge of a 6-foot drop, out by the ropes course. Hang a quick U-turn and dash back in between two arrowed posts for a short, steep climb.

0.2 Déjà vu—the trail doubles again, only this time sending you down an 8-foot drop. U-turn again and ride back into the woods once more. Cross a pair of bridges, then hit some solid tech 3 roots, rocks, logs, and whatnot.

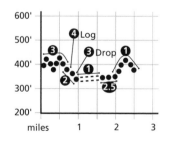

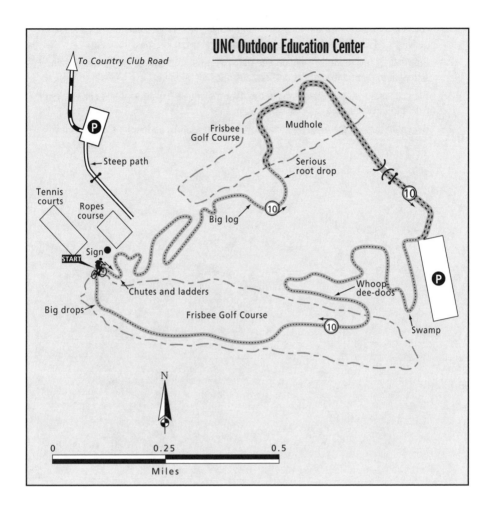

UNC Outdoor Education Center

To Country Club Road

P

Frisbee Golf Course

Mudhole

Serious root drop

Steep path

Tennis courts

Ropes course

Big log

10

10

Sign

START

Chutes and ladders

Big drops

Frisbee Golf Course

Whoop-dee-doos

P

10

Swamp

N

S

| 0 | 0.25 | 0.5 |

Miles

0.5 Tech 3+ log hop, a 2-foot concrete ledge drop, then some long tech 2 contouring and stream crossings.

0.8 Tech 4 log move, this one angled and slightly off-camber.

1.0 Trail makes a dive downslope toward the golf course. A smooth but daunting 2-foot log drop crosses the entire trail. It's an easy move at speed, but it's just plain scary. Ride it or walk it, 'cause the bust is bad. Turn right when you hit the golf course, following a grassy doubletrack.

1.2 Track bears right, following edge of woods. There's often a major mudhole here.

1.4 **Caution:** Just after you pass under a bridge, watch carefully for a chain strung across the trail. It's really difficult to see, and it'd be a nasty surprise.

1.5 Look for sign (MTB TRAIL) and singletrack on the right, just as the track reaches a small parking lot. Tech 3 stream crossing, then some cool pyramids, logs, and mud.

2.0 Drop a long section of tight whoop-dee-doos, then pop out onto the golf course again. Turn right and head toward the only obvious opening up the hill.

2.4 The last section of track descends in two big waves down toward good old pin 14. With little effort, you can sail the crests of these slopes.

2.5 Bear right through the opening at the bottom of the slopes, and return to the trailhead.

11 Southern Village

For such a short trail, this track sure makes you feel like you're really mountain biking. You'll enjoy slipping through the trees, climbing up through the rocks, and popping over the roots. This is an excellent introductory trail for your novice friend, and it's right at the edge of town. For more of a workout, drop your seat, stand the whole way, and lap it five or six times.

Location: Southern Village community, just on the south edge of Chapel Hill and Carrboro.
Distance: 1.7-mile loop.
Approximate riding time: 15 to 30 minutes.
Difficulty rating: Tech 1+. Mostly smooth hardpacked track with some roots and rocks mixed in.
Trail surface: 1.7 miles of singletrack.

Highlights: Pretty little trail within an easy bike ride of downtown and several new apartment complexes. Nice initial offering for first-timers.
Land status: City park.
Maps: Trail map available from Chapel Hill Parks and Recreation Department.

Finding the trailhead: From Chapel Hill, take South Columbia Street south out of town, which becomes U.S. Highway 15/501 South when it crosses the North Carolina Highway 54 bypass. In about 0.5 mile, turn right into the entrance for Southern Village. Drive around the square, turn right just past the church, and look for the trailhead sign straight back at the edge of the parking lot.

Miles and Directions

0.0 From the Southern Village parking lot, enter past the trail sign. Turn left to start the loop. Twisty, smooth track with some small roots.

0.4 Cross Dogwood Acres Road (trail is clearly signed), then hit a testy tech 2 root section.

0.5 Pass under power lines.

0.7 Respectable tech 3 climb up and around rocks and rootballs. Good place for beginners to challenge themselves (and maybe develop some falling skills).

0.8 Continue straight for the loop. The spur left darts out to Merritt Drive.

0.9 Fairly flat, tech 1 track with a few little humps and twists.

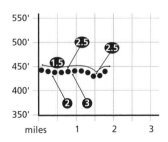

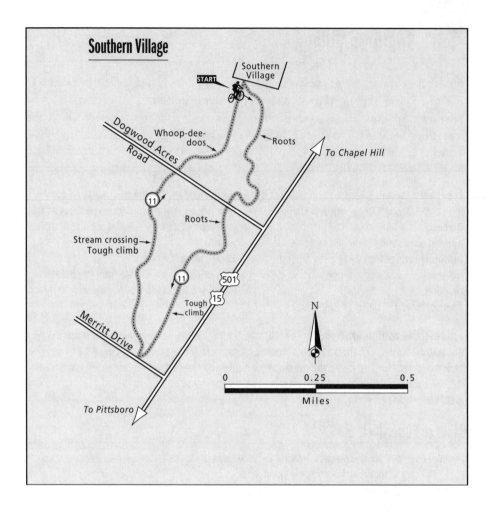

Southern Village

START

Southern Village

Dogwood Acres Road

Whoop-dee-doos

Roots

To Chapel Hill

11

Roots

Stream crossing
Tough climb

11

501

15

Tough climb

Merritt Drive

N

To Pittsboro

0   0.25   0.5

Miles

1.0 Tricky little rooty downhill (tech 2.5), followed by a small stream crossing and a steep rooty tech 3 climb.

1.1 Go straight under power lines. Signs clearly mark where trail picks up.

1.2 Straight across Dogwood Acres Road again. Signs clearly mark where trail picks up. From here trail hits a few small whoop-dee-doos, runs through a little mud, and twists back and forth through the pines.

1.5 Cross wide muddy stream, then follow main trail right, through a cut in a pile of fallen pine trees.

1.7 Turn left and roll back out at the trailhead.

12 San-Lee Park

Another creation by Donn Otti and the crew of Sanford Area Mountain Biking Association (SAMBA), this track uses every bit of available terrain for a joyous ride full of swooping turns, roller-coaster drops, unexpected switchbacks, and mad dashes through the woods. Every rider, from newbies to experts, will enjoy this trail. Reversing it at the end totals a little more than 10 miles, providing a serious workout. There is a nice shaded stream to relax beside after the ride. The lake provides opportunities for fishing and boating.

Location: San-Lee Park, ten minutes from downtown Sanford, thirty-five minutes from Raleigh.
Distance: 5.1-mile loop.
Approximate riding time: 45 minutes to 1.5 hours.
Difficulty rating: Tech 2 overall. Lots of small rocks and roots. Occasional tough, rocky switchbacks push it to tech 3 in places.

Trail surface: 4.8 miles of prime Piedmont singletrack; 0.2 mile of pavement; 0.1 mile of gravel road.
Highlights: Primo singletrack; roller-coaster rides down across the numerous bridges and back up; extremely high fun factor.
Land status: County park. Winter hours 8:00 A.M. to 5:00 P.M.; summer hours 8:00 A.M. to 8:00 P.M.
Maps: USGS Sanford.

Finding the trailhead: From Raleigh take U.S. Highway 1 South toward Sanford. Take exit 78 (Deep River Road) and turn left at the top of the ramp, then make an immediate right onto Lower Moncure Road. Go 9 miles, then turn left onto Lick Creek Road. Follow it to the end, then turn right onto Poplar Springs Church Road. Go 2 miles, then turn right onto Pumping Station Road. The park entrance is about 2 miles on the left. Park in the gravel lot just inside the gate.

Miles and Directions

0.0 From parking lot take the steep paved road uphill toward the RV camping area. You'll come out at a small parking area, with the lake and a dock down to the right. Straight ahead is a chained gravel road, with a sign for RV campground and bike trail. This is the way, obviously.

0.3 As you enter the RV camping area, look for the trailhead sign and a mailbox on your right, just by the first RV parking spot. Sign your name on the sign-in sheet stashed in the mailbox, so we can prove just how often the trail is used.

0.4 First of many brakes-free zones down across small wooden bridge. Note that every bridge on this trail has a smooth transition on both sides. The drop in may be steep, but stay away from that brake lever and you'll really enjoy yourself.

0.9 Turn right as singletrack dumps you onto old doubletrack with sign that says NO HORSES! This starts a zippy little speed zone that drops you down across another bridge, short switchback climb, another bridge, then a tougher steep climb.

1.6 Bridge crossing. Rocks after bridge can be tricky at speed (tech 2+).

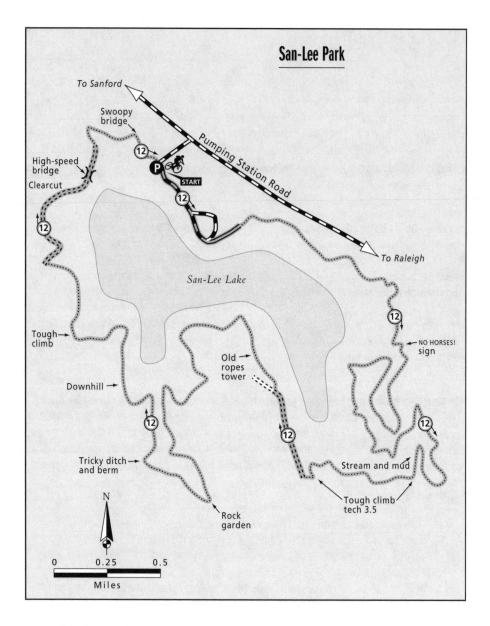

San-Lee Park

To Sanford

Swoopy bridge

Pumping Station Road

High-speed bridge

Clearcut

START

To Raleigh

San-Lee Lake

Tough climb

Old ropes tower

NO HORSES! sign

Downhill

Tricky ditch and berm

N

Stream and mud

Tough climb tech 3.5

Rock garden

0   0.25   0.5

Miles

2.1 Mondo downhill switchback section (three in a row), with big roots and big rocks; call it a tech 3 to clean it.

2.2 Second open-water stream crossing, then a long gooey patch for some serious mud-dogging. Be first in line here, or be ready to eat some mud pie.

2.3 Toughest climb on the trail: steep, extremely tight and rocky switchbacks that keep coming and coming. Very tough to pick a clean line. Even advanced riders may dab here. Solid tech 3+ to clean.

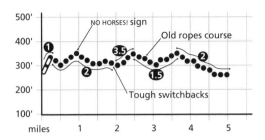

2.5 At the top of this painful climb, turn right onto an old doubletrack. This is a good place to stop and cheer/harass those still working the climb. Plus, you'll want to recharge here for the downhill that awaits.

2.8 Watch for singletrack that peels off to right. If you suddenly find yourself busting through limbs and bushes on the doubletrack, you probably need to back up.

2.9 Cruising downhill continues. Watch for a pillow-sized rock in center of trail: excellent launch site for the vertically inclined. Pass old, rotten ropes course and tower. **Note:** Stay *off* the tower, as it's a deathtrap, no fooling. And one idiot killing himself here could close the whole trail.

3.5 Turn left at sign for new singletrack section. Immediate tech 2.5 contouring, tough off-cambers, and slick rocks.

3.7 Tech 3 rock garden.

3.9 Cross a steep-sided ditch, with a tricky bermed turn on the far side. Shortly after, turn left because this new section feeds back into the main trail.

4.1 Trail tops out and feeds into an old doubletrack. Best dose of speed yet, dashing through the woods and under the power lines.

4.4 Tough climb beside clearcut, up through a bunch of chicken heads.

4.8 Fast downhill through clearcut and then a fast drop across bridge. Watch for steep exit at bridge and bad erosion gully as you drop down.

4.9 Top out, then drop into the last roller coaster of the trail, zooming across one last fast bridge.

5.1 Exit trail, crossing wide stream over long wooden and steel bridge. Drop onto grass for breather, return to vehicle, or turn around and go back in for a second helping.

13 Devil's Ridge

The operators of Devil's Ridge have spent a lot of time building and polishing this trail, and it really shows. The berms and bridges are solid, the signage is excellent, and the trail always seems freshly raked with little or no debris or litter. You can crank through this entire course and never catch so much as a stick in your wheel. It's smooth, fast, and not too technical—a perfect spot for introducing new riders or practicing for the next race. Beware that this place can be a serious mudfest after a rain, and a puddle that looks 2 inches deep can swallow you and your bike whole.

Note that two separate courses share the woods here: the mountain bike course and a motorcycle hare scramble course, which do not share any tracks, though they do cross numerous times. The scramble course is much deeper and wider and has obviously been dug by motorcycles. Although this place can seem like a bit of a maze, the two courses generally cross at ninety-degree angles, so when in doubt, go straight and keep following the red arrows. If you're supposed to turn, it's clearly marked. The owners ask that bike riders stay completely off the motocross course located up top.

Location: Fifteen minutes west of Sanford.
Distance: 4.2-mile loop.
Approximate riding time: 45 minutes to 1.5 hours.
Difficulty rating: Tech 1+ overall. Toughest technical move is the tech 3+ climb to the clearing near the end. A few tech 2+ root sections. Otherwise, most of the trail is very clean, if awfully twisty.
Trail surface: Clean, hardpacked singletrack.
Highlights: Lots of roots, twists and turns, and short surprising climbs. Serious mud after a rain. As a bonus, on many Sundays you get to watch the motocrossers show you what "big air" really means.
Land status: Private land but very friendly to mountain bikers. Track is always open to ride, except during motorcycle races and hunting season.
Maps: USGS White Hill (for topo details only; no trails shown).

Finding the trailhead: From Raleigh, take U.S. Highway 1 South to Sanford. Seven miles after US 1 and U.S. Highways 15/501 merge, turn right at the light (just past the Food Lion shopping center) onto Center Church Road (sign: DEVIL'S RIDGE MOTOCROSS). Go 0.5 mile and turn right onto Henley Road; go 2 miles and turn right onto Dycus Road. Drive 1 mile and turn right onto Blackstone Road, then after another 0.3 mile, turn left onto Kings Farm Road. The course is 1 mile up on the right and is well marked; just pull in and park. If the gate is closed, it's okay to park on the road and ride in.

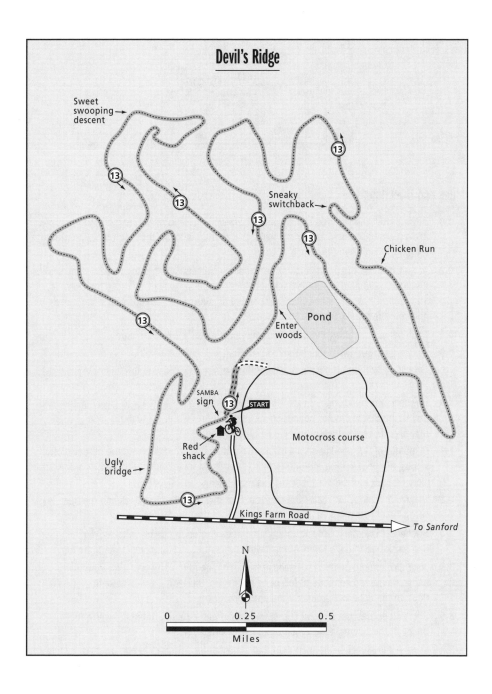

Devil's Ridge

Sweet swooping descent

13

13

13

Sneaky switchback

13

13

Chicken Run

13

Pond

Enter woods

SAMBA sign

13 START

Red shack

Ugly bridge

Motocross course

13

Kings Farm Road

To Sanford

N

0   0.25   0.5

Miles

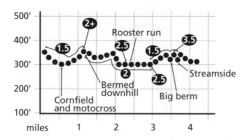

Miles and Directions

0.0 Begin trail at the little red shack, near the SAMBA sign. Head down the dirt road that parallels the motocross starting gate. When the road turns follow the (sometimes faint) trail toward the left end of the pond.

0.2 At the corner of the pond, look for an opening going straight into the woods. It crosses the motorcycle hare scramble track once or twice on the way in, so it can look kind of torn up. But hold the faith another 30 feet or so, and you'll pick up a clear singletrack and some red arrows.

0.3 Trail runs you up along the far side of the pond. All tech 2 track to here.

0.5 Sweet descent down through the Chicken Run, with some nice air potential tacked on the end. Watch for the racing rooster in this section; I've had him outrun me twice along here.

1.0 Downhill switchback right, in the same steep, rooty terrain. It's easy to miss this turn and end up on the scrambles course, so be sure to drop right at some roots, then skid across a slick bridge, and you'll pick up the arrows again.

1.8 Climb out of the woods into the clearing. Head straight across toward the next section of woods, and look for the red arrows to lead you in. More excellent tech 2 track, with occasional tech 3 root sections. Lots of sweeping curves carved *just* right.

2.1 Trail feeds into an old road for a short section, then a quick twist back into the trees for several cool root drops in a row.

3.0 Sweeeeeet swooping descent through the trees, five or six curves that'll let you lean over and just carve through them. At night, with lights, this section alone is worth the trip.

3.3 Long drop on old doubletrack hands off a lot of speed to carry over a short wooden bridge. At the top continue to follow wide track up, then a big sweeping bermed turn down to the right and around. Good speed zone.

3.6 Short, steep descent twisting through the trees, with a hard left and an ugly, wobbly bridge at the bottom. Play it right or end up in the ditch.

3.8 Cross a gas-line clearing, then drop through some tech 3 rocks to end up down by the stream. Ugly, root-filled climb back up from the stream is a tech 3 grind that'll test your slow-speed skills and grit.

3.9 Pop out of the woods just below the main park gate. Turn left to follow track as it dips in and out of the woods a few times on its way back to the start—or just bail for your vehicle if one lap was enough.

4.2 Return to the starting point at the red shack.

Launching at Devil's Ridge.

14 Governor's Creek

This is mostly easy spinning around smooth berms and over rounded humps. There are some short, rocky climbs and a couple of fast drops. Recent changes in land ownership forced some major rerouting of this trail. But as usual, Donn Otti and crew did a great job of using what was already available and adding cool new track wherever possible. If you knew Governor's before, you'll recognize many pieces of track, though some of them are heading in the opposite direction now. This is always a fun trail to ride, with numerous opportunities for some adrenaline injection along the way. Excellent new signage makes it almost impossible to miss a turn.

Location: Fifteen minutes west of Sanford.
Distance: 4.4-mile loop.
Approximate riding time: 30 minutes to 1 hour.
Difficulty rating: Tech 2 rooty track, with some tech 3 roots and rocks.
Trail surface: 100 percent singletrack.

Highlights: Short, quick humps and dips for lots of little air; fast slaloming; rock slabs.
Land status: Popular mountain bike race course. Open to the public to use at your own risk.
Maps: USGS White Hill.

Finding the trailhead: From Raleigh, take U.S. Highway 1 South to Sanford. Seven miles after US 1 and U.S. Highways 15/501 merge, turn right at the light (just past the Food Lion shopping center) onto Center Church Road (sign: DEVIL'S RIDGE MOTOCROSS). Follow this to the end, then turn left onto South Plank Road. Take a quick right onto Stanton Hill Road, then another quick right onto Underwood Road. The trailhead and parking area are 0.5 mile ahead on the right. Occasional signs for Mountain Bike Park are along the way.

Miles and Directions

0.0 From the parking area follow the trail as it skirts the edge of the woods and heads out along the road.

0.1 Trail clearly turns right into woods. Immediate assault of tech 2.5 roots and drops at speed. Some big dips and some smooth cruising tossed in as well. Red arrows on the trees clearly mark the trail throughout.

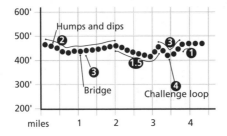

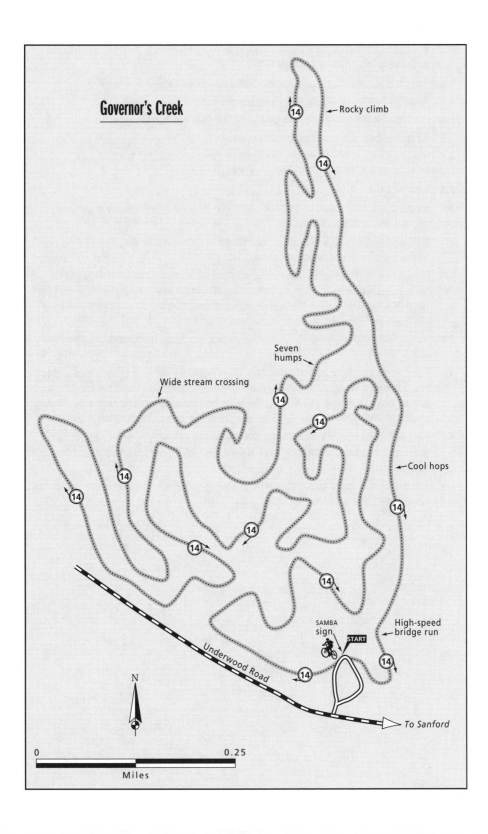

Governor's Creek

Rocky climb

Seven humps

Wide stream crossing

Cool hops

High-speed bridge run

SAMBA sign

START

Underwood Road

To Sanford

N

0   0.25

Miles

0.6 Trail drops into and out of a rocky 6-foot ditch; you're probably traveling at a good clip, so finding a clear path is essential.

0.9 Cross bridge, with tough rooty, eroded climb to follow. Call it a tech 3 to clean it.

1.4 Funky off-camber pyramid with a sharp left afterward.

1.6 Climb beside dry streambed. Trail cuts left at top onto new track.

1.8 Paralleling field and road, new track flows easily through the woods.

2.2 Heading up old doubletrack (this used to be a sweet downhill, but times change . . .), follow trail as it cuts left back onto new track again.

2.6 Wide, shallow stream crossing.

3.0 Tough, tech 3.5 rooty section that twists and humps around the trees. Good place to spin out and whack your knee.

3.2 Cool descent that starts with seven dips/humps in succession twisting through trees, then a fast off-camber run down the hill.

3.6 Pop off new track at the entrance to the old (and signed) Advanced Loop. Though the monster log has been cut through (continuous stacking during the races just made it too much of a liability, I guess), the tech 3+ rock garden below and the rooty climb to follow still make you work for it.

3.8 Tech 2 track parallels the clearcut, with some excellent hopping opportunities along the way.

4.0 Trail enters clearcut for a short piece, then dives back into the woods down a steep drop, over a bridge, then right into a mean rooty switchback climb. Serious speed can mount quickly, and freaking out and missing the bridge would be a really bad choice. So either go slow, or drop it brakes-free and just hang on. About an 8 on the fun/fear scale.

4.2 Easy tech 1 track, with a sweet dip/hump combo that can set you up for some easy, sweet air. Once you find the spot, you'll know it, and you'll probably go back for a few more flights.

4.4 Trail swings out toward road, hitting a bit of loose, sandy track. Trail then curves back around and delivers you to the parking area.

Triad

The Triad of Greensboro, Winston-Salem, and High Point dishes out a wide variety of trails for mountain bikers to enjoy. You can find smooth cruising at Country Park, rootier track through the watershed on Owl's Roost, and respectable technical challenges at Hobby Park.

15 Owl's Roost

Owl's Roost is by far the most serious of all the Watershed trails. Although this track starts innocently enough, serious technical challenges lurk along the lake's edge. Lots and lots of roots, often downhill, are often laced together into long, gnarly, off-camber welcome mats. A slick, 20-foot, smooth-bellied gully waits after the worst of the roots for a weightless roller-coaster drop—you'll need to do it several times. Then there's a monstrous log pyramid, on an uphill no less, squatting at the top of the last hill. After all that, you can return on a fast grassy doubletrack to bypass some of the rougher terrain.

Location: Along Lake Brandt, on the north side of Greensboro.

Distance: 9.9-mile lariat.

Approximate riding time: 1.5 to 2.5 hours, depending on whether the woods thrashes you.

Difficulty rating: Tech 3 overall. Initial drop to the lake is a tech 2, but many difficult root sections later on. Major pyramid near the end

of the loop is a tall, tech 4 monster. Dabbing somewhere is almost a certainty.

Trail surface: 8.2 miles of singletrack; 1.7 miles of doubletrack.

Highlights: Roots, sneaky and snaky; huge log pyramid; big mud; 20-foot gully drop; lots of bunny hops; logs.

Land status: Greensboro watershed property.

Maps: USGS Lake Brandt.

Finding the trailhead: From Interstate 40 in Greensboro, take exit 127 onto U.S. Highway 220 North. US 220 winds through and around Greensboro, and merges with Wendover Avenue at some point. Watch for the US 220 North exit off Wendover; US 220 at this point is called Battleground Avenue. Follow Battleground Avenue through a multitude of lights for 10 long miles. Then turn right at a light onto Owl's Roost Road, just after a big brown sign for Bur-Mil Park. Make an immediate left onto Bur-Mil Club Drive. Follow this entrance road in, then park in the parking lot just past the golf driving range. Trailhead sign is at the edge of the parking lot toward the driving range.

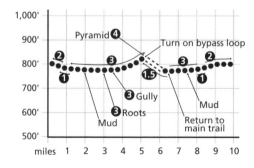

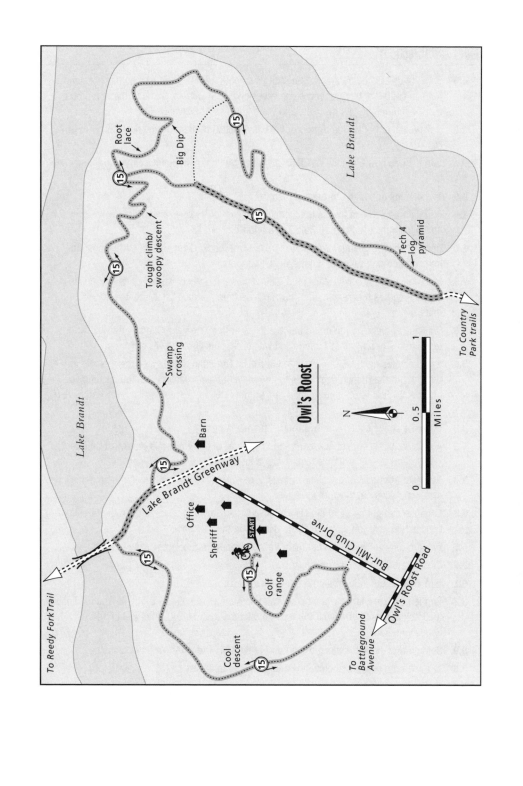

Owl's Roost

Lake Brandt

Lake Brandt

To Reedy Fork Trail

Root lace

Big Dip

Tough climb/ swoopy descent

Swamp crossing

Barn

To Country Park trails

Tech 4 log pyramid

N

0   0.5   1
Miles

Lake Brandt Greenway

Office

Sheriff

START

Golf range

Bur-Mil Club Drive

Owl's Roost Road

To Battleground Avenue

Cool descent

Miles and Directions

0.0 Begin at the signed trailhead. Starts off as smooth, tech 1 track, with some twists and turns, a couple of bridges, and some occasional tech 2 roots. Some of the root drops may be intimidating for newbies, and the bridges can be awfully slick.

0.2 Trail breaks out of woods by soccer field. Trail picks up ahead to the right and is clearly signed.

0.3 Turn right as new entrance trail Ts into existing trail. Cool, hopping slalom run through the trees.

0.9 Trail flattens and starts to parallel the lake.

1.6 Turn right as trail hits a wide doubletrack. Track to left crosses lake over long walkway and will connect you over to Bald Eagle and Reedy Fork.

1.9 Turn left onto singletrack as it breaks up over the bank. Clear sign for Owl's Roost Trail. Immediate tough series of humps, dips, and roots.

2.3 Mud. Thick, goopy, nasty, black mud. Sometimes the walkboards across are complete, and sometimes they're not. After you climb up from the mud pit, it's roots and more roots.

3.3 Continue straight, as the return trail branches in from the right. Shortly after, watch for a tech 3 rooty descent that's often filled with slick mud. This one will slam you.

3.6 Trail branches right, just as you hit a large gully. The main trail has a decent bridge at the bottom, but the branch right leads to an excellent roller-coaster drop. Trail hits the lip, plunges 20 feet to the bottom, and zips up the far side. Just pedal like crazy and have a blast.

3.9 Continue straight. Alternate bypass trail branches right.

5.2 A burning, uphill switchback leads you to the feet of a log pyramid that must be 5 feet tall. Up and over is a doable tech 4 with a lot of speed and a big lunge.

5.3 Turn right at choice of doubletrack trails. Fast, smooth return run, though the pine needles are slippery in the corners.

6.4 Continue straight as tread changes to singletrack. Trail right leads back to the lakeside trail, just in case you need to hit the Big Dip on the way back.

6.7 Turn left as you T back into the main trail. Get ready for the roots again.

7.7 Cross the Black Swamp once again.

8.1 Turn right as the trail ends onto the service road.

8.3 Turn left onto singletrack, just before you reach the long walkway over Lake Brandt. Follow the track across the bridge if you want to take the road ride to either Bald Eagle or Reedy Fork Trail.

9.0 Some jumps available along the bottom of the trail. Then starts a bit of climbing.

9.6 Turn left onto new entrance trail heading back to trailhead.

9.9 Return to trailhead.

16 Reedy Fork

Here is an easy, fun ride that anyone will enjoy; a good introductory trail. It's mostly smooth, level cranking with enough roots and other drops to make you pay attention. You'll at least see the beavers' handiwork, if not the fat little buggers themselves.

A short tale: While resting at the far end of the trail, we chanced upon a litter of puppies that someone had dumped there. The four starving little guys devoured all my Clif bars. We couldn't leave them, so we made a sack out of a sweatshirt and stuck them inside, then finished the ride back. By the time we reached the truck, we had found homes for all four of them with fellow riders.

Score: mountain bikers—4; irresponsible jerks who leave puppies to starve (and for whom a special hell is reserved)—0.

Location: Along Lake Brandt, on the north side of Greensboro.
Distance: 6.8 miles out-and-back.
Approximate riding time: 45 minutes to 1.5 hours.
Difficulty rating: Tech 1.5 overall. Some tougher roots and a tech 3 drop onto a bridge that'll make you pay attention.

Trail surface: 6.8 miles of singletrack.
Highlights: Bridges; logs; some fun hops and drops; stream crossings; beaver construction.
Land status: Greensboro watershed property.
Maps: USGS Lake Brandt.

Finding the trailhead: From Interstate 40 in Greensboro, take exit 127 onto U.S. Highway 220 North. As you progress through town, this turns into Battleground Avenue. Follow US 220 past Lake Higgins. Turn right onto North Carolina Highway 150, then right onto Lake Brandt Road. Look for parking area and trailhead on your left just as you approach the Lake Brandt dam.
To reach Reedy Fork from the Owl's Roost Trail, take Strawberry Road to Alley Road to Lunsfords Road to Lake Brandt Road.

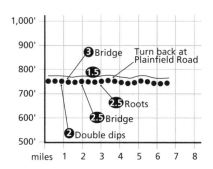

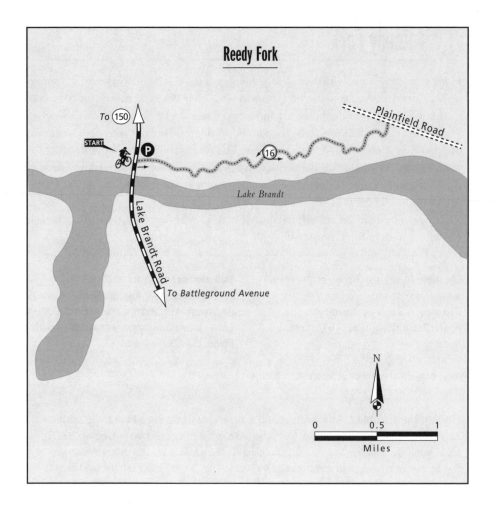

Reedy Fork

Miles and Directions

0.0 Trail starts out as smooth, tech 1+ hardpack, running beside a wide, slow-moving stream. Trail gradually gets muddier.

0.3 More mud, then a bit of a swamp ride. Scary, tech 3 bridge to cross.

0.5 Bear right, following red arrows. Tread back to hardpack.

1.0 Trail lays out a cool double dip for you. Just after, a short alternate loop branches back to the left.

1.2 Twisty drop down to a narrow bridge: tech 3+. Then bear left following arrows.

1.4 Begin the only bit of real climbing. Other end of alternate loop branches in from left.

2.1 Another narrow bridge, flanked by rooty banks: tech 2+.

2.3 Turn right and cross a small bridge. Trail gets swampy again.

2.9 Tech 2+ roots. Sign posted for the other direction: REEDY FORK TRAIL.

You never know what you'll find on the trail at Reedy Fork.

3.2 Cross an old, overgrown road and bear right to pick up the singletrack again.

3.4 Trail ends at Plainfield Road. Drink, check the woods for puppies, then head back.

4.5 Cross bridge, then turn left.

4.7 Cross another bridge, then a bit of fast contouring.

5.8 Double dips.

6.3 Bear left at this Y.

6.8 Return to parking area.

17 Bald Eagle

This is a fine, flat cruising trail, slaloming through the trees, hitting the hops, and running the streams. It's a warm-up for either of the other trails in Bur–Mil and an excellent intro ride for beginners. Just tool along, or get in the big ring and crank, whichever you want.

Location: Along Lake Higgins, on the north side of Greensboro.
Distance: 6.8 miles out-and-back.
Approximate riding time: 30 minutes to 1 hour.
Difficulty rating: Tech 2. Lots of bunny hops, small logs, and narrow creek crossings. A few short, off-camber rooty climbs provide a little tech 3 action. Dab-free ride very possible.
Trail surface: 6.8 miles of singletrack.
Highlights: Fast singletrack cruising; bunny hops; small logs; lake views.
Land status: Greensboro watershed property.
Maps: USGS Summerfield.

Finding the trailhead: From Interstate 40 in Greensboro, take exit 127 onto U.S. Highway 220 North. As you progress through town, this turns into Battleground Avenue. Follow US 220 past Lake Higgins. Just after crossing Lake Higgins, turn left onto Hamburg Mill Road. Turn left shortly into the second parking area for the marina. The trailhead is clearly signed at the edge of the parking lot.

Miles and Directions

0.0   Leave from the marina parking lot. Trail entrance clearly signed and starts right off with some fine, tech 1+ track that twists and turns through the trees. Flat contour running. Multiple creek crossings are bridged or lined with corduroy.

0.8   Cross an opening, which is a gas line right-of-way.

1.6   Cross Carlson Dairy Road. Watch for fast traffic. Trail clearly picks up on other side with more of the same fun, easy track.

2.0   Cross over a long wooden bridge. Bunny hop opportunities abound.

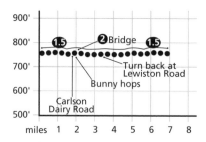

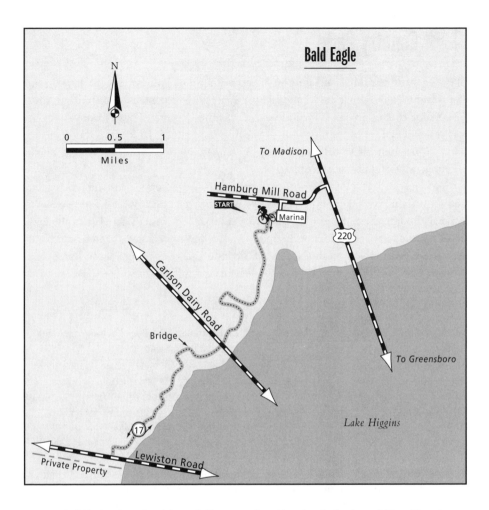

3.4 Trail hits Lewiston Road (paved). Turn around at this point. At the time of this writing, the trail across the road was private property and closed to bikes. Look for updated signs.

5.2 Cross Carlson Dairy Road.

6.8 Return to parking area.

18 Country Park

This is a good beginner and intermediate cruising trail. You can get a warm-up on the paved greenway that circles the lake, or you can send your less-than-adventurous honey out to the greenway while you get a little singletrack into your system. A well-maintained set of trails (if awfully confusing), Country Park offers lots of small, tech 2 roots and other challenges, along with a few big logs and lots of high-speed, twisting-through-the-trees cruising.

This place is a literal maze of trails. There are lots of intersections and cross-trails, and I'd be lying if I said you'll be able to follow my directions with no problems. In general, though, the route given here runs a counterclockwise loop between the lake and the cemetery. Try to follow the main track when in doubt; bearing to the right will generally keep you on the outside of the loop. You can't really get too lost, unless you get into the military park, so if you start to see lots of confederate statues, turn around.

Location: Jaycee Park, on the north side of Greensboro.

Distance: 4-mile loop.

Approximate riding time: 45 minutes to 1.5 hours.

Difficulty rating: Tech 2. Lots of buff cruising track; some tech 3 logs; lots of roots and small drops.

Trail surface: 3.6 miles of singletrack; 0.4 mile of dirt doubletrack.

Highlights: Logs; roots and rocks; tight single-track cruising; the typical stuff.

Land status: Guilford county park.

Maps: USGS Greensboro; Greensboro Area Bike and Trail Map, available from Greensboro Parks and Recreation and area bike shops.

Finding the trailhead: From Interstate 40 in Greensboro, take exit 128 and turn north onto East Lee Street. Follow signs for U.S. Highway 220 as this road changes names to Muro Boulevard, then Fisher Street, then finally Battleground Avenue. After a few miles, turn right onto Pisgah Church Road, then hang an immediate left at the entrance sign for Jaycee/Country Park. Turn left onto Forest Lawn Drive, then right into the parking lot for the Lewis Center (large brick building). A ballfield is at one end of the parking lot, and Safetyland (a surreal play/driving town setup for kids) is on one side. Trailhead is at the corner between the two.

Miles and Directions

0.0 Trail begins at the back of the parking area between the fence to Safetyland and the ballfield. Cross a small ditch and hang an immediate right at the first T you hit. Trail starts off with clean, hardpacked tech 1+ singletrack.

0.3 Turn left at the T. Small bridge and clearing off to right.

0.4 Pass a green, wooden swing and white arrows on the trees, then bear right at the Y into a small meadow. Shortly after, you'll cross a small playground area, and the trail bears uphill.

0.5 Bear right at this Y and follow the white arrows for a good, tech 2 climb.

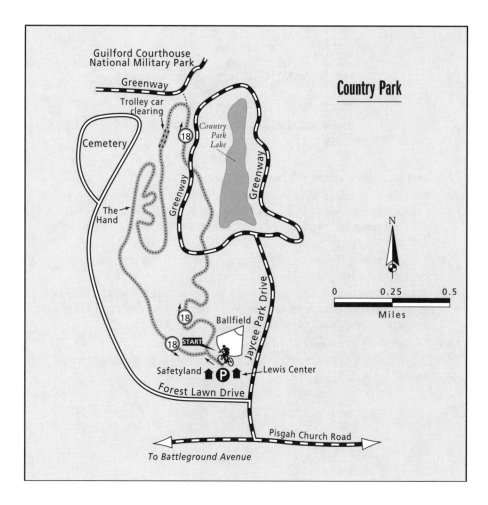

0.6 Trail crosses the paved lake greenway. Cross the greenway, ride over a sizable wooden bridge, then immediately turn right onto more singletrack.

0.8 Nice 12-inch drop, then bear left uphill at the Y, heading away from the lake.

0.9 Ride up a long set of landscape-timber steps. Cross the paved greenway again, ride through a gap in the wooden fence, and cut straight across another playground area to pick up singletrack on the other side.

1.1 Turn left at this T (right takes you to the military park).

1.5 A 12-inch log-drop leads you into a five-way intersection. Turn sharp right, and you'll start to see the cemetery off to your right. Track is very twisty, mostly tech 1+, with some large tech 3 logs along the way.

2.1 Cross one small wooden bridge, then a second bridge constructed of an old Ping-Pong table. Head uphill, still by the cemetery.

2.2 Trail enters a clearing and turns into dirt doubletrack behind an old brick building. Track leads past several old trolley cars and crosses a gravel path that leads to the cemetery.

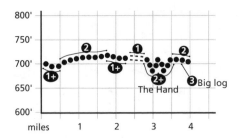

2.6 Drop back into the woods; trail returns to singletrack.

2.7 Trail leads to "the Hand," an intersection with five or six possibilities. Turn sharply right for a steep, fast, tech 2+ drop, then a quick U-turn and a return to the Hand. Turn right again and repeat the drop/U-turn process. Return to the Hand once more and turn right again onto the next track.

3.1 Trail loops out once more, running back along the edge of the cemetery fence, then returns to the Hand.

3.2 Turn right at the Hand one last time, following the sign for Long Trail of Peace. Bear right at the immediate Y that follows, following the red ribbons. Cross a little humpty bridge, then start cranking though some fast, twisty, tech 2 cruising track.

3.6 Nice, 24-inch log to practice your moves on—a tech 3 to clean it.

4.0 Trail comes back up along the Safetyland fence. Bear right at the Y, and pop back out into the parking area.

19 Hobby Park

This trail has got it all: huge berms, rock gardens, streams, big logs, pyramids, a serious drop through a rock- and log-infested erosion gully, and a climb that gives you the option of lung-busting or heart-breaking fun. It's Disneyland for the two-wheeled set—not a trail for first-timers or for anyone who really hates falling. This trail will test your technical skills (and courage) from all angles. Beginners will be scared—often. Intermediates will probably crash—often. Advanced folks can pound through it for an experience like riding a jackhammer.

The trail changes occasionally and often isn't well marked. When in doubt, follow a general clockwise direction or head uphill to return to the airfields and parking area.

Location: Winston-Salem, just south of Interstate 40.
Distance: 6.6-mile loop.
Approximate riding time: 45 minutes to 1.5 hours.
Difficulty rating: Tech 3+. Hobby Park tosses out one tough technical move after another. Jumps abound for some good air-time potential. Descent through the rock garden is a tech 4 number, particularly because it's tough *not* to carry a bunch of speed into it.

Trail surface: All singletrack (except for final run up the paved derby track); mostly hard-pack with some sand and loose surface.
Highlights: Lots of jumps; cool log pyramids; fast, crazy downhills; multiple brakes-free zones; heart-breaking climb.
Land status: City park.
Maps: Sketch available on the North Carolina Mountain Bike Authority Web site at members. aol.com/NCMBA/home.html and also at www.mbinfo.com.

Finding the trailhead: From Interstate 40 (*not* Business 40) in Winston-Salem, take exit 189, Stratford Road West (U.S. Highway 158). Go about 3 miles and turn left onto Clemmonsville Road, then take an immediate left into the well-marked park entrance.

Miles and Directions

0.0 Start from parking lot. Enter in past park sign and over a 3-foot red-clay hump. Trail starts with multiple bunny hops over sandy track littered with big rocks.

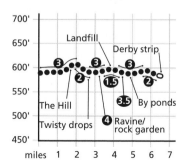

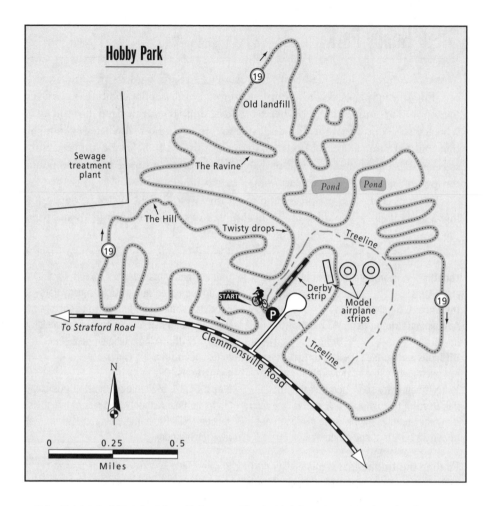

0.1 Quick left, right, left, at three Ys in a row. If in doubt, follow clearest track and end up back near the parking lot. First of many extremely sweet brakes-free sections.

0.4 Ignore trail that peels in from right.

0.7 Turn right at four-way intersection. Lots of dips to dance over.

0.9 Sharp turn back left by orange fencing. Straight is a shortcut that avoids climbing Poop Plant Hill, but also misses some excellent zipping through the trees. Your choice, but I think it's worth it; besides, you ought to pay to play.

1.4 Several more grin-inducing brakes-free zones. Last one drops you onto a long wooden walkway. Start calling up your reserves now, 'cause the biggest climb of the ride is just around the corner.

1.7 Poop Plant Hill. A choice of tracks is now offered up this painful climb: snaking back and forth for prolonged agony or straight up the throat for a quick victory or demise. Call it a tech 3 but a mean one. Follow main track straight. Shortcut reenters from right by orange fence.

Grinding up Poop Plant Hill at Hobby Park.

1.9   Sharp left turn. Straight leads to back of derby grandstands.

2.4   Track enters clearing behind derby track, follows left along the edge, then drops back into the woods. Tasty brakes-free zone, several short wooden bridges, and lots of twisty root-drops lead you back down by the poop plant.

3.2   Turn left at T, shortly after running into and back out of the field again. Stop, cinch your shorts, and prepare for the rock garden. This tech 4 descent tosses you a respectable rock ledge, then a large log, then drops you into a high-walled erosion gully that can be ridden high on the side. Ugly, but sweet: sort of like my bulldog.

3.5   Bear left as you enter the landfill. In summer this place is a sticker-filled wasteland and is best bypassed by going right. Decent chance to stretch your legs a bit otherwise. Follow track as it cuts across landfill then doubles back. Bypass peels in from right.

4.6   Sharp right turn drops you down toward lower pond.

4.7   Turn left at edge of lower pond to cross dam. Turn right at far end of dam for a 5-foot weightless drop.

5.0   Turn right at T. Look for boards nailed across a huge rootball for some optional serious technical action.

5.1   Cross bridge and follow dam between upper and lower pond.

5.5   Follow track across short section of field near airplane circle. Track reenters woods, then skirts along edge of field through a sandy hemlock grove.

5.8   Bear left at Y to drop down near Clemmonsville Road.

5.9   Follow track straight for one last chance at some speed (opening to left leads back to parking lot if you've had enough already). Track leads out into field for some smooth, fast cruising. Circle around airplane strip to enter bottom of derby track.

6.6   Zip down the derby track, then groan up the other side for a last bit of sweat before you return to the parking lot.

Charlotte, Statesville, and Morganton

The Queen City hosts a bevy of singletrack beauties. We included only four because of legal reasons, but there are several other open trails in the area. Catawba River Front, Renaissance Park, and Cane Creek are all located on public property, whereas Beech Springs is a private venture. South Mountain outside Morganton is as brutal a trail as you'll find anywhere. Signal Hill is Statesville's only legal ride (that we could find, at least).

20 Catawba River Front

This is a top-notch ride, only fifteen minutes from Charlotte. Catawba is the kind of trail that's doable for a determined beginner yet still challenging for an advanced rider. For the uninitiated the climbs will require some pushing, and the rooty drops will keep you on your toes or your face, depending on your concentration and ability. You'll get lots of fast downhill action that slips back and forth through the trees. Speed comes quickly in many spots, but be warned that most of the downhills end with a sudden turn at the river's edge. Opportunities for air abound with dozens of dips and humps to fly from, including the River Monster—a 5-footer that'll show you its ugly side if you don't show proper respect.

Location: On the banks of the Catawba River, about fifteen minutes west of Charlotte.
Distance: 8.5-mile loop.
Approximate riding time: 1.5 to 2.5 hours.
Difficulty rating: Tech 3 overall. Roots everywhere for a near constant pounding except along the power line, and then you get rocks and gullies. Lots of knee-high jumps, at least

one double, and a monster launch pad down by the river.
Trail surface: 7.3 miles of singletrack; 1.2 miles of dirt doubletrack.
Highlights: Switchy downhills; jumps; bermed turns; slalom course; mudholes.
Land status: County park.
Maps: USGS Mount Holly.

Finding the trailhead: From Charlotte, follow Interstate 85 South to exit 29, Sam Wilson Road. Turn right at the top of the ramp, then hang an immediate (and I mean immediate) left onto Performance Road. Turn left again onto Mores Chapel Road, then right onto Heavy Equipment School Road. Follow this until the road ends at a metal gate and the trailhead.

Miles and Directions

0.0   From the parking area ride straight past the gate onto a wide, dirt doubletrack. Follow this track as it curves under the power lines and up the hill.

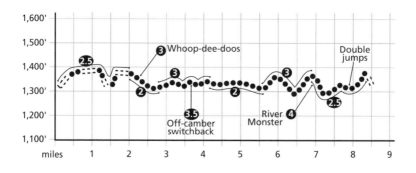

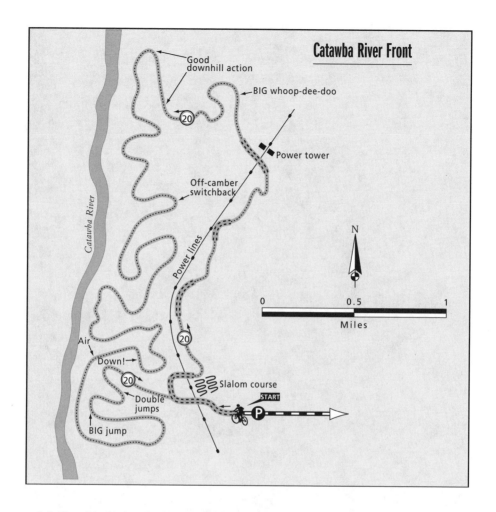

0.4 Turn right, back under the power lines, as you reach the top of the hill. Track takes you to the edge of the woods, where some tasty singletrack picks up (tech 2+, small rocks and roots).

0.8 Pop out of the woods and run under the power lines. Watch for immediate singletrack on the right darting back into the woods. Ride the woods for about 200 yards, jump out onto the power-line track again for a steep downhill, then back in for more sweet single-track.

1.5 Back out on the power-line doubletrack again. Turn left just before two big power-line towers and cross over to the singletrack on the other side.

1.8 Sweet, twisty track leads you into a cool gully for some roller-coaster action, then over some big ol' whoop-dee-doos. Bear right if you're given the option. (Several faint, older tracks peel off; just follow the clearest trail.)

2.2 Fast downhilling through the trees, heading toward the river.

The Excitable Boy has good reason to be.

2.4 Turn left as you bottom out at the river (or just go straight if you want to swim awhile). Trail works back and forth with good use of terrain, some big dips, tree tunnels, and several surprise mudholes—a little bit of everything.

3.1 Climb, turn right at the T, and head back to the river.

3.3 Climb some more, turn right at this T, too, and head back to the river.

3.6 Turn right once more for another trip back down the hill. Challenging, off-camber switchback to maneuver (tech 3+).

3.8 Big dip with a bridge in the middle, then a steep climb, and another trip back to the river.

4.1 Turn left, up away from the river. You'll cross several old roads and doubletrack trails; just keep following the clear track, and you'll eventually end up back by the river once again.

5.7 Bear right at this Y, dropping down across some old drainage pipes, then into a tough, granny-gear climb.

6.0 Bear right as you pop out of the woods back up near the power lines. Look for an immediate right back into the trees. Get ready for the best downhill yet, a fast descent that swoops through the trees, with several surprise switchbacks.

6.2 Turn left as you reach the river again.

6.9 Slip along the river for a while, climb up, then roar back down to challenge the River Monster, a 5-foot behemoth of a jump that deserves respect and some good suspension.

7.7 Cool set of double jumps, each with a tight, bermed turn afterward.

8.1 Return once more to the power lines. Head downhill on the doubletrack to return to the parking area, or take the challenge of the slalom course hidden out in the middle of the field among the high weeds (beware the steep jumps).

8.5 Return to the parking area.

21 Renaissance Park

This little secret singletrack gem lies hidden only a long wheelie's ride from the Charlotte Coliseum. Don't be fooled, as we were, into expecting a smooth, cruising trail set up for Buffy on her Huffy, though. What begins with a friendly dirt path quickly turns into rock-and-root-strewn singletrack of surprising meanness. Pyramids and log crossings abound. Ugly, tech 3+ descent halfway in requires concentration, courage, or the sense to walk it.

Location: Next door to the Charlotte Coliseum, in downtown Charlotte.
Distance: 4.7-mile loop.
Approximate riding time: 45 minutes to 1.5 hours.
Difficulty rating: Tech 2.5 overall. This track is very temperamental and can change from a tech 1 cruiser to a tech 3 root/rock/log playground with no warning. Many of the rooty sections will be overwhelming for beginners.

Trail surface: 4.4 miles of singletrack; 0.3 mile of gravel doubletrack.
Highlights: Big pyramids; lots of humps and root drops; treacherous roots; view of coliseum; located almost in downtown Charlotte!
Land status: City park.
Maps: Sketches available on the North Carolina Mountain Bike Authority Web site at members.aol.com/NCMBA/home.html and at www.mbinfo.com.

Finding the trailhead: From Interstate 77 in Charlotte, take exit 5 onto West Tyvola Road. Go about 3 miles; pass the Charlotte Coliseum on your left. Go another mile or so, then turn left into the first Renaissance Park entrance.

Miles and Directions

0.0 Start from end of parking lot, near Dumpster and dirt piles. To start with Loop 1, hop on track along the edge of the parking lot, and head toward the park entrance. As parking lot ends look for obvious singletrack cutting straight through grassy field.

0.6 As it nears Tyvola Road, this singletrack suddenly changes from smooth, tech 1 hardpack to a rooty, eroded track full of drops and washouts. Beginners should keep their eyes open for the transition.

0.8 Cross short wooden bridge. **Caution:** Bridge is often slick with mud and will slap you down faster than you can blink.

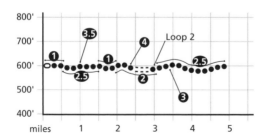

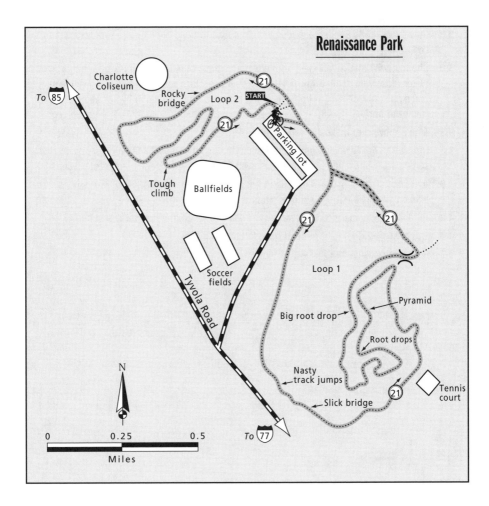

Renaissance Park

1.0 Trail wanders by second park entrance and edge of tennis courts, then reenters woods just past courts, offering up a nice 3-foot drop with a fat tech 3+ rock perched right at the lip for a world-class launching pad.

1.4 Trail varies from sweeping tech 1 track to a series of large log pyramids, short drops, and tough, rooty climbs. Temperament seems to change almost constantly.

2.3 Nastiest drop on the trail; sometimes marked with a DANGER sign or note. This is a 6-foot-high drop, with large roots snaking across its surface and even larger gaps in between the roots; call it a tech 4, mainly for the biff potential. Cut the roots as straight as possible, avoid the gully in the middle, use a little speed, resist the impulse to brake, and you should sail over it. Otherwise, walk it and hone your skills on the smaller versions along the trail.

2.5 Cross another bridge and immediately turn left by a large, unmarked wooden post. Trail winds through a bit more singletrack, then drops you onto a gravel road. Follow road straight.

2.8 Gravel road ends at edge of parking lot. Turn right to head back toward your vehicle and Loop 2 trailhead.

3.0 Shortcut to Loop 2 bears right from edge of parking lot onto singletrack back into woods. Watch closely for small arrow pointing to trailhead. Once you're in the woods, ignore several small trails peeling in from left. If you miss this entrance, go in by arrows near the Dumpster and bear right.

3.3 Tech 3 move over makeshift rocky bridge.

3.5 Opening to right reveals Charlotte Coliseum through the trees. Track from here dishes out some sweet drops, humps, and logs, served from a bed of smooth, fairly fast singletrack.

3.9 Trail turns sharply right across a short bridge, just after a series of major bunny hops. Watch that you're not still airborne when the turn shows up.

4.2 Tortuous, loose, rocky climb. Here's where you pay for all that fun you've just had.

4.6 End of Loop 2. Turn right to head back to the parking lot.

4.7 Return to parking area.

22 Beech Springs

This is an excellent trail. It's a blast to ride with enough roots, rocks, jumps, and drops to satisfy the thrasher quotient in just about anyone. Devil's Drop gives you a choice of three insane descents with other treacherous drops at the Rock Dam and Gravity Cavity. And although novices will, or should, choose to dismount at a few spots, they should take heart knowing that most of the tough moves have bypasses cut.

Beech Springs is a shining example of a professionally designed and maintained mountain bike park. Besides the incredible riding, additional features include picnic benches for reviving and reliving the ride, and an information center filled with ads, maps, lost keys, notes for riding partners, waivers, and info sheets. Hats off to Mike Andrews for having the foresight and the simple good grace to provide us with such a wonderful green playground.

Location: Twenty minutes north of Charlotte.
Distance: 4.7-mile loop.
Approximate riding time: 40 minutes to 1.5 hours.
Difficulty rating: Tech 3 overall, though it ranges widely. Ribbons of lazy tech 1 single-track wind gracefully through the trees in places. Elsewhere along the trail Devil's Drop, Gravity Cavity, and the Rock Dam all push tech 4 with more logs, humps, and pyramids scattered about.
Trail surface: Pure singletrack in all its incarnations: sandy, boggy, hardpacked, loose, rocky, and eroded. Just what you wanted and more.
Highlights: BMX playground at trailhead with tons of jumps; big ravine drops; several tricky rock moves; one big-ass rooty descent.
Land status: Private land set up solely for mountain bikers. Fee: $2.00 per rider per day, a bargain wherever you come from. Contact Mike Andrews at (704) 782-6134 for information or just to say thanks.
Maps: Trail map available at trailhead information shed.

Finding the trailhead: From Charlotte take Interstate 85 North and exit on Poplar Tent Road (exit 52) heading west. Turn right at the top of the ramp. Go roughly 100 yards and turn right onto Goodman Road. Beech Springs Mountain Bike Park is clearly marked on the left about 1 mile down the road.

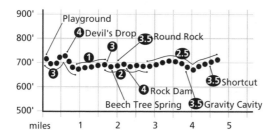

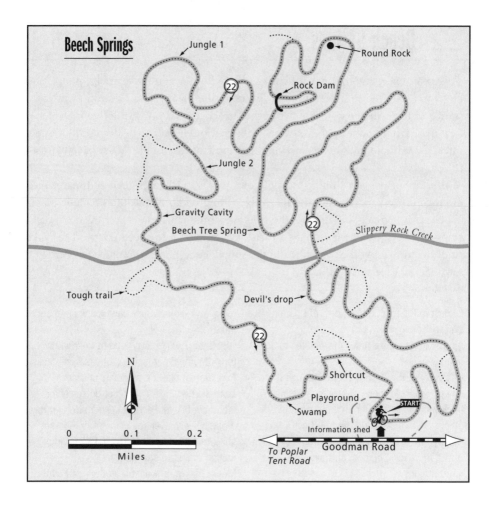

Miles and Directions

0.0 Start from the info shack. Drop through the BMX humps, and start following the red arrows around to the right. (**Note:** Be sure to sign a waiver and drop off your $2.00 in the shack first, so someone will know if you don't make it back, and so you won't look like a cheapskate if you stack at the dam and never make it back.)

0.1 Cross small wooden bridge, then follow arrows straight. Sign: NO HORSEBACK RIDING.

0.2 Turn left for TOUGH TRAIL OPTION, or stay straight for the main trail. Option trail is full of logs, roots, and twisty drops (solid tech 3), and main trail gives up some fast hardpack cut by narrow gullies. I enjoyed them both, so it's up to your own tastes. Same mileage either direction.

0.4 Follow red arrows straight on main trail. Option trail to right isn't really worth it, and you'll miss some really excellent water bars in the process.

0.5 At OPTION: DEVIL'S DROP, turn left. I recommend this option highly, though only if you enjoy screaming 80 feet down a steep, root-encrusted hillside. Otherwise continue straight and wait for your more foolhardy companions to join you by the stream at the bottom. Note that trying to bail out or even brake hard in the middle of any of these descents will result in serious penalties. Do not look at the padded tree in the middle of the first descent, lest it suck you into its woody embrace. Cross stream at bottom (via stream bottom or bridge) and follow arrows left. Ignore all other trail options as you start to climb.

1.4 Track flattens to tech 1, runs into old farm road, and turns sharply left by the yellow flagging. Following descent runs fast over some off-camber washouts (tech 3), then into three or four big, fun, sweeping turns.

1.7 Pass Beech Tree Spring. The clear, cool spring bubbles from the ground by the foot of a massive, silver-skinned giant. Picnic table makes for a nice break spot, if you need one already. Follow red arrows straight along edge of field.

1.8 There are multiple paths and bridges across this muddy area. Hug the right side, and follow red arrows uphill.

2.0 Trail turns left at edge of field, then drops back in past Round Rock. Tech 3+ move to ride up and over Round Rock (wheelie drop is probably your best choice).

2.1 Follow main trail to left. LOG OPTION trail to right adds a little length, but not much else.

2.2 ROCK DAM BYPASS to left. The Rock Dam to right is a nasty, tech 4 drop down through some hungry-looking rocks. This is a very worthwhile move but pay heed to the CAUTION sign. Trip mileage includes the bypass trail to the left.

2.8 Turn right for JUNGLE 1 OPTION trail. Additional dosage of rooty, twisty track dotted with 12-inch drops.

3.0 Turn right again when Jungle 1 Ts back into main trail.

3.2 Turn left for JUNGLE 2 OPTION. Trail holds an excellent pair of 2-foot rock drops to leap from.

3.7 Turn left as Jungle 2 Ts back into main trail. This brings you to the top of Gravity Cavity, a 15-foot-deep network of gullies that offers sick drops, wall riding, and some serious, tech 3 and 4 roller-coaster action. Bypass trail along right side of gully provides an easy return for the multiple passes you'll have to take here. Turn left again at bottom of Gravity Cavity.

3.8 Cross Slippery Rock Creek, then turn left. TOUGH TRAIL 2 OPTION to right is fairly rough track with a tough and ugly climb woven in. I'd opt to stay on the main track.

4.2 Tough uphill rock move, as you enter a small clearing with fence on your right. Sign for SWAMP, though I never saw one.

4.4 Sign: SHORTCUT IF YOU CAN. Who could resist a dare like that? Turn right, and prepare for an ugly tech 3+ descent, followed by some gully drops and short, tough climbs. Be careful crossing the slick wooden bridge at the bottom.

4.7 Return to parking area. Excellent hump/big drop/hump combo just before exiting woods—sort of like Mother Nature handing you a cookie as you leave her playground.

23 Cane Creek

A number of trails lace the land around the lake. The directions given here lay out two loops: The first is a beginner's loop with a minimum of technical challenges, though it does contain some huge, skanky, horse-induced mudholes. The second loop offers a number of tricky rock gardens and stream crossings that can slap you down in a big way if you don't play them right. An excellent pair of jumps bookend the grassy area just before the dam. For an interesting—if somewhat unsavory—wildlife experience, keep an eye out for the buzzard tower.

The park offers several other really nice features. There are picnic facilities all over the place and a snack bar down by the beach. The bathhouses contain free showers and flush toilets. If you ask nicely at the office, they'll let you use a hose to wash your bikes off. And for a measly $2.00, you can go swim in the lake and wash the dust from your weary bones.

Location: Waxhaw, twenty minutes south of Charlotte.
Distance: 11.9-mile loop.
Approximate riding time: 1.5 to 3 hours.
Difficulty rating: Tech 1+ overall. Occasional short tech 2 rock/root sections on beginner loop. Several tech 3 and 3.5 rock gardens and stream crossings on intermediate loop.

Trail surface: 11.3 miles of singletrack; 0.5 mile of grassy doubletrack; 0.1 mile of gravel doubletrack.
Highlights: Easy cruising on beginner's loop; lake views; rock gardens; tricky stream crossings; serious mudholes.
Land status: County park.
Maps: USGS Waxhaw; map available at park office.

Finding the trailhead: From Charlotte, take Interstate 77 South to Interstate 485. Exit onto North Carolina Highway 16 South, and go about 8 miles to Waxhaw. At the stoplight in Waxhaw (there's only one), turn left onto North Carolina Highway 75 (Waxhaw Highway). Go about 0.5 mile, and bear right onto Old Providence Road by the brown sign for Cane Creek Park. Somewhere along the way this turns into Old Waxhaw-Monroe Road. After 2 miles or so turn right onto Providence Road. Cross North Carolina Highway 200, go another 2 miles, then turn right onto Harkey Road. Cane Creek Park is 1 mile on the right.

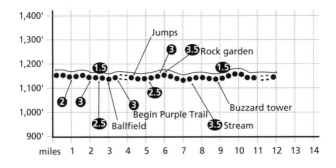

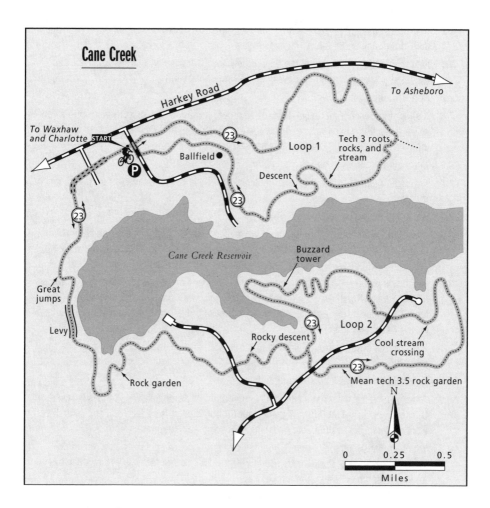

Cane Creek

Miles and Directions

0.0 From the parking area ride back up past the park office. Turn right onto the second red trail entrance, the one closest to Harkey Road. You'll follow the red blazes for this entire loop. Mileage starts at this point.

0.3 Bear left at this Y, following the red blazes. Track is tech 1+ hardpack, with a few tech 2 roots. You'll find some small bunny hop opportunities along the way, but other than that it's a cruiser.

0.7 First of several mondo mudholes, like equine-induced bomb craters. These things can swallow you.

1.0 Trail runs near Harkey Road, then you get a short but fun twisty descent into several small tech 2 rock gardens.

1.4 Pass through a power-line opening.

1.5 Turn right to follow blazes. Straight leads to private property.

1.8 Red trail turns right onto a short section of pea-gravel doubletrack, runs down near the lake, then back under the power lines again.

2.0 First real technical offering of the day: a tasty, tech 3 trail salad of roots and rocks, surrounding a shallow stream and a fat, skanky mudhole. Yum!

2.2 Red trail turns left at this T.

2.5 A short, fun descent into a small ravine and over some tech 2+ roots leads you to a four-way intersection. Go straight to follow the red blazes; left and right are *orange,* which all look the same if you're wearing sunglasses.

2.6 Turn right to follow red blazes.

2.7 Turn right again to follow red blazes. A noticeable tech 2 climb leads you up past a picnic table.

2.8 Go straight to follow red blazes.

2.9 A quick right turn leads you out into a grassy field. Hug the right side of the field as you go around the baseball diamond. There's no real trail across the field, but you will still see some red blazes. Trail clearly picks up and enters the woods past the ballfield.

3.5 Trail drops you back out onto the park entrance road. Turn right on the hardtop, heading toward Harkey Road. Go 30 feet, then turn left onto the start of the second (purple) loop. The welcoming mat of tech 3 roots and rocks will let you know that you're no longer on the beginner's loop.

3.7 Trail crosses a wide, grassy field and a gravel road, then heads back into the woods for more fun.

4.0 Turn right at the T to follow the purple blazes.

4.2 Bear left at the Y toward the lake. You'll enter another small grassy field that's bracketed by two excellent 3-foot jumps. The play-out for both jumps is perfect, and you'll surely want to spend some time here polishing your soaring techniques.

4.3 When you finish jumping around, bear left along the top of the lake's dam, then left again at the far end, following the purple blazes. Lots of smooth, twisty-turny track follows, with some occasional mudholes.

5.1 Long technical section: a tech 2+ rock garden, then a rocky descent, a rocky climb, and a zippy downhill. Expect some serious grin inducement and possibly the first big bust of the day.

5.6 Turn right just before the edge of a parking lot. Shortly after, bear right again, around the end of a chain-link fence and past an RV camping area.

6.0 Hit a paved service road. Trail picks up across the road, maybe 15 feet up to the left, and starts with a banging tech 3 descent/mudhole/climb combo.

6.2 Turn right at the T, then pass under the power lines. Not long after, you'll dive into a choice tech 3+ root/rock garden that runs along the edge of a stream. You'll eventually return from across the stream here on the blue trail.

6.5 Hit another paved service road. Jag left, then right back into the woods.

6.6 Continue straight at this intersection. Purple trail ends and red blazes begin. Watch for a mean, tech 3 rock garden.

7.5 Excellent stream crossing, with many options, from a smooth, tech 2+ nose-in to a tech 3+ leap off a root lip. Shortly after, cross a second stream over a short log bridge; bridge is ridable, but the gaps between the logs are treacherous.

7.6 Continue straight past branch to the right (both ways are blazed red).

7.7 Turn right as you hit a gravel road. Ride down past a wooden cabin, cross the hardtop road, and pick up the green trail on the other side.

7.8 Bear right at the Y and run along the edge of a field for a 100 yards or so, then dart back in among the trees.

8.7 Go under the power lines. Be sure to check out the tower on a sunny day, as it's often a roosting spot for a dozen black buzzards. Not especially attractive fellows, but an important part of the food chain all the same.

8.9 Sharp right turn onto the blue trail.

9.2 Tech 3+ rocky stream crossing, then a right turn to put you back onto the purple trail and into the rock garden from mile mark 6.2.

9.5 Cross the hardtop service road again. Trail picks up just to the left across the road.

9.9 Bear left as you return to the RV campground, going around the fence and back into the woods.

10.8 Bear right, and ride back across the dam. Get ready for those wonderful jumps that wait for you again on the far side.

11.9 Cross the wide, grassy field, grind your way up one last tech 3 rocky climb, and return to the park entrance road. Parking area is down to your right.

24 South Mountain

The South Mountain Trail climbs up to series of ridges that encircle a large cove. Ridgeline running isn't usually that tough, but this is a severe trail. Imagine the longest, rockiest, most painful single climb you've made in recent years. Now imagine it a dozen or more times in the space of 18 miles; not a pretty picture. But the descents are worth it: crazy-fast over loose rocks with dozens of water bars. Even the paved section runs a ridgeline, and we hit 40 miles per hour coasting it at one point. If you think you can hammer *anything* for 18 miles, then come to South Mountain, but consider yourself warned about spending the night on the mountain.

> "This section is 'strainuous.' And this other section is 'strainuous' too." —Lady at the park desk. We scoffed. Now we believe.

> "The mountain must stop; but we can continue." —David T, the Mango Medic

Location: South Mountain State Park, 32 miles southwest of Morganton.

Distance: 17.7-mile loop.

Approximate riding time: 4 to 6 hours.

Difficulty rating: Tech 3 overall. The saddles are flat and smooth, easy tech 1 rides. But most of the downhills are steep, covered with loose rocks, and littered with water bars of various construction. At least one tech 4 rocky section.

Trail surface: 15.7 miles of old Forest Service road/doubletrack; 2 miles of pavement.

Highlights: Formidable climbs; outrageous, rocky descents full of water bars; long-range views; wildlife; waterfall.

Land status: North Carolina state park. The only one to offer any real mountain biking. Thank you, South Mountain, for your foresight and consideration. We love these mountains, too. **Note:** The park closes between 6:00 P.M. and 9:00 P.M., depending on the season. Check at the office for closing time, because you'll be sleeping in the car if you don't get out before the gates are locked.

Maps: USGS Morganton South, Benn Knob; North Carolina State Parks Map Guide by Graphics, 2000; park map available at ranger station.

Finding the trailhead: Traveling on Interstate 40 West, south of Morganton, watch for the SOUTH MOUNTAIN STATE PARK sign. Take exit 105 and turn onto North Carolina Highway 18 South. Follow this for about 10 miles, then turn sharply back right onto Sugar Loaf Road. Go another 5 miles, then turn left at the Citgo station onto South Mountain Park Road. After another 2 miles, turn right onto a gravel road at the sign for South Mountain State Park. Follow the gravel road to the park entrance. The Headquarters Trail starts just at the edge on the parking lot.

Miles and Directions

0.0 Start from the parking lot. Turn left onto the Headquarters (HQ) Trail, up past the gate and the white house with the barking dogs. Flat, tech 1 gravel doubletrack. Be sure to sign in at the gate so the rangers will know how much we love their trail, and so they'll know if you don't make it back out.

0.2 Amphitheater down to left.

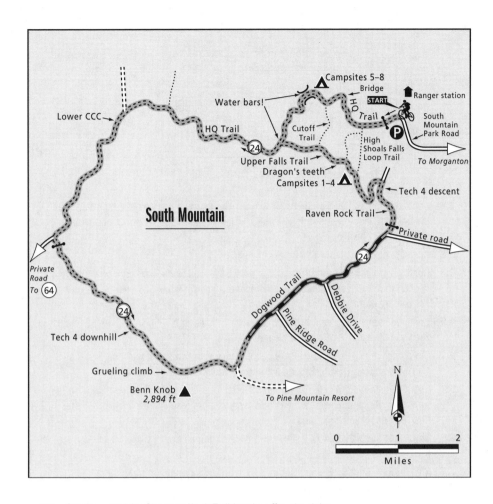

0.3 Continue straight. Chestnut Knob Trail breaks off to the right.

0.4 Small downhill with your first taste of water bars. Trail leads across a small wooden bridge.

0.5 Turn right uphill at this Y. Sign says TO SITES 5–8. Ride up steep, hardpacked gravel double-track with heavy erosion cuts and quick elevation gain.

0.7 Pretty cascade and swimming hole in stream down to left.

0.9 Wooden bridge.

1.3 Short descent, then cross another bridge. And now, my friends, the pain begins. Don't even look up; just start climbing. Tread is hardpacked dirt doubletrack sprinkled with loose chicken heads. This is one long, mean, tech 3 climb.

2.5 Turn right at this major intersection. Signs point right for Headquarters Trail, Shinny Trail, and Lower CCC Trail, and left for Upper Falls Trail, sites 1 through 4, and High Shoals Falls. Rest at this intersection until you're sure your heart won't explode. Then follow the trail right. Short climb, then the first of many scary descents with some wicked water bars and some serious speed.

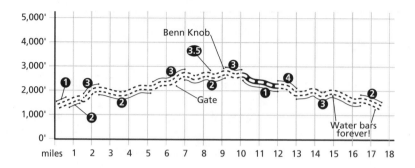

3.0 Continue straight. Jacobs Trail (walking only) breaks off to the left. Along the ridgetops, the trail is a wide-open dirt doubletrack. On the slopes, it's loose, rocky, and either deadly fast or heartbreakingly steep.

3.6 Continue straight. Shinny Trail breaks to right.

4.4 Continue straight. Old road (Horseridge Trail) breaks off to the right. By now you'll have noticed that you're surrounded by an emerald paradise. Relax and enjoy it—when you're not holding on for dear life.

4.9 Continue straight. Fox Trail breaks to left. Very difficult, tech 3+ climb; cluttered enough to keep you always searching for a cleaner line.

5.2 Top a ridge, then the bottom just falls out. Here's your first set of really big water bars with an excellent waist-high berm set in the middle: 8.5 on the fun meter.

5.7 Enormous steep, rocky climb (what else?). Get in granny early or plan on standing the whole way. Remember that you can ride every one of these climbs; it's just a matter of how much pain you can stand.

6.6 Turn left at the big yellow gate. Track straight is signed NO BIKES; I think it leads to a private road.

7.1 Sign for park boundary; double orange blazes. Flat, wide-open cruising terrain for a nice long while. Then back to falling down the mountain.

7.8 White sign: PARK BOUNDARY. NO GUNS. What a reassuring thought. Following downhill is a serious gravity run. It's steep, way fast, and sketchy as can be with lots of loose rocks that shift as you hit them. It was a squirrelly tech 4 descent, and we were all glad to survive it.

8.9 Unbearably long, hemorrhaging climb. Then a long saddle, then some more climbing. Then another flat, then some more climbing. This hill is all about pain and determination.

9.2 Continue straight. Singletrack to right signed NO BIKES probably leads to Benn Knob.

9.7 Turn sharp back left at this intersection, following sign for BIKES. Descent is fast and furious (like you expected something else). Then you get another serious granny-gear climb.

10.1 Trail dumps you onto Dogwood Trail, a paved road, which continues to run up and down the same ridgeline you've been on. You can *cook* on this puppy; I hit 40 miles per hour coasting!

10.7 Continue straight. Pine Ridge Road to right.

11.2 Continue straight. Debbie Drive to right, then Fern Lane. Incredible view that probably reaches 100 miles on a clear day.

12.0 Continue straight past gate onto Raven Rock Trail. Paved road turns right. Now that

The ride gets rocky at South Mountain.

you've had a taste of something more civilized, it's back to a steady diet of loose, sketchy downhills covered with chicken heads. Continual tech 3+ assault.

12.4 Trail cuts back sharply left. Now you get an even nastier downhill than the last one: a tech 4 field of loose boulders and mean water bars, tilted to a severe angle. Some of these water bars are 4 feet tall with some really ugly landing zones behind them. This is not a place for front brakes or for the faint of heart.

12.9 Trail turns back left again, this time onto Upper Falls Trail. Raven Rock continues straight with a NO BIKES sign. Continued descent snakes through a deep, dark, rhododendron forest with the ever-present water bars here and there.

13.4 Cross stream (Jacob's Fork), and ride past campsites 1 through 4. Portable toilet conveniently located here.

13.5 Turn left at this T. Right branch is one side of Falls Loop Trail (hiking only).

13.8 Tech 4 descent with dragon's teeth outlining the water bars. Hit the gaps in the teeth or jump them. Straight on is a bad idea.

14.1 Turn left again. The last real climb of the ride, and it's the ugly runt of the litter. If none of the other climbs broke you, this one just might do it. Trail straight ahead was the other side of Falls Loop Trail (hiking only).

14.5 Continue straight past the Cutoff Trail (hiking only) to the right.

15.1 Enter at the large, signed intersection where you started the loop, and hang the sharp right turn back onto Headquarters Trail. Swallow hard and hang on, 'cause you've probably never dropped a run like this before. Nearly 30 water bars on the way down, coming at you at warp speed. Just hang on, keep your butt back and your front wheel pointed downhill, and you'll probably be okay.

16.3 Cross bridge at bottom, near campsites 5 through 8. Only one last climb to make, and this one's a baby compared with the monsters you've already survived.

16.8 And one last serious descent. A number of big water bars, then a sizable boulder to launch from, backed up by a huge water bar that will probably send you for the record jump of the ride.

17.2 Bear left as trail drops you down to the lower intersection. Easy, flat run from here on out.

17.7 Return to parking lot. If you don't have a cooler full of cold drinks, you should probably go lie in the stream for a while.

25 Signal Hill

This is an excellent singletrack playground, particularly considering that it's one minute off the interstate. The builders have made excellent use of a limited space with a trail that twists and swoops over humps and bumps without seeming congested or slow. Lots of tight turns, multiple dips, and a half dozen excellent jumps along the back stretch keep it interesting. The trail is clearly marked and fairly easy to follow. Any time you're running past Statesville, take your bike and check it out; it's probably the best half hour you'll spend all day.

Location: Statesville.
Distance: 4.8-mile loop.
Approximate riding time: 30 to 45 minutes.
Difficulty rating: Tech 2 overall. Some tech 2+ roots and a tech 3 off-camber climb. But although the trail is relatively smooth, there are lots of dips, humps, and jumps that could spell disaster for beginners or anyone else liable to grab a handful of brakes at an inappropriate time.

Trail surface: Singletrack—nothing but singletrack.
Highlights: Humps; jumps; dips; roots; typical singletrack fare.
Land status: County park.
Maps: USGS Statesville East; map posted at trailhead.

Finding the trailhead: From Interstate 77 in Statesville, take exit 50 for Broad Street. Head east on Broad Street, passing a bunch of retail sprawl. Turn left at the third light onto Signal Hill Road. The park is less than a half mile on the right. The trailhead starts at the edge of the parking lot, just behind the information sign.

Miles and Directions

0.0 Trail begins just behind the information sign. Be sure to sign in on the sheet provided. Follow the hardpack track to the right, up behind the shopping center, then dive into the woods and start playing.

0.4 Lots of dips, one after another. Trail snakes down a little ravine and twists back and forth over some small roots for a constant tech 2 ride.

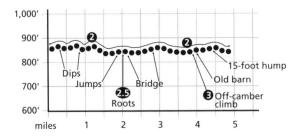

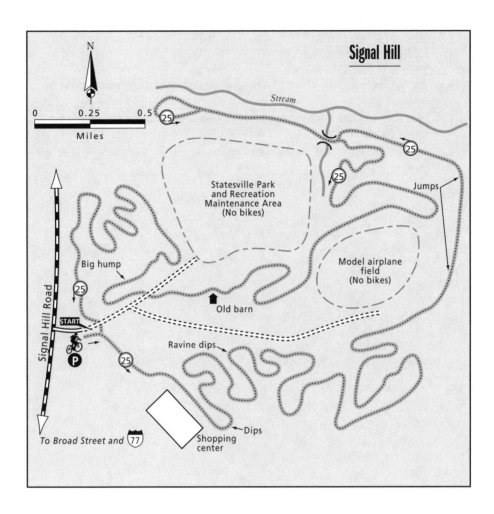

1.0 Trail runs the edge of the woods behind a red brick building. By now you've been grinning constantly for a mile, and there's more to come.

1.6 Bear right as the trail runs along the edge of the model airplane field. This leads you to five or six cool jumps along the back stretch. Good play-out after each jump; just stay out of the rough grass on either side.

2.2 Turn right across a fairly wide wooden bridge, then bear left along the edge of a field. Maintenance buildings up to your left, stream down to the right. Close trees make for some fun, tight gates to thread.

2.5 Trail loops for a short climb, then takes you back across the field on the same track you took in.

2.8 Recross the bridge and hang a right onto some freshly cut track.

3.2 Come out near the airplane field again. Cool, bermed sweeper turn shortly after.

3.4 Bear left at the Y, just at the far edge of the airfield.

3.9 Mean, off-camber, tech 3 climb. Pass an old tin-sided barn, and ride over a funky little bridge/pyramid, then cross a gravel service road; trail clearly picks up on other side of the road.

4.2 Get cranking to zip up a sudden 15-foot-tall hump, then drop off the back side and hit another 6-footer.

4.3 Trail closely parallels Signal Hill Road, heading toward a small power station and back toward the parking lot.

4.8 Return to parking lot, and probably set off on another loop because you haven't had your fill of fun yet.

Uwharrie National Forest

U wharrie National Forest sits alone in the middle of the Piedmont, its 1,000-foot peaks perching over the rest of the rolling hills. Through the diligent efforts of the Uwharrie Mountain Biking Association (UMBA), three loops of dedicated mountain bike trail are now open with as many as three more slated for construction. The Rattlesnake Loop was recently opened but I haven't had a chance to ride it yet. I hear it's a bear. Off-road vehicle trails are open in the upper section of the forest, and they are legendary in their brutality.

26 Uwharrie–Supertree

If you just want to enjoy the downhill and don't want to bother with long climbs or gnarly track, then you need to make several loops around Supertree. Once you start descending, it gets fast as hell with wide-bermed turns swooping through the trees and a dozen or more magnificent water bars for some supreme air. An easy return back up Wood Run Road sets you up for multiple trips around, sort of like a free pass to your favorite ride at the carnival.

Location: Uwharrie National Forest, 40 miles southeast of Asheboro, 30 miles east of Charlotte.

Distance: 7.7-mile lariat.

Approximate riding time: 45 minutes to 1.5 hours.

Difficulty rating: Tech 2. Supertree is fairly smooth, though multiple, knee-high water bars on the descent can up the ante a bit—particularly if you're cooking—and a few of the landing zones are a bit dicey. Wood Run Road is a tech 1 run, just long enough to give your legs a good warm-up and cool-down.

Trail surface: 1.5 miles of singletrack; 2.2 miles of dirt and gravel doubletrack; 4 miles of gravel road.

Highlights: Fast swoopy descent with big water bars; easy climb and return.

Land status: Uwharrie National Forest.

Maps: USGS Morrow Mountain; *Uwharrie Lakes Region Trail Guide,* by Don Childrey (excellent reference for all biking, hiking, and off-road vehicle trails in the area). Maps are posted at trailhead.

Finding the trailhead: From Asheboro take U.S. Highway 220 South. Exit onto North Carolina Highway 24/27 toward Troy. After you pass through Troy, go another 10 miles on NC 24/27, and watch for the Uwharrie National Forest–Wood Run Trails sign on the right. If you cross the Pee Dee River, you went too far.

From Charlotte take U.S. Highway 74 East. Exit at Albemarle Road, which is NC 24/27. Follow NC 24/27 through Albemarle and over the Pee Dee River. Park entrance is on the left.

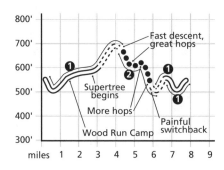

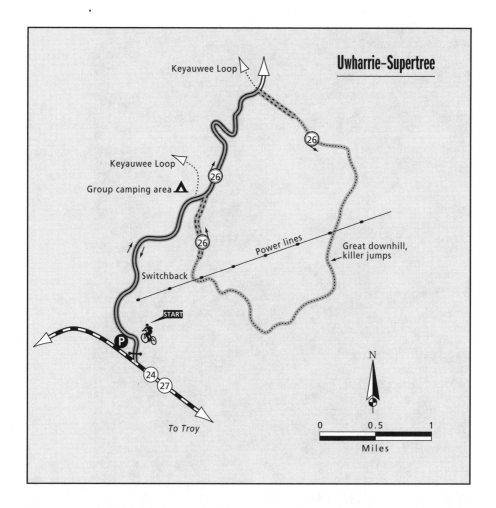

Miles and Directions

0.0 From the parking area ride in past the gate onto Wood Run Road (gravel). Easy, wide-open cruising for the next several miles.

1.4 Continue straight past the Wood Run campsite.

2.6 Turn right at this signed intersection onto the entrance to Supertree Loop. Tread starts off as gravel doubletrack, but don't despair, 'cause there's plenty of fun stuff farther on.

3.2 Bear left at this split, following the UMBA sign. Tread is still gravel doubletrack.

4.1 Doubletrack ends and true singletrack begins. Pass under the power lines and cross Dutchman's Trail (hiking only).

4.3 And now Supertree delivers. You get one teaser downhill with a few hops, a short climb, and then a long, raging descent. Numerous smooth-topped water bars along the drop with excellent launching potential. Beginning riders really need to keep their speed down, unless they want some impromptu flying lessons.

In retrospect, landing it would have been a much better alternative than bailing.

5.6 Trail turns sharply right as it hits the bottom and changes to dirt doubletrack. Some loose, fast running with a few small hops and some sharp corners.

5.8 Trail pops out to run along under the power lines for a bit. Cross a small stream then hit a respectable switchback and climb to get back out of the bottom. Tread changes from dirt to gravel doubletrack.

6.3 Turn left as you pop back out onto Wood Run Road, just across from the campsite.

7.7 Return to the trailhead and parking area.

27 Uwharrie–Keyauwee

Keyauwee offers up a little bit of everything: fast, snaky singletrack; sketchy down-hills; mean, rocky climbs; big whoop-dee-doos. It's the kind of trail that makes you work for your fun but still feels like a bargain. The good folks at UMBA did a great job with this one. At the end of Keyauwee, you can run right into Supertree Loop for some more serious downhilling, extending the ride by another 3 miles.

Location: Uwharrie National Forest, 40 miles southeast of Asheboro, 30 miles west of Char-lotte.
Distance: 8.9-mile lariat.
Approximate riding time: 1 to 2 hours.
Difficulty rating: Tech 2+. Keyauwee is a solid tech 2 singletrack for most of its length with a handful of tech 3 rocks and roots sprinkled along both the climbs and descents.

Trail surface: 3.9 miles of singletrack; 0.7 mile of doubletrack; 4.3 miles of gravel road.
Highlights: Sweet rocky downhills; water bars; long-range views.
Land status: Uwharrie National Forest.
Maps: USGS Morrow Mountain; *Uwharrie Lakes Region Trail Guide,* by Don Childrey (excellent reference for all biking, hiking, and off-road vehicle trails in the area).

Finding the trailhead: From Asheboro take U.S. Highway 220 South. Exit onto North Carolina Highway 24/27, and head toward Troy. After you pass through Troy, go another 10 miles on NC 24/27, and watch for the Uwharrie National Forest–Wood Run Trails sign on the right. If you cross the Pee Dee River, you went too far.
From Charlotte take U.S. Highway 74 East. Exit at Albemarle Road, which is NC 24/27. Follow NC 24/27 through Albemarle and over the Pee Dee River. Park entrance is shortly on the left.

Miles and Directions

0.0 From the parking area ride in past the gate onto Wood Run Road (gravel). Easy, wide-open cruising for the next mile or so.

1.4 Turn left as you hit the opening for Wood Run campsite. Turn just before the portable toi-let, hug the side of the clearing, and run right up to the entrance sign for Keyauwee Loop. Trail starts off with a tough, tech 2+ rooty section, sort of an entrance toll.

1.6 Bear left at the Y. Track straight is blocked off; may be an old hiking trail.

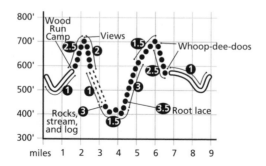

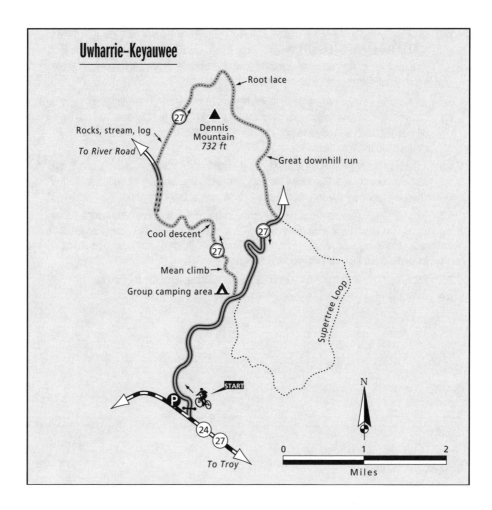

Uwharrie-Keyauwee

Root lace

27

Dennis
Mountain
732 ft

Rocks, stream, log

To River Road

Great downhill run

Cool descent

27

27

Mean climb

Group camping area

27

Supertree Loop

START

P

N

24
27

To Troy

0   1   2

Miles

1.8   Hit a long, painful, rocky climb. This one will have you howling *No más!* by the time you reach the top.

2.0   Climb finally ends, and you get an adrenaline-boosting descent along the edge of an old clearcut. Fast run with lots of loose chicken heads and a few small bunny hops through some tight undergrowth. Nice view from the top.

2.3   Trail flattens and feeds into an old gravel doubletrack.

2.7   Another pretty long-range view to left.

3.0   Trail gets a bit fast and loose as it changes from doubletrack to gravel road.

3.3   Turn right onto clear singletrack that peels off and drops down into the trees. UMBA sign is hidden in bushes, but trail entrance is very clear. Immediate, tech 3 descent over some big rocks, ending in a tech 3 stream crossing with a respectable log to back it up. Last time through we found a huge rattlesnake lying by this log, so keep your eyes peeled and your feet on your pedals.

3.6   Keyauwee mellows and offers some gentle tech 1+ up-and-down for a while. Red blazes mark the trail.

3.9 Triple set of shallow dips set into an otherwise smooth section of trail, just to remind you not to take things for granted. These hungry little suckers are just deep enough to grab your front wheel and either toss you on your face or bring delicate parts of your anatomy into painful contact with your bike stem.

4.4 Tech 3 stream crossing leads you into a long, ugly, and off-camber climb.

4.7 Straight at this crossroads, continuing on Keyauwee. Cross the Uwharrie Trail (hiking only). Long, tech 3+ root lace just after the intersection, then some more off-camber climbing dotted with tech 3 rocks.

5.8 A little flat, tech 1+ cruising leads you to the start of a rip-roaring downhill. Descent is fast and more than a little loose in spots with some great whoop-dee-doos and a few small logs as incentive to improve your hopping skills. Excellent run!

6.3 Turn right as Keyauwee drops back onto Wood Run Road. If you've had enough, follow Wood Run (and the following trail notes) back to the trailhead. The gravel can get really loose in the corners, so take it easy or be ready to drift. If you still want more, hang an immediate left instead and dive into Supertree.

7.5 Pass the Wood Run camp on your right. Continue straight for the trailhead.

8.9 Return to the trailhead and parking area.

Boone

B oone sports several cool rides right within town limits. But the real riding is in the Wilson Creek area, about twenty minutes southeast of town, in the heart of Pisgah's Grandfather Mountain district. The entire Yancey's Ridge, Schoolhouse Ridge, and Wilson Creek system probably contains more than 35 miles of phenomenal track.

28 Woodruff Ridge

This is one crazy—if short—downhill. If you like it fast and ugly, this is your place. Beginners should avoid this place; everyone else should use (or abandon) caution. Extremely tough stream crossings, narrow and unpredictable lines, and a pair of boulder drops make for some serious launch (and damage) potential. The waterfall below the parking area provides the perfect place to soak your wounded pride and body after the ride.

Location: Globe, about 15 miles south of Blowing Rock.
Distance: 7.5-mile loop.
Approximate riding time: 45 minutes to 1.5 hours.
Difficulty rating: Singletrack starts off as tech 2, then jumps to tech 3+ on the downhill with several tech 4 stream crossings and a pair of tech 4+ boulder drops.

Trail surface: 1.8 miles of singletrack; 0.5 mile of gated Forest Service road; 5.2 miles of gravel road.
Highlights: Hard-core descent; technical creek crossings; steep narrow track; big rocks; beautiful lush undergrowth and big trees.
Land status: Pisgah National Forest.
Maps: USGS Globe; USDA Forest Service Wilson Creek Area Trail Map.

Finding the trailhead: From Blowing Rock turn off Main Street (U.S. Highway 321 Business) onto Globe Road. Follow this twisting gravel road south for about 6 miles until you hit the tiny town of Globe. Turn right onto Anthony Creek Road (North Carolina Highway 1362). Go about 2 miles, and watch for a parking spot on the right on an inside curve. Very nice campsite and excellent waterfall on Anthony Creek to the right. Trailhead is just across the road on the left.

Miles and Directions

0.0 From the parking area turn right, continuing up Anthony Creek Road (NC 1362). Follow this gravel road up to the hamlet of Gragg.

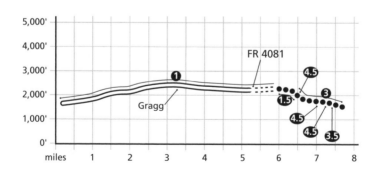

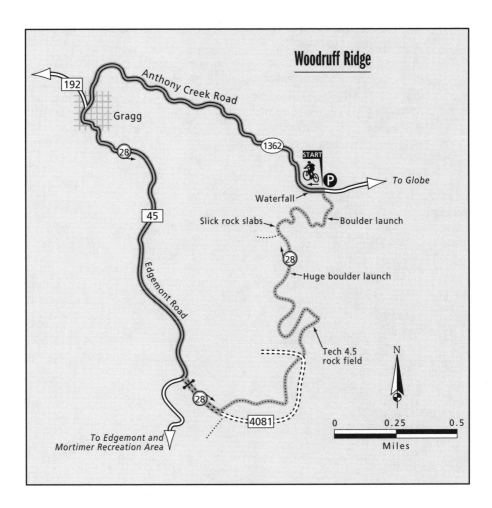

Woodruff Ridge

192

Anthony Creek Road

Gragg

28

1362

START

P

To Globe

Waterfall

Slick rock slabs

Boulder launch

28

Huge boulder launch

45

Edgemont Road

Tech 4.5
rock field

N

28

4081

To Edgemont and
Mortimer Recreation Area

0   0.25   0.5

Miles

3.2   At Gragg, turn left onto Edgemount Road (Forest Road 45).

5.2   Turn left onto Forest Road 4081 (gated Forest Service road).

5.7   Turn left onto dirt singletrack. Starts off with some slight downhill, fairly level, tech 1+ track. Don't be fooled though; this is like the first sip of grain alcohol punch: deceiving and deadly.

5.9   Cross old logging road. Begin some narrow contour running.

6.2   Drop down a narrow ledge back onto FR 4081 and turn right just for a bit. Watch for immediate sharp left back onto the singletrack. Here starts the downhill assault with an initial salvo of tech 4 roots. Then you get an extremely dicey tech 4+ rock field, followed by a pair of tech 3 stream crossings.

6.8   A 3-foot-high boulder planted in the middle of the trail for a *big* rock move (tech 4+). This puppy can launch you 12 or 15 feet down the trail with a narrow, sketchy landing zone. While you're celebrating your successful landing, don't bust in the pair of bad, tech 3 stream crossings that follow.

7.1 Trail bears right; old, unused track crosses stream to left. Just after, watch for some slippery and downright dangerous rock slabs, tech 4+, that carry some serious bust potential. Then more crazy speed, roots, and rocks.

7.3 Second rock launching pad, though this one is only a tech 3+ and good for only 8 to 10 feet of air time.

7.5 Drop down onto the road, and return to parking area.

29 Long Yancey

This trail offers you everything you can handle and more. It starts with Short Yancey's long, brutal climb, then throws in some even nastier ones later for good measure. Along the way, it hands out insane switchbacks that go on for days, boulder fields, incredibly tight tunnel running, whoop-dee-doos, and a hair-raising gravel road run. The swimming hole along Forest Road 45 is a required stop, along with Coffey's General Store.

Smart riders will leave a shuttle vehicle at Coffey's and avoid the 4-mile gravel road climb back to the start. You won't be missing out on much other than a whole lot of pain.

Location: Roseborough; about twenty-five minutes south of Blowing Rock.
Distance: 17-mile loop.
Approximate riding time: 3 to 5 hours.
Difficulty rating: Tech 3 overall. Several tech 4 descents of various flavors and textures will have you shaking in your shoes. Several tough technical climbs and creek crossings. It would not be kind to take novices on this trail.
Trail surface: 3.1 miles of singletrack; 4.6 miles of old Forest Service road; 9.3 miles of gravel road.

Highlights: Rocky climbs; crazy rocky descents; whoop-dee-doos; rhododendron tunnel running; creek crossings; huge erosion gully; high-speed gravel road run; excellent swimming hole; Coffey's General Store.
Land status: Pisgah National Forest.
Maps: USGS Globe; USDA Forest Service Wilson Creek Area Trail Map.

Finding the trailhead: From Blowing Rock or Boone, take the Blue Ridge Parkway south. Turn left onto North Carolina Highway 1511 (Roseborough Road), near Grandmother Mountain and the town of Linville. Follow NC 1511 for 7 miles or so past the tiny town of Roseborough. Watch for a wide parking area on the right, just before a short concrete bridge over Webb Creek. Forest Road 192 heads uphill across the road.

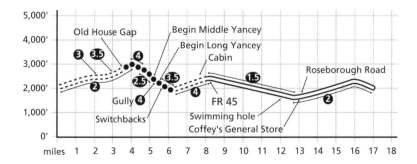

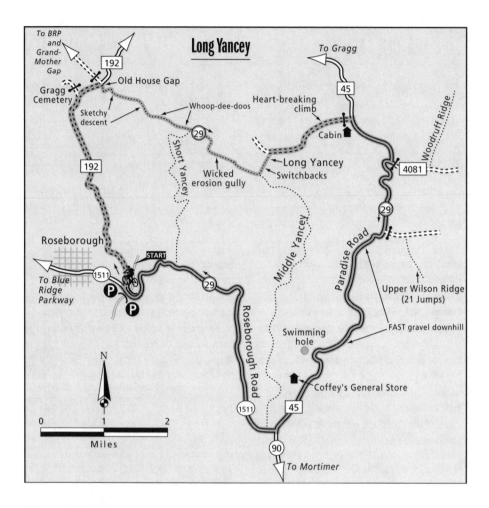

Miles and Directions

0.0 Like all the Yancey Ridge trails, this one leaves the parking area, crosses Roseborough Road, and starts up FR 192. It's the first of many long, painful climbs, though this one is probably the worst. Ignore all the various side trails and turnoffs until you reach Old House Gap. Just find a good gear and keep chugging.

2.0 Tech 3 rock garden. Only one good line, and that switches back and forth all over. Red-blazed trail down left toward the stream.

2.6 Shallow cave to the right. Gorgeous cascade and swimming hole down left at the stream.

2.7 Steep and painful tech 3+ rocky climb. Believe it or not, we once met a small Ford station wagon coming down the trail at this spot! What were those guys drinking?

2.8 Continue straight past gated road on the left. Sign: ROAD CLOSED. FOOT TRAFFIC WELCOME. I believe this leads to the old Gragg Cemetery.

There are many creeks in the Wilson Ridge area.

3.2 Enter intersection at Old House Gap. Turn right up short incline onto singletrack; stub of brown USDA Forest Service sign can be found if you look hard. Gated road to the left leads up to the Blue Ridge Parkway. Gravel road straight is continuation of FR 192, which leads to Gragg.

3.4 Bear left uphill at this Y. Trail tops along a ridgeline, then drops with several sweet whoop-dee-doos.

4.6 Go straight onto Middle Yancey. Get set for a mean, rocky climb that's no fun at all. Turn back right leads to Short Yancey.

5.0 Major erosion gully with steep sides and big drops. Lines wander and often just disappear, so be prepared to hop a lot. Call it a tech 4 move to clean the whole thing.

5.4 Fast contour running leads you to a couple of awfully skanky mudholes. Then some faster, rooty descending.

5.6 Turn sharply back left onto Long Yancey (straight is continuation of Middle Yancey). You'll run through a long, tight rhododendron tunnel filled deep with leaves, then hit a crazy section of steep, tech 3+, 180-degree switchbacks.

5.9 Follow Long Yancey as it bears left, down over some whoop-dee-doos, out on a finger, then down some more. Turn right at the T that follows. More insane switchbacks, these filled with rocks and roots.

6.1 Straight across Wilson Creek. This wide stream crossing is doable, but tough, with a mean little boulder field on the far side: Call it a tech 4.

6.2 Second stream crossing is more ridable but shouldered by a tech 4+ climb. After pushing your way up this, you get dropped onto an old doubletrack beside an old cabin. Then the series repeats itself for a while: rock, stream, more rocks, bigger stream, fall down, get up, more rocks.

7.0 Begin the worst climb of the ride: just a steep, eroded, long dirt road. Don't look up, just keep grinding.

7.6 Pass a white gate and pop out onto Forest Road 45, Paradise Road (gravel). Another cabin sits just to the right. And now's a good time for a break, before the long drop back. Gravel road descent that follows is fast and crazy with loose, deep gravel and erosion bumps filling the inside corners, 180-degree switchbacks, and occasional drainage ditches. Watch for auto traffic.

8.5 Continue straight down FR 45. Gated road to left leads to Woodruff Ridge Trail.

9.4 Continue straight down FR 45. Gated road to left leads to Upper Wilson Ridge Trail (21 Jumps).

12.0 Cross concrete bridge. Wilson Creek provides a gorgeous, deep, cool swimming hole. This is a required stop if you've been cranking all day in the heat. At some unknown point, FR 45 has changed into North Carolina Highway 90.

13.0 Stop at Coffey's General Store. Go through the doors here, and take a step back in time. They even sell those tiny, ice-cold bottles of Coca-Cola. The folks here are real friendly and have great stories to tell. Ask politely, and they'll let you park your shuttle vehicle across the road and save yourself the next 4 miles of climbing, an option I highly recommend.

13.2 Turn right at the Edgemont Baptist Church onto Roseborough Road.

17.0 Return to the parking area near Roseborough.

30 Short Yancey

You pay your money up front for this ride; that means starting out with an unrelenting 3.2-mile climb. But such pain buys you a buffet of downhills to enjoy on the way back: smooth, fast, dirt cruisers; eroded and fickle hardpack; sick, tilted boulder fields; and slippery gravel screamers. Although novices might walk a section or three, anyone with the grit to make the opening climb will enjoy this trail thoroughly.

Location: Roseborough; about twenty-five minutes south of Blowing Rock.
Distance: 9-mile loop.
Approximate riding time: 2 to 3 hours.
Difficulty rating: Tech 2 overall. Several tech 3 rock sections on both climb and descent. The first drop after Old House Gap is a long, nasty tech 4 that will chew you up and spit you out if you're not careful.

Trail surface: 4.8 miles of singletrack; 3.2 miles of old Forest Service road; 1 mile of gravel road.
Highlights: Whoop-dee-doos; screaming descents of various flavors; big berms; hemlock coves.
Land status: Pisgah National Forest.
Maps: USGS Globe; USDA Forest Service Wilson Creek Area Trail Map.

Finding the trailhead: From Blowing Rock or Boone, take the Blue Ridge Parkway south. Turn left onto North Carolina Highway 1511 (Roseborough Road), near Grandmother Mountain and the town of Linville. Follow NC 1511 for 7 miles or so past the tiny town of Roseborough. Watch for a wide parking area on the right, just before a short concrete bridge over Webb Creek. Forest Road 192 heads uphill across the road.

Miles and Directions

0.0 From the parking area, cross Roseborough Road, and start up FR 192, an old, rocky, tech 2 doubletrack. And thus begins one long, painful climb. Ignore all the various side trails and turnoffs until you reach Old House Gap. Just find a good gear and keep chugging.

2.0 Tech 3 rock garden. Only one good line, and that switches back and forth all over. Red-blazed trail down left toward the stream.

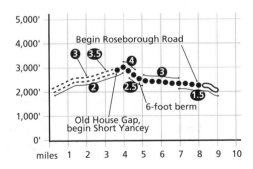

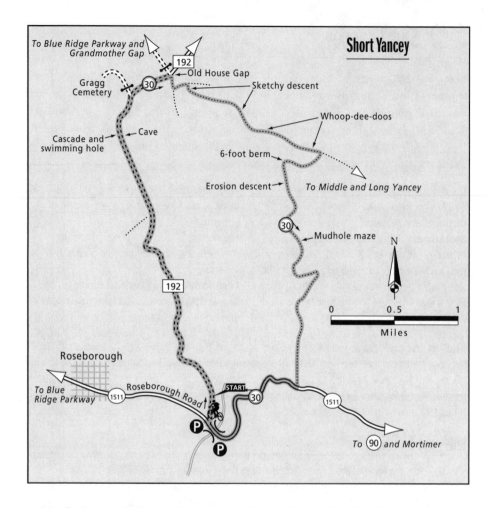

Short Yancey

To Blue Ridge Parkway and
Grandmother Gap

192

Old House Gap

Gragg
Cemetery

30

Sketchy descent

Whoop-dee-doos

Cascade and
swimming hole

Cave

6-foot berm

Erosion descent

To Middle and Long Yancey

192

30

Mudhole maze

N

0   0.5   1
Miles

Roseborough

To Blue
Ridge Parkway

1511

Roseborough Road

START

30

1511

To 90 and Mortimer

2.6 Shallow cave to the right. Gorgeous cascade and swimming hole down left at the stream.

2.7 Steep and painful tech 3+ rocky climb.

2.8 Continue straight past gated road on the left. Sign: ROAD CLOSED. FOOT TRAFFIC WELCOME. I believe this leads to the old Gragg Cemetery.

3.2 Enter intersection at Old House Gap. Turn right up short incline onto singletrack; stub of brown Forest Service sign can be found if you look hard. Gated road to the left leads up to the Blue Ridge Parkway. Gravel road straight is continuation of FR 192, which leads to Gragg.

3.4 Bear left uphill at this Y. Trail tops along a ridgeline, then drops with several sweet whoop-dee-doos.

3.8 Turn sharp right, downhill. Sign straight says NO BIKES. NO HORSES. The following downhill is certainly scary and probably dangerous. It's loose, fast, and filled with some nasty, hungry-looking rocks. It's a tech 4 descent for certain. After it flattens and clears up, you get a long, fast tech 2 tunnel run that's smooth and sweet with some great whoop-dee-doos.

Climbing up Short Yancey. DAVID TOLLERTON PHOTO

4.4 Turn sharply back right at this T. More fast descending with a long series of sweeping inside turns.

4.9 Berms keep getting bigger and bigger until you hit one monster that stands 6 or 7 feet tall. More whoop-dee-doos to follow, then a sketchy, eroded, tech 3+ descent with lines that wander and disappear unexpectedly.

5.8 Super mudhole maze with holes that are hub-deep. Thread your way through or guess which is the shallow one.

6.5 Climbing through a thick rhododendron tunnel. Pass an old road to the right, then bomb another rocky, tech 3 downhill. Big, tight switchback into a mean-spirited climb.

7.3 Flat, tech 1+ contour running through a majestic hemlock grove.

7.9 Turn right when you drop back out onto Roseborough Road. Now, for one last shot of adrenaline: a long, fast gravel downhill with a huge switchback in the middle. Watch for car traffic.

9.0 Return to the parking area. Nearby Webb Creek is the perfect spot for cooling your feet, head, or entire body.

31 Wilson–Schoolhouse Ridge Loop

This is a true Jekyll-and-Hyde ride. Wilson Ridge is a cultured sort of trail, a smooth, dirt-faced roller coaster for most of its length, with whoops and jumps to delight even the most jaded bike pilot. The locals lovingly refer to this section of trail as 21 Jumps. Schoolhouse Ridge, however, is its homicidal, crackhead cousin. Blind turns through the mountain laurel suddenly drop you into 4-foot erosion gullies, ravines, and packs of sick root drops that would like nothing more than to break your bones. It's a sadistic piece of riding. Put the two together, and you've got something to alternately delight and terrify just about anyone. And believe it or not, the locals recently rerouted Schoolhouse to take out some of the worst stuff. Watch for a lot of debris and downed trees, courtesy of the winter storms.

> "Dooooode! That was hard core, man!"—Excitable Boy
> "You forgot to mention the climb, Timm."—Mud Pie

Location: Mortimer, about forty minutes south of Blowing Rock, 1.5 hours north of Morganton.

Distance: 11-mile loop.

Approximate riding time: 2 to 3 hours.

Difficulty rating: Tech 3 to 4.5. Wilson Ridge has only one tough rooty section, with lots of easy cruising and airlifts. Schoolhouse Ridge, on the other hand, is a war zone, filled with expert-level root drops and erosion gullies.

Trail surface: 5.6 miles of singletrack; 5.4 miles of gravel road.

Highlights: Twenty-one (or more) gorgeous jumps; ridge running; horrific root drops and ravines.

Land status: Pisgah National Forest, Grandfather Mountain District.

Maps: USGS Globe; USDA Forest Service Wilson Creek Area Trail Map.

Finding the trailhead: Follow Interstate 40 to Morganton. Take exit 105, North Carolina Highway 18 North, into Morganton. As soon as you get into town, continue straight onto North Carolina Highway 181, as NC 18 takes a funky break off to the right. Follow NC 181 north 12 miles, then turn right onto Brown Mountain Beach Road (there are clear signs for NC Bike Route #2). Go 4 miles, and turn left onto Ralph Winchester Road (Forest Road 1328) by a brown sign for Brown Mountain Beach. Follow FR 1328 to its end (only 8 miles, but it feels like 50) and a T with North Carolina Highway 90. Turn left, and immediately pass Mortimer Recreation Area, the place to leave a shuttle vehicle, if you're so fortunate. Follow NC 90 for 5 miles up the mountain, past Edgemont and Coffey's General Store, then past Forest Road 4068. After a particularly steep section in the road, watch for an unmarked dirt road and parking area on the right, with a metal gate at the far end (if you pass Forest Road 4081, you've gone too far). Park here, and ride past the gate into a small meadow. The entrance to Wilson Ridge is immediately to your right; look closely, as it's sometimes overgrown.

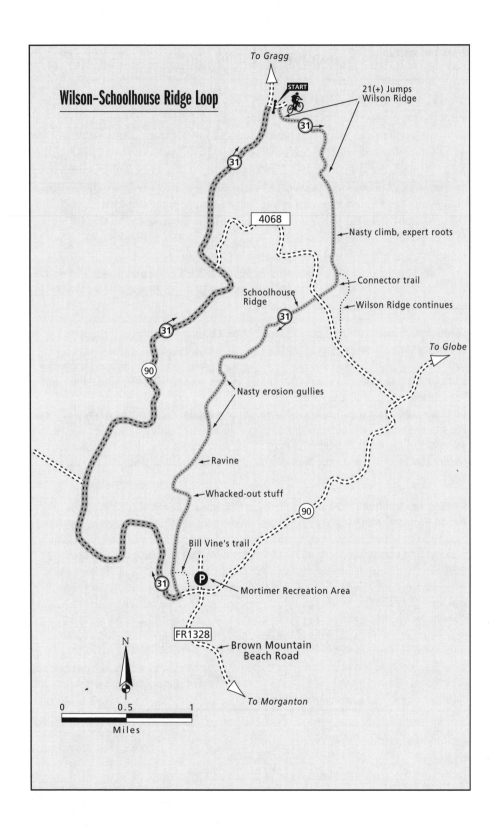

Wilson-Schoolhouse Ridge Loop

To Gragg

START

21(+) Jumps
Wilson Ridge

31

31

4068

Nasty climb, expert roots

Connector trail

Schoolhouse
Ridge

31

Wilson Ridge continues

90

31

To Globe

Nasty erosion gullies

Ravine

Whacked-out stuff

90

Bill Vine's trail

31

P

Mortimer Recreation Area

FR1328

Brown Mountain
Beach Road

To Morganton

N

0   0.5   1
Miles

Miles and Directions

0.0 From the entrance off NC 90, ride around the metal gate out into a small meadow. Hug the right side, and immediately hit the (unsigned) entrance to Upper Wilson Ridge, better known as 21 Jumps. Buffed launching ramps start almost immediately, with clear landings and plenty of run-out. Easy, tech 2 track. Not an especially fast descent, just fun to the core. Watch for a couple of deep mudholes that span the trail.

0.8 Short but steep climb, up over some of those fine water bars.

1.0 Continue straight past an old road on the right. More descending and more water bars, but this time it's a bit dicey and loose—steeper, too.

1.5 Long, rooty, ego-crushing climb, topped off with an ultramean tech 4 root lace at the base of a big tree. Then a 30-foot-long puzzle of roots, hungry for front wheels and kneecaps.

1.9 Turn right at this T, onto the connector trail, for a quick trip down to FR 4068. The connector is steep and rocky, a sketchy tech 3.5 run with lots of hops and drops, washouts and berms.

2.3 Drop onto FR 4068 (gravel), and cut straight across for the entrance to Schoolhouse Ridge. Picks up with some fairly flat ridgeline running, and lots of nice, gooey mudholes—perfect for decorating your buddies' jerseys. Here's the bailout point for anyone who just wants to play on 21 Jumps without risking the wrath of Schoolhouse. Just turn right onto FR 4068, run it out till you hit NC 90 again, then turn right and ride a mile or two back up to your vehicle.

2.6 Easy descent through a saddle, then a long, rambling climb.

2.8 Split left at this Y, following a smooth, tech 1 hardpacked doubletrack. Easy downhill contouring follows, with some gorgeous swoopy berms and more chances for some fine air. This section bypasses some of the old trail that was completely bombed out.

3.4 Still cooking along the contours, 1- to 2-foot drops start to crop up, but at this speed you can just sail off them with only a grin.

3.9 Uphill climbing through a rhododendron tunnel. Cool scenery, but a painful climb all the same, over slippery roots and leaves.

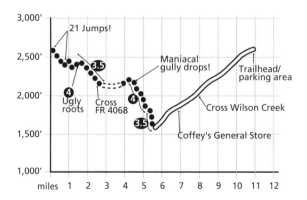

4.2 Trail peaks at the top of the ridge by a nice campsite. Cut left through the campsite to pick up the new singletrack on the other side. Here's a good place for the application of both body armor and prayers of safety. The descent down Schoolhouse starts off steep as hell, with a nasty switchback in the rhodo leaves, then a long series of tech 4 root drops, ledges, and deep erosion gullies. Lots of serious crash-and-burn potential, so be sure or walk it.

4.5 Surf down a crazy gully-run, with menacing drops one after another. Your only hope to ride this is to just let it roll, jump the deepest spots, and hope for the best.

5.1 The pounding finally slacks off as the trail runs out along a finger through some tight rhododendron tunnels. At a small clearing, choice of straight on Schoolhouse to the road, or sharp left to drop down Bill Vine's trail into the campground. Schoolhouse is fast and rooty. Bill Vine's is very narrow, with slippery off-camber sections through the rhododendron. Both are interesting choices.

5.3 From Schoolhouse, you drop suddenly out onto NC 90, with Mortimer Recreation Area down to the left. Bill Vine's trail drops you onto the campground road. Turn left to return to the parking area.

5.5 Return to parking area at Mortimer. Celebrate your survival appropriately. If you are unfortunate enough not to have a shuttle vehicle waiting, turn left onto NC 90, and get ready for a long, long gravel road ride.

6.5 Continue straight on NC 90, past the Edgemont Baptist Church and the intersection with Roseborough Road.

7.0 Pass Coffey's General Store, the perfect spot to refuel yourself before the grind back to the top.

8.0 Cross over Wilson Creek on a wide, concrete bridge. On a hot summer day, nothing beats this swimming hole.

9.1 Continue straight past FR 4068.

11.0 Turn right into the trailhead/parking area for Wilson Ridge.

Pisgah National Forest

Pisgah National Forest is the Queen Mother of eastern singletracking. If Tsali is the Autobahn of riding, then Pisgah is the Eco-Challenge. The trails here will thrash you, thrill you, scare the bejeebers out of you, and send you home with a grin that will make people worry about you. These woods contain some of the most beautiful trails—as well as some of the most hideous goat paths—that you can find anywhere. Enjoy, but be aware that the Queen often demands a sacrifice—in blood.

32 Little Avery Loop

Don't know if you're up for Pisgah's charms? This short loop offers a chance for some easy speed, some respectable roots, and an advanced stream crossing before the quick return back to the start. If all that does is whet your appetite for further adventure, then check out the Buckhorn Gap Loop or parts of Big Avery Creek. This is a good trail on which to gauge an unknown rider's skills before venturing on to the serious riding that awaits up above.

Location: Pisgah National Forest, Davidson River Campground area, forty-five minutes south of Asheville.
Distance: 2.2-mile loop.
Approximate riding time: 30 minutes to 1 hour.
Difficulty rating: Tech 2. Excellent introductory ride to give someone a small taste of what Pisgah has to offer. Some rocks, a tech 3+ root section, and a seriously mean tech 4+ stream crossing to keep newbies from getting too cocky.
Trail surface: 1.8 miles of singletrack; 0.4 mile of gravel road.
Highlights: Fast cruising; rocks and roots; stream crossing.
Land status: Pisgah National Forest.
Maps: USGS Pisgah Forest; USDA Forest Service Pisgah District Trail Map; National Geographic Trails Illustrated Pisgah Ranger District.

Finding the trailhead: From Asheville take Interstate 26 East (actually south) to North Carolina Highway 280 South. Follow NC 280 for about 15 miles to the town of Brevard. Turn right onto U.S. Highway 276, which leads up into the heart of the Pisgah National Forest. About 2 miles in, pass the Pisgah Ranger Station, and turn right onto Forest Road 477 (gravel road), following the sign for the Pisgah Horse Stables. Go about another 2 miles, pass the gated road for the horse stables on your right, then watch for the second parking area on the right. Look close, and you'll see the sign for Buckhorn Gap Trail.

Miles and Directions

0.0 Head in from the parking area onto Buckhorn Gap Trail. A smooth, tech 1+ run, maybe the smoothest run you'll find in Pisgah. Small dips and root drops along the way.

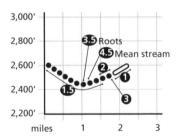

Little Avery Loop

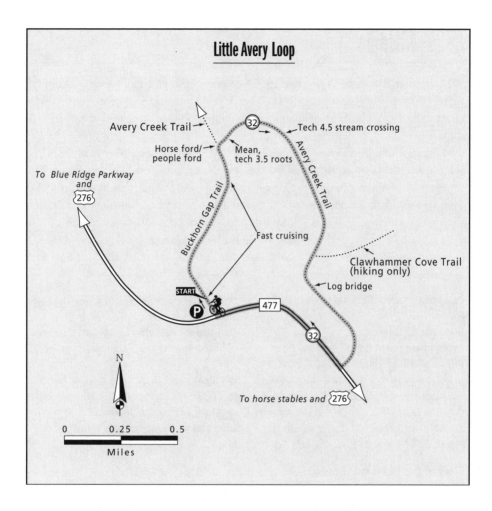

0.9 Turn sharply back right onto the lower section of Avery Creek Trail. Watch for a particularly mean section of tech 3+ roots.

1.3 Extremely tricky tech 4+ stream crossing with a nasty, root-strewn lead in. Several log bridges both before and after.

1.5 Small waterfall on your right.

1.6 Continue straight past Clawhammer Cove Trail (hiking only) on your left.

1.7 Tough, tech 3 climb up some slippery water bars.

1.8 Turn right as you come out onto FR 477. Watch for cars.

2.2 Return to the parking area.

33 Kitsuma

Kitsuma is an awesome ride—period. Once you climb past the dozen or so initial switchbacks (which, strangely enough, are kind of fun in their own right), you're faced with a torpedo run down along knife-edge ridgelines that drop forever. You'll drop a ridge, switchback, then contour run until the next ridge peels off, over and over again. Most of the trail is smooth and buff, but screaming down an 18-inch-wide track along a sixty-degree fall line brings its own form of adrenaline. The return trip is 5 miles of easy cruising on an abandoned and gated section of old U.S. Highway 70, with excellent views of the ridgeline you just descended. I can't do it justice; just ride this trail and it'll instantly be one of your top-five favorites.

"That was some sick singletrack. I dug it." —David T
"Man! Mom is fast for an old lady." —Laura Lou

Location: Between Black Mountain and Old Fort.

Distance: 10.3-mile loop.

Approximate riding time: 1.5 to 2.5 hours.

Difficulty rating: Tech 2+ overall. Most of the singletrack is smooth, fast, and clear. However, a number of the downhill switchbacks rate a tech 3 to tech 4. The real difficulty here is that the trail is so fast and so bloody narrow in places, it's barely wider than your tires. You

could sleep on the return trip if you could only keep pedaling.

Trail surface: 5 miles of singletrack; 3.8 miles of abandoned highway; 1.5 miles of pavement.

Highlights: Knife-edge ridge running; fast contour runs; switchbacks aplenty; tight mountain laurel thickets; incredible views.

Land status: Pisgah National Forest.

Maps: USGS Old Fort.

Finding the trailhead: From Asheville take Interstate 40 to exit 66 for Ridgecrest. Turn left (north) at the top of the ramp. Just over the bridge turn right onto Dunsmore Avenue. Follow this road straight, past a stop sign, and onto King George Road. Follow King George to the end and a small parking area with a sign for Kitsuma Peak Trail and Old Fort Picnic Area.

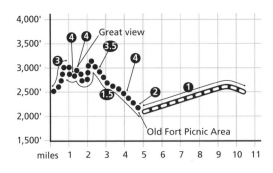

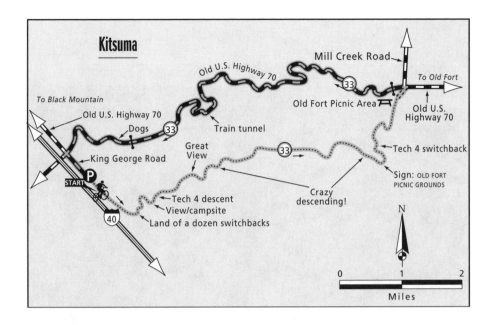

Kitsuma

Old U.S. Highway 70 · To Black Mountain · Old U.S. Highway 70 · Dogs · 33 · Train tunnel · King George Road · Great View · START · P · 40 · Tech 4 descent · View/campsite · Land of a dozen switchbacks · Crazy descending! · 33 · Mill Creek Road · To Old Fort · 33 · Old Fort Picnic Area · Old U.S. Highway 70 · Tech 4 switchback · Sign: OLD FORT PICNIC GROUNDS · N · 0 · 1 · 2 · Miles

Miles and Directions

0.0 Trail begins by sign for Kitsuma Trail and Old Fort Picnic Area. Tread starts as grassy doubletrack. The semis on I-40 will be rolling by only 20 feet away, but you'll soon leave them far behind and below.

0.3 Trail cuts sharply left uphill: true singletrack with a steep, tech 3 rocky and rooty climb. Yellow blazes lead you through the first two switchbacks.

0.5 Another eight switchbacks in a row. All of them are tight, with some sporting mean tech 3 roots and others wide open. Fairly flat, tech 1+ riding in between.

0.9 Switchback 11 brings you by a rocky ledge with views of Black Mountain and Montreat. In June the blooming mountain laurel walls the trail with pink-and-white blossoms.

1.0 Trail enters a small campsite clearing and continues on the other side across some large rock slabs. The first descent of the ride starts here, and it's probably the toughest: a seriously steep, eroded, tech 4 drop that requires you to just let it go and hang on.

1.2 Round a corner and start dropping again. This time you're running an 18-inch-wide trail across a sixty-degree fall line, then through a tight switchback, with little room for error.

1.3 Gorgeous view over the entire valley. After you pocket the camera, get ready for a very sketchy, tech 4 switchback, followed by some narrow, slippery, off-camber contour running. Trail here is only a tech 1+, but then again it's only about as wide as your tires, and the drop off the side is pretty imposing.

1.7 Pair of switchbacks up, both very tight, for a last bit of elevation gain. Then the bottom drops out, and you're zooming down a saddle through extremely tight laurel thickets. Sometimes all you can do is drop your head and follow your wheel. From here out Kitsuma hits a really sweet rhythm: fast saddle, ridgeline run, tight switchback, scorching

Take time to appreciate the view of Kitsuma Trail on the return trip.

contouring, then into the next saddle. It's a 9 on the fun scale and just doesn't seem to end.

3.5 Tight, tech 3+ switchback. You're simply bombing it at this point, so keep an eye peeled for the sudden turns.

3.9 Trail turns left at sign: OLD FORT PICNIC GROUNDS. Watch out for the off-camber contouring just after this, as my back wheel dropped over the edge three times within 50 feet.

4.0 Another extremely tight, tech 4 switchback. Contouring that follows holds a huge inside berm. Try really hard not to look over the side as you're running, 'cause the drop will make you woozy. Watch for a nasty washout along the way.

4.3 Fly over a crazy, tech 3+ rootball in the middle of the trail and try to land on a 10-inch-wide ledge on the other side. It's a screamer, whether you make it or not.

4.6 Trail flattens and starts running beside a small creek. Tech 2 trail gives you a few small roots to bunny hop.

4.9 Kitsuma finally ends, dumping you out into the Old Fort Picnic Area. You'll find bathrooms and water here, along with some wide-eyed picnickers who may either offer you some cake or grab their children and prepare to run. Follow the gravel access road straight out to the hardtop.

5.0 Turn left at this four-way intersection, onto old US 70 (paved) with a DEAD END sign posted.

5.3 Pass a white metal gate. Follow this abandoned section of US 70 up into the hills. In June and July watch for thickets of ripe blackberries to sweeten the ride back.

6.7 Just past a landslide on the road, you get an excellent view of the Kitsuma ridgeline off to the left. You'll be astonished at how high and narrow it looks, which is just the way it felt screaming down.

8.3 As you pass some concrete guardrails on your left, look over the edge and you'll find a cool railroad tunnel that runs right underneath you.

9.1 Pass another white gate and continue straight on old US 70.

9.4 As you finally finish climbing, watch for the pair of dogs who live at the trailers on the left: The small one likes to bark and chase you, and you'll be surprised how fast the little bugger is. The big, gentle pitbull just keeps a quiet eye from atop his wrecked car throne.

10.0 Turn left at this intersection onto King George Road and follow it to the end.

10.3 Return to the trailhead.

34 Mo' Heinous

This downhill should be attempted only by riders who are either very secure in their bike-handling skills or don't mind crashing and bleeding (I'm still carrying the scars from this one). The locals rated the entry to Mo' Heinous a tech 4+ on a scale of 5, which should give you reason to pause right there. The initial drop-in requires total commitment; this deep, steep-sided gully offers only one choice of lines and no exit except out the bottom. After the initial scare, the trail slips through some very tight and sudden switchbacks, over a number of major water bars, then starts to drop again. The next few miles are insanely fast, down old Forest Service road doubletrack, around blind corners, and over more water bars. This ride is brutal, sick, and pounding, and will have even the most jaded of hammerheads working to unclench their brake hands and clean that wide-eyed, posttrauma look from their faces.

Location: Bent Creek Research Forest, twenty minutes south of Asheville.

Distance: 9.9-mile loop.

Approximate riding time: 1.5 to 2.5 hours.

Difficulty rating: Tech 3+ overall. Initial drop on Mo' Heinous is a tech 4+. Lower Sidehill offers a festival of tech 3 rooty hops to gradually bring your pulse back down into the normal range. This is a black diamond run; make no mistakes.

Trail surface: 5.2 miles of singletrack, 2.1 miles of old Forest Service road and doubletrack, 2.6 miles of gated gravel road.

Highlights: Wretched, unforgiving climb; incredibly steep eroded descent; horrendous water bars; steep rocky drops; high-speed, contour-hugging singletrack and doubletrack.

Land status: Experimental forest.

Maps: USGS Dunsmore Mountain; USDA Forest Service Pisgah District Trail Map; National Geographic Trails Illustrated Pisgah Ranger District.

Finding the trailhead: From Asheville take Interstate 26 East (south, actually) to North Carolina Highway 191 South. Go about 2 miles, then turn right at the light onto Bent Creek Ranch Road (from here, you'll just follow the signs for Lake Powhatan). This road soon runs into a development and branches; bear left onto Wesley Branch Road. Go another 2 miles and look for the Hardtimes Trailhead sign on your left, along with a dirt parking area. Get out, get geared up, and get ready to ride.

Miles and Directions

0.0 Begin from Hardtimes Trailhead. Obvious entrance to Expresso Trail is straight across Wesley Branch Road (the paved road you just drove up). Expresso will wake you up quickly with a short tech 2+ rocky climb and an uphill log pyramid.

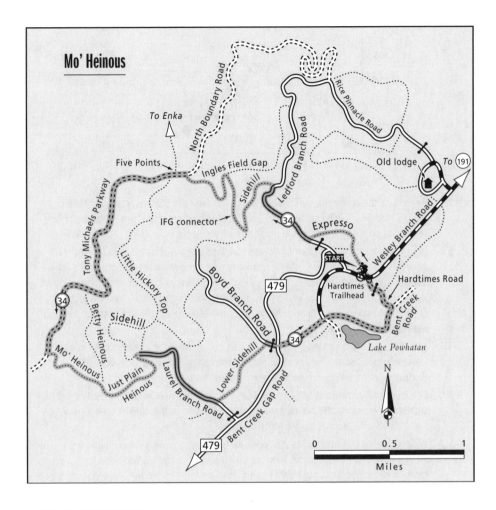

Mo' Heinous

0.2 Bear right at the Y.

0.4 Trail drops you out onto Ledford Branch Road (gravel), just past the gate. Turn right, and head uphill.

1.3 Sharp left turn back onto Sidehill, just in the middle of a curve in the road. Trail entrance is clearly signed, but it's still easy to miss. Watch for a picnic area just across from the entrance. Sidehill starts with some easy tech 1+ cruising and a gorgeous 3-foot-tall berm. Climb that follows is long but not too tough if you stay in the clear line.

2.0 Top a rise and hit a funky intersection of trails. Take the first available right, a sharp turn back that starts climbing up the Ingles Field Gap (IFG) connector trail (signed). Another right farther on is the continuation of Sidehill. If you didn't like the last bit of climbing, you'll hate this next section. It's a good bit steeper with a number of tech 2 and tech 3 rock sections to grind and twist your way through.

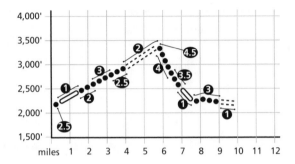

2.7 Turn left as the connector trail intersects IFG Trail. Now the climbing gets *really* steep, though at least it's fairly smooth and buff. Serious pain potential here. Watch for riders screaming on the way down, who won't believe you're climbing IFG.

3.6 Drag yourself up the last pitch of IFG, and fall into an exhausted heap at Five Points. After your medic has resuscitated everyone in your group, turn left onto the dirt double-track that is the Tony Michaels Parkway. Don't take the singletrack to your immediate left signed for Little Hickory Top, and definitely do not go straight across onto the lost trail to Enka. This next bit of climbing, although long, will seem like a picnic compared with the torture of climbing IFG.

4.2 Pass through a gap and dive into a really bad poison ivy (or is it poison oak?) section. Either way, don't stop here for a rest or bathroom break. Trail gets very rocky after this (tech 2+), which makes for even more miserable climbing.

5.0 Continue straight past the left turn for Betty Heinous. This spot is usually marked with a small cairn of stones. Do not mistake this for Mo' Heinous. If it doesn't look incredibly sketchy at the beginning, it's not Mo' Heinous.

5.7 Turn left for the entrance to Mo' Heinous, the big kahuna of Bent Creek. Initial entry is an eroded gully that pitches about forty-five degrees down, switches back and forth a few times, then really starts to get ugly. We're talking big loose rocks, tight switchbacks, steep water bars, and way, way too much speed for such tight, rocky stuff. This trail can be a serious meat grinder, so watch it.

6.2 Though you probably didn't notice, Betty Heinous fed in from the left. And now you get some real speed: 30+ miles per hour on some steep, sketchy track that we call Just Plain Heinous. Tread fades into old dirt doubletrack, littered with big rocks and water bars; generally, there's only one clear line, unless you can bunny hop a long, long way.

7.0 Watch for a big stinky mudhole filled with rocks that lurks on the inside corner. It's a serious faceplant waiting to happen.

7.1 Turn right at the four-way intersection onto Laurel Branch Road (gravel). Watch your speed on the run-out from here, 'cause you'll still be high on adrenaline and the gravel is really loose.

7.5 Sharp left turn back onto Lower Sidehill Trail (signed). Trail climbs a bit, tops out in a little meadow, then descends over a bone-jarring series of water bars and root drops into a tight, twisty rhodo tunnel.

Most of the rides in the Bent Creek area begin at the Hardtimes Trailhead.

8.6 Turn right as Lower Sidehill dead-ends onto Boyd Branch Road (gravel). Go straight past the big rocks and the gate at the end of Boyd Branch, cross Bent Creek Gap Road (gravel; watch for cars), and pick up dirt doubletrack on the other side.

9.1 Cross Lake Powhatan Road (paved) and continue straight on dirt/gravel doubletrack past Lake Powhatan and a small water treatment plant.

9.7 Turn left onto Hardtimes Road (gravel).

9.9 Pass gate and return to Hardtimes Trailhead.

35 Little Hickory Top

Little Hickory Top is an excellent ride for someone who wants to venture up onto the high trails, but who isn't up for the speed of Ingles Field Gap (IFG) or the technical challenges of Betty and Mo' Heinous. This loop gives you a long warm-up with plenty of time to build your courage for the trip back down. Enough rocks, roots, berms, and hops still make it feel like an adventure.

Location: Bent Creek Research Forest, twenty minutes south of Asheville.

Distance: 10.3-mile loop.

Approximate riding time: 1 to 2.5 hours.

Difficulty rating: Tech 2 overall. Little Hickory Top throws a few tech 2+ and 3.5 rocky sections in your way, and Lower Sidehill is littered with tech 3 roots.

Trail surface: 3.2 miles of singletrack; 6.7 miles of gated Forest Service road; 0.2 mile of gravel road; 0.2 mile of pavement.

Highlights: Streams; roots; some large rocks; relatively easy climb to the top; Lake Powhatan for a dip after the ride.

Land status: Experimental forest.

Maps: USGS Dunsmore Mountain; USDA Forest Service Pisgah District Trail Map; National Geographic Trails Illustrated Pisgah Ranger District.

Finding the trailhead: From Asheville take Interstate 26 East (south, actually) to North Carolina Highway 191 South. Go about 2 miles, then turn right at the light onto Bent Creek Ranch Road (from here, you'll just follow the signs for Lake Powhatan). This road soon runs into a development and branches; bear left onto Wesley Branch Road. Go another 2 miles and look for the Hardtimes Trailhead sign on your left, along with a dirt parking area. Get out, get geared up, and get ready to ride.

Miles and Directions

0.0 Start from Hardtimes Trailhead. Turn left onto Wesley Branch Road (the paved road you drove in on).

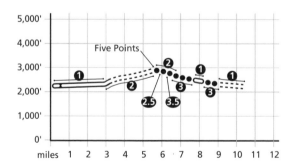

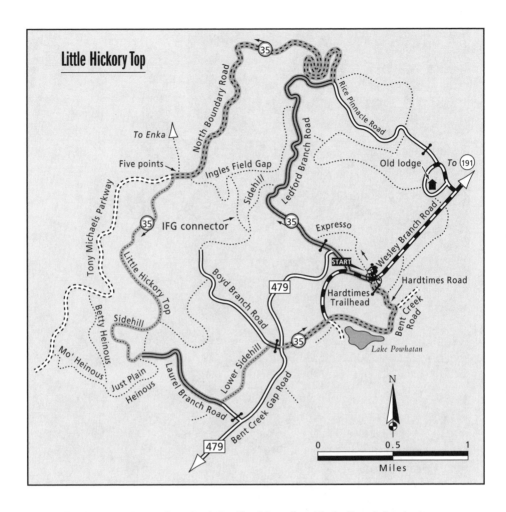

Little Hickory Top

To Enka

Five points

North Boundary Road

Ingles Field Gap

Sidehill

Ledford Branch Road

Rice Pinnacle Road

Old lodge

To (191)

Tony Michaels Parkway

(35) IFG connector

(35)

Expresso

Wesley Branch Road

Little Hickory Top

Boyd Branch Road

START

479

Hardtimes Trailhead

Hardtimes Road

Bent Creek Road

Betty Heinous

Sidehill

Lower Sidehill

(35)

Lake Powhatan

Mo' Heinous

Just Plain Heinous

Laurel Branch Road

Bent Creek Gap Road

N

479

0   0.5   1

Miles

0.2 Continue straight onto Bent Creek Gap Road (gravel), as Wesley Branch Road enters Lake Powhatan Park.

0.4 Continue straight again past the metal gate onto Ledford Branch Road (gravel) as Bent Creek Gap Road bears left. Tread is hardpacked gravel doubletrack.

2.7 Turn left at this intersection onto the North Boundary Road (gravel). This old forest doubletrack is a combination of dirt and pea-gravel. Several unmarked trails and old roads peel off of this road; ignore them all until you reach Five Points. SHELTERWOOD sign explains selective logging techniques used to encourage secondary growth of birch and ash.

3.8 North Boundary Road narrows to tech 2, dirt singletrack. Track is eroded and loose in many spots, making for tough climbing. And it keeps on climbing.

4.2 Nice view to right—if you can pick your weary head up.

5.4 A short, fun descent brings you to the clearing known as Five Points. From here, bear ahead to the left onto Little Hickory Top Trail (signed). IFG falls back to the left, the Tony

Timm soars on Little Hickory Top. DAVID TOLLERTON PHOTO

Michaels Parkway continues straight, and the lost trail to Enka turns right. Now all your climbing pays off. After just a tad more uphill, Little Hickory Top starts to drop, a hard-packed tech 2 singletrack. You'll run through a big dip, then hop onto some sweet track that hugs the contours as it drops through the forest.

5.7 Big berm to zoom around. Don't be afraid; just let go of the brakes and zip around the edge.

6.1 Watch for a section of tech 2+ rocks, a big switchback, then some big, nasty tech 3+ rocks. Novices should use some caution here.

6.4 Trail narrows and runs a tight edge through a cool rhododendron tunnel.

6.7 Two choices for Sidehill Trail at the Y. Stay straight for a bit of climbing.

6.9 Continue straight past this unsigned branch to the left. Trail starts to drop again, getting fast and a bit sketchy through some loose, tech 3+ rocks. Careful of the slick rocks when crossing the streams.

7.3 Little Hickory Top really hits its stride, switching back and forth, with some root drops, small water bars, and several more big berms.

7.5 Continue straight through this four-way intersection onto Laurel Branch Road (gravel). This is a good spot to catch your breath and make sure your friends all make it down in one piece.

7.9 Sharp left turn back onto Lower Sidehill Trail (signed). Trail climbs a bit, tops out in a little meadow, then descends over a bone-jarring series of water bars and root drops into a tight, twisty rhodo tunnel. The last section of Lower Sidehill is a continual tech 3, so novices need to stay on their toes.

9.0 Turn right as Lower Sidehill dead-ends onto Boyd Branch Road (gravel). Go straight past the big rocks and the gate at the end of Boyd Branch, cross Bent Creek Gap Road (gravel; watch for cars), and pick up dirt doubletrack on the other side.

9.5 Cross Lake Powhatan Road (paved) and continue straight on dirt/gravel doubletrack past Lake Powhatan, up over the curb, and down past a small water treatment plant.

10.1 Turn left onto Hardtimes Road (gravel).

10.3 Pass gate and return to Hardtimes Trailhead.

36 Ingles Field Gap

This is a superb adrenaline run that will slap a grin on your face to last the rest of the day. There are downhills that score about a 9 on the fun factor and sweet, swooping descents, surprisingly smooth, with several 3- to 4-foot-high inside berms. Lots of bunny hopping potential and some huge air potential near the end of Ingles Field Gap (IFG). Advanced riders can crank this entire ride with plenty of time to warm up before hitting the steeps. Intermediates (and even really determined beginners) will find the climbs doable (if painful) and the descents exhilarating, and will probably declare this their favorite ride so far.

Location: Bent Creek Research Forest, twenty minutes south of Asheville.

Distance: 11.5-mile loop.

Approximate riding time: 1.5 to 2.5 hours. You may want to allow some extra time because a single run around One Dog just won't be enough, and the jumps at the bottom of IFG will call you back like a siren's song (quite possibly to your destruction).

Difficulty rating: Tech 2+ overall. This loop runs a wide gamut of technical requirements. Ledford Branch and North Boundary Roads are tech 1. Sidehill and IFG are buff, tech 2 roller-coaster runs, but they throw a few dicey, tech 3 rocky sections at you that require finding that one clean line to prevent dabbing (or dashing). Nothing too tough overall, but a number of spots that can really leave you tweaked if your attention wanders (or if you panic and grab a handful of brake) at the wrong time.

Trail surface: 9.6 miles of singletrack; 1.8 miles of gravel road; 0.1 mile of gravel doubletrack. Singletrack is extremely buff hardpack in most places, loose and rocky in a few others.

Highlights: Incredibly smooth swooping descents; huge berms; big water bars and whoop-dee-doos; fast gate runs.

Land status: Research and demonstration forest.

Maps: USGS Dunsmore Mountain; USDA Forest Service Pisgah District Trail Map; National Geographic Trails Illustrated Pisgah Ranger District.

Finding the trailhead: From Asheville take Interstate 26 East (south, actually) to North Carolina Highway 191 South. Go about 2 miles, then turn right at the light onto Bent Creek Ranch Road (from here, you'll just follow the signs for Lake Powhatan). This road soon runs into a development and branches; bear left onto Wesley Branch Road. Go another 2 miles and look for the Hardtimes Trailhead sign on your left, along with a dirt parking area. Get out, get geared up, and get ready to ride.

Miles and Directions

0.0 Begin from Hardtimes Trailhead. Obvious entrance to Expresso trail is straight across Wesley Branch Road (the paved road you just drove up). Expresso will wake you up quickly with a short tech 2+ rocky climb and an uphill log pyramid.

0.2 Bear right at the Y.

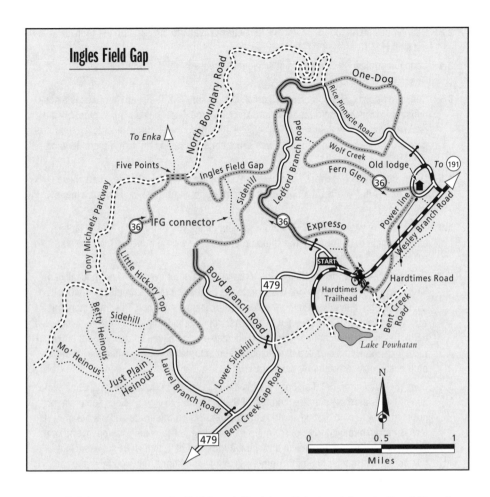

Ingles Field Gap

To Enka

Five Points

Ingles Field Gap

North Boundary Road

Ledford Branch Road

One-Dog

Rice Pinnacle Road

Wolf Creek

Fern Glen

Old lodge

To 191

36

Sidehill

IFG connector

36

Expresso

Power line

Wesley Branch Road

Tony Michaels Parkway

Little Hickory Top

Boyd Branch Road

START

479

Hardtimes
Trailhead

Hardtimes Road

Bent Creek Road

Betty Heinous

Sidehill

Mo' Heinous

Just Plain
Heinous

Lower Sidehill

Laurel Branch Road

Bent Creek Gap Road

Lake Powhatan

N

479

0   0.5   1

Miles

0.4 Trail drops you out onto Ledford Branch Road (gravel), just past the gate. Turn right, and head uphill.

1.3 Sharp left turn back onto Sidehill, just in the middle of a curve in the road. Trail entrance is clearly signed, but it's still easy to miss. Watch for a picnic area just across from the entrance. Sidehill starts with some easy tech 1+ cruising and a gorgeous 3-foot-tall berm. Climb that follows is long but not too tough if you stay in the clear line.

2.0 Top a rise, and hit a funky intersection of trails. Choices are straight for a hiking-only trail, sharp right back uphill for the IFG connector, and another right for Sidehill; the trails are clearly signed. Take the second right turn to continue on Sidehill and start descending immediately. This downhill is fast and very smooth if you stay in the line. However, the line switches back and forth, and if you get out of it, you'll be in some nasty tech 3 rocks at an unhealthy speed, so pay attention. This run is about an 8 on the fun scale.

2.5 Sidehill ends and runs straight into Boyd Branch Road (gravel).

2.6 Turn right off Boyd Branch onto continuation of Sidehill. Two entrances here, only one of which is signed, that join back together shortly. Tread here is old dirt doubletrack.

2.8 Doubletrack starts to fade, and clear singletrack breaks to the left. Turn left to follow the fun stuff.

3.4 Continue straight on Sidehill. Faint singletrack breaks to the left, which is the Upper/Lower Sidehill connector.

3.9 Continue straight at the intersection onto Little Hickory Top. The sharp left back is a continuation of Sidehill. Unfortunately, now it's climb time. Little Hickory Top is probably the easiest climb to Five Points, but you've still got to gain about 400 vertical feet, so be prepared for some grinding. Starts off with some contour running through a rhododendron tunnel.

4.5 Nasty, slippery tech 3+ rocks to navigate. Particularly in the middle of a climb, these guys are a bear. After, you get a tough uphill switchback to grunt through, then some more rocks.

5.0 Some relatively easy (tech 1+) contour running brings you to a big dip, with a large drainage pipe in the bottom. The climb up the far side will be a pusher for just about everyone.

5.2 Finally, a short downhill run brings you to an intersection of five trails, known locally as Five Points or Four Corners. IFG is ahead to the right and breaks immediately downhill. If it looks like the entrance drop on a roller coaster, it's the right trail. This track starts off very steep, very fast, and very smooth (tech 2, tops), launching you through a 4-foot-high berm. Beginners and cautious riders should keep a good check on their speed; otherwise, they chance gaining terminal velocity, then completely wigging when they zoom up on a nasty rock section or off-camber turn.

5.8 Continue straight on IFG. Trail back right is the IFG connector down to Sidehill. This section of IFG is even sweeter than the first, if that's possible. Some sections seem almost polished, they're so buff, and several stream crossings on the inside corners are hairy tech 3 moves through large, loose, sharp rocks. Some sections are wide open, and others hold only a single 2-inch line through the rocks. All of it, though, is gut-wrenchingly fast. Watch for another one of those magnificent inside berms, followed by a rare outside-corner berm.

6.4 Watch for set of three 10-inch tombstones grouped together in the middle of a steep, descending curve. Excellent launching potential for the vertically inspired. Great faceplant potential for the overly cautious or maneuverability challenged.

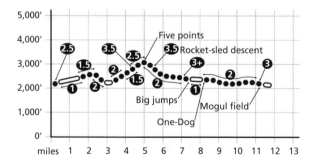

Tony slips along Wolf Creek. DAVID TOLLERTON PHOTO

6.6 Zip through a small opening that contains a short wooden bench (useful after the climb up IFG, but that's another ride). Final descent down IFG back to the road is exceptionally steep and fast (tech 3+) with three serious whoop-dee-doos tacked onto the very end.

7.1 Exit off IFG and turn left onto Ledford Branch Road (gated; gravel).

7.8 Continue straight through four-way intersection, up over the embankment for the entrance to One-Dog Trail (unsigned). Left is the North Boundary Road, and right is Rice Pinnacle Road. What lies ahead is perhaps the most enjoyable mile of singletrack I've ever discovered. The first descent on One-Dog gains speed steadily, switching through the trees, then the bottom drops out for a magnificent brakes-free zone. Easy climb after, with a respectable tech 3 suspended log to climb, jump, or avoid. Then another high-speed slalom run through the trees; big, sweeping right turn at bottom of hill can sling-shot you into next section if you nab the line just right. (**Note:** Just across from the big turn lives a big black dog, for which the trail is named. Though he's supposedly fenced, this escape artist has twice come out of the trees at me like a hairy cruise missile. Doesn't seem mean, just touchy about unannounced visitors. Keep an eye out for him.)

8.6 Trail slips and twists through a dark, mysterious pine forest, on a track as smooth as poured concrete. Several nice bunny hops in here, but beware of the pine-branch spears. Bear left at T just after pines.

8.9 Turn left as you T into Rice Pinnacle Road (gated; gravel). Take an immediate right onto the first singletrack you see (it's only about 50 feet or so), then up and over a knee-high dirt hump.

9.1 Turn right at the T onto Wolf Creek Trail (unsigned).

9.3 Three intersections follow close together; turn left at each one. Last turn puts you onto Fern Glen Trail (unsigned), which slips and twists tightly through the trees for a gradual downhill.

10.3 Turn right as you T into an old logging road.

10.5 Bear right uphill onto a dirt doubletrack under some small power lines. This, of course, is called the Power Line Trail.

10.9 Turn right onto Wesley Branch Road (paved; beware of cars). After only 30 yards or so, turn left onto singletrack under some more small power lines. **Warning:** Do not jump the first jump under the lines, no matter how enticing it looks. The landing zone is a mogul field that will slap you down fast.

11.4 Turn right onto Hardtimes Road (gravel).

11.5 Pass the gate and return to Hardtimes Trailhead.

37 Sidehill Loop

This is a fun loop for someone who isn't up for the climb to the top of the ridge. It's also a good introductory run for beginners who want to try their hand at some true singletrack. Descents vary from rail smooth to loose and sketchy. Water bars and roots on Lower Sidehill will have you hopping whether you like it or not. This is an excellent, fun ride that doesn't cost you a lot.

Location: Bent Creek Research Forest, twenty minutes south of Asheville.
Distance: 7.6-mile loop.
Approximate riding time: 1 to 1.5 hours.
Difficulty rating: Tech 2. Mostly buff singletrack with some tech 3 rocks along the descents on Sidehill and some tech 3 roots and water bars on Lower Sidehill.
Trail surface: 5 miles of singletrack; 1.3 miles of doubletrack; 1.3 miles of gravel road.

Highlights: Smooth swooping descents; berms; water bars; tricky root drops.
Land status: Research and demonstration forest.
Maps: USGS Dunsmore Mountain; USDA Forest Service Pisgah District Trail Map; National Geographic Trails Illustrated Pisgah Ranger District.

Finding the trailhead: From Asheville take Interstate 26 East (south, actually) to North Carolina Highway 191 South. Go about 2 miles, then turn right at the light onto Bent Creek Ranch Road (from here, you'll just follow the signs for Lake Powhatan). This road soon runs into a development and branches; bear left onto Wesley Branch Road. Go another 2 miles and look for the Hardtimes Trailhead sign on your left, along with a dirt parking area. Get out, get geared up, and get ready to ride.

Miles and Directions

0.0 Begin from Hardtimes Trailhead. Obvious entrance to Expresso Trail is straight across Wesley Branch Road (the paved road you just drove up on). Expresso will wake you up quickly with a short tech 2+ rocky climb and an uphill log pyramid.

0.2 Bear right at the Y.

0.4 Trail drops you out onto Ledford Branch Road (gravel), just past the gate. Turn right, and head uphill.

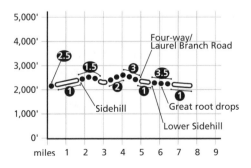

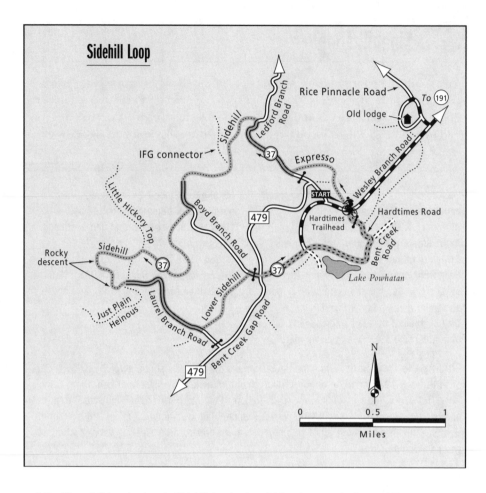

Sidehill Loop

Rice Pinnacle Road

Old lodge

To 191

Ledford Branch Road

Sidehill

IFG connector

37

Expresso

Wesley Branch Road

START

Hardtimes Road

479

Hardtimes Trailhead

Little Hickory Top

Boyd Branch Road

Bent Creek Road

Rocky descent

Sidehill

37

Lake Powhatan

Just Plain Heinous

Lower Sidehill

37

Laurel Branch Road

Bent Creek Gap Road

479

N

0   0.5   1

Miles

1.3 Sharp left turn back onto Sidehill, just in the middle of a curve in the road. Trail entrance is clearly signed, but it's still easy to miss. Watch for a picnic area just across from the entrance. Sidehill starts with some easy tech 1+ cruising and a gorgeous 3-foot-tall berm. Climb that follows is long but not too tough if you stay in the clear line.

2.0 Top a rise, and hit a funky, but clearly signed, intersection of trails. Choices are straight for a hiking-only trail, sharp right back uphill for the IFG connector, and another right for Sidehill; take the second right turn to continue on Sidehill, and start descending immediately. This downhill is fast and very smooth if you stay in the line. However, the line switches back and forth, and if you get out of it, you'll be in some nasty tech 3 rocks at an unhealthy speed, so pay attention. This run is about an 8 on the fun scale.

2.5 Sidehill ends and runs straight into Boyd Branch Road (gravel).

2.6 Turn right off Boyd Branch onto continuation of Sidehill. Two entrances here, only one of which is signed, which join back together shortly. Tread here is old dirt doubletrack.

2.8 Doubletrack starts to fade, and clear singletrack breaks to the left. Turn left to follow the fun stuff.

3.4 Continue straight on Sidehill.

"Everything out here is Sidehill."—A common quote heard in Bent Creek

3.9 Intersection with Little Hickory Top Trail. Turn sharply left back uphill to continue on Sidehill. Trails are clearly signed, but be sure not to miss the turn when your head is hanging as you drag yourself up the last climb.

4.1 Continue straight on Sidehill. Unsigned singletrack breaks to the left, marked by a cairn of stones. From here Sidehill starts descending fast, alternating smooth buff sections with hairy tech 3 fields of chicken heads. Hold the line, stay off the brakes, and scream yourself silly.

4.8 Continue straight at this four-way intersection onto Laurel Branch Road (gravel). Watch your speed on the run-out from here, 'cause you'll still be high on adrenaline and the gravel is really loose.

5.2 Sharp left turn back onto Lower Sidehill Trail (signed). Trail climbs a bit, tops out in a little meadow, then descends over a bone-jarring series of water bars and root drops into a tight, twisty rhododendron tunnel.

6.3 Turn right as Lower Sidehill dead-ends onto Boyd Branch Road (gravel). Go straight past the big rocks and the gate at the end of Boyd Branch, cross Bent Creek Gap Road (gravel; watch for cars), and pick up dirt doubletrack on the other side.

6.8 Cross Lake Powhatan Road (paved), and continue straight on dirt/gravel doubletrack. As you pass Lake Powhatan itself, the gravel track turns into Bent Creek Road.

7.4 Turn left onto Hardtimes Road.

7.6 Pass gate and return to Hardtimes Trailhead.

38 Betty Heinous Loop

Betty Heinous, although not quite in the same league as her big brother Mo', is a fast, hair-raising run that will have you alternately grabbing all the brakes you can and letting them go to hope for the best. This loop includes a brutal climb up Ingles Field Gap (IFG), the bonzai run down Betty, root-hopping along Lower Sidehill, then a final grind up one side of Sidehill and a bobsled run down the other. Don't make the mistake of thinking this is a girly run, no matter what the name says.

Location: Bent Creek Research Forest, twenty minutes south of Asheville.
Distance: 12.8-mile loop.
Approximate riding time: 1.5 to 2.5 hours.
Difficulty rating: Tech 3 overall. Betty and Just Plain Heinous are a surly lot and can slap down even the most confident of riders with a nasty combination of speed, tech 3 rocks, and a tech 4 erosion gully. Lower Sidehill is a tech 3 rootfest. IFG isn't too technical; it's just one mean climb.

Trail surface: 8.9 miles of singletrack; 1.4 miles of old Forest Service road/doubletrack; 2.5 miles of gated gravel road.
Highlights: Screaming contour running; heart-breaking climb; big berms; stream crossings.
Land status: Experimental forest.
Maps: USGS Dunsmore Mountain; USDA Forest Service Pisgah District Trail Map; National Geographic Trails Illustrated Pisgah Ranger District.

Finding the trailhead: From Asheville take Interstate 26 East (south, actually) to North Carolina Highway 191 South. Go about 2 miles, then turn right at the light onto Bent Creek Ranch Road (from here, you'll just follow the signs for Lake Powhatan). This road soon runs into a development and branches; bear left onto Wesley Branch Road. Go another 2 miles, and look for the Hardtimes Trailhead sign on your left, along with a dirt parking area. Get out, get geared up, and get ready to ride.

Miles and Directions

0.0 Start from Hardtimes Trailhead. Go past gate at bottom of parking area onto Hardtimes Road.

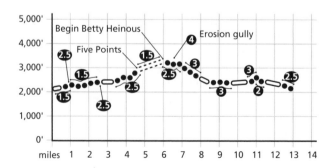

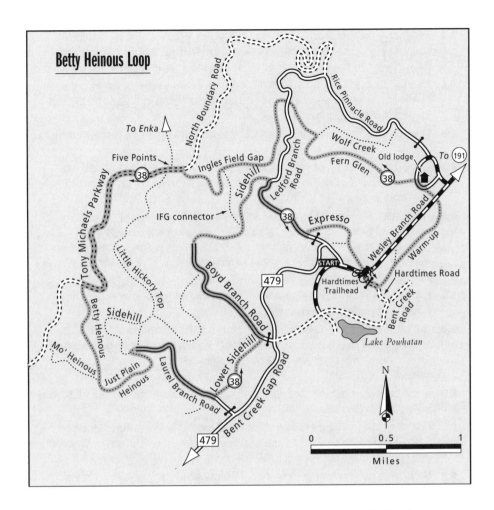

Betty Heinous Loop

0.1 Turn left onto the second singletrack you see, which is the Warm-up Trail. This little tech 1+ track offers a bit of everything, including a short climb, a stream crossing, a couple of fun logs to work over, and a zippy descent back and forth down through a gully.

0.8 Continue straight across Wesley Branch Road (paved). Trail on this side is much rockier (tech 2+).

0.9 Turn left onto a paved walkway. Small wooden bridge back to right.

1.0 Continue straight past the ruins of an old Boy Scout lodge. Track turns into a wide tech 1 gravel doubletrack.

1.2 Turn left onto the first true singletrack you see, which is known as Fern Glen. Tread is somewhat soft clay and pine mix; smooth tech 1+ track with some tech 2 roots.

1.9 Turn left at the T, up and over a series of small, slippery water bars. Track quickly turns into an old logging road, filled with large egg-sized gravel. Steep switchbacks are a bear to climb.

2.4 Turn right onto Ledford Branch Road. Tread is hardpacked gravel doubletrack.

2.6 Turn sharply left back onto IFG Trail (signed). This first section of climbing is brutally steep, running up over several big whoop-dee-doos. **Warning:** Watch for riders coming down this trail, as they'll have little chance to slow down before flattening you.

3.1 Hit a tiny clearing with a small wooden bench. You can say a prayer of thanks to the builder as you rest here. Following track teases with some flats through an old clearcut, then starts climbing again.

3.9 Continue straight and continue climbing. Branch left is the signed IFG connector down to Sidehill.

4.3 Again, continue straight past this left branch (another connector to Sidehill, this one unnamed and unsigned). The next climb is again brutally steep, but it's very smooth, and—more important—it's the last one.

4.5 Finally reach Five Points. After a long rest and a search for your missing lung, saddle back up and bear left onto the unsigned doubletrack, which is known as the Tony Michaels Parkway. Do not take the immediate left onto Little Hickory Top, and whatever you do, don't take the unsigned singletrack straight ahead, which is the lost trail to Enka. It'll be a long ride home if you do.

5.1 Pass through a gap and enter a really bad poison ivy field. Trail gets rockier and more eroded, always climbing a slight grade.

5.9 Turn left at the entrance to Betty Heinous. This turn is usually marked with a small cairn of stones. Initial drop is very steep, with a tech 2.5 covering of loose chicken heads. Serious speed here carries you abruptly into a sharp right turn at the bottom, so pay attention.

6.2 A little flat contour running and even a dash of uphill. But don't fret, because the bottom is just about to drop out.

6.3 Fast, steep contour running through some tech 3 rock fields and an extremely sketchy tech 4 erosion gully. You won't be able to stop in time for the gully, so just try to bounce from one side to the other and hop over the cracks.

6.9 Mo' Heinous peels in from the right, though you probably didn't see it. Now Just Plain Heinous takes over with crazy speed (30+ miles per hour) over some tech 3+ rocks and a number of big water bars. You'll be getting air whether you want it or not, so just relax and hold on.

7.7 Watch for a big stinky mudhole filled with rocks that lurks on this inside corner. It's a serious faceplant waiting to happen.

7.8 Turn right at this four-way intersection onto Laurel Branch Road (gravel). Watch your speed on the run-out from here, 'cause you'll still be high on adrenaline and the gravel is really loose.

8.2 Sharp left turn back onto Lower Sidehill Trail (signed). Trail climbs a bit, tops out in a little meadow, then descends over a bone-jarring series of water bars and root drops into a tight, twisty rhodo tunnel.

9.3 Turn left as Lower Sidehill dead-ends onto Boyd Branch Road (gravel). Follow Boyd Branch to the end.

10.3 As Boyd Branch Road ends, continue straight onto the entrance for Sidehill Trail (signed). Climbing Sidehill this direction is a test of grit and handling skills, as you slowly grind your way up the slope, dodging loose baby heads and downhill-bound riders.

Into the big woods. DAVID TOLLERTON PHOTO

10.8 Finally top a rise and hit intersection with the IFG connector trail. Take the second left to continue on Sidehill. This run down Sidehill is fast and sweet, a smooth tech 2 run with a huge 3-foot berm on one inside corner for some serious screaming fun. IFG connector cuts sharply back left and starts climbing.

11.5 Sidehill drops you out onto Ledford Branch Road (gravel). Turn right to descend back to the trailhead.

12.4 Just before you hit the gate at the end of Ledford Branch, turn left onto a short section of singletrack, which is a spur off Expresso.

12.6 Bear left at the Y to continue on Expresso and return to the trailhead. Watch for a tech 3 pyramid and some dicey tech 3 rocks just before you drop down to the hardtop.

12.8 Trail drops you out onto Wesley Branch Road, just across from Hardtimes Trailhead.

39 Explorer

Here is another fine intermediate ride from Bent Creek's tamer south side. Explorer is a perfect choice for introducing someone to the exquisite pleasure of zooming downhill. It doesn't require too much effort to gain the top, then you get a gorgeous run back down that could vary from mild to wild, depending on your speed and aeronautics. A stream crossing at the bottom is the perfect way to end the run before an easy return trip back to the arboretum. This is an excellent ride overall if you just want to spin for an hour and still get in a little downhill time.

Location: Bent Creek Research Forest, twenty minutes south of Asheville.
Distance: 8.7 miles out-and-back.
Approximate riding time: 45 minutes to 1.5 hours.
Difficulty rating: Overall, tech 2+. Lots of easy contour cruising both up and down with some respectable water bars and a few hungry rocks to avoid.

Trail surface: 4.9 miles of singletrack; 0.6 mile of gravel road; 3.2 miles of doubletrack.
Highlights: Excellent 2-mile downhill; stream crossing; water bars; rhododendron tunnel.
Land status: Experimental forest, USDA.
Maps: USGS Dunsmore Mountain; USDA Forest Service Pisgah District Trail Map; National Geographic Trails Illustrated Pisgah Ranger District.

Finding the trailhead: From Asheville take Interstate 26 East (south) to North Carolina Highway 191 South. Go about 2 miles, then turn right at the light onto Bent Creek Ranch Road (from here you'll just follow the signs for Lake Powhatan). This road soon runs into a development and branches; bear left onto Wesley Branch Road. Go roughly 1 mile, and look for the North Carolina Arboretum on your left. Enter the gates, hang an immediate right, and follow this paved road around to the greenhouse parking lot. By the way, the greenhouse is usually open for visitors and has clean rest rooms, a hose, and a water cooler. Just be considerate, and don't track lots of crud in after your ride. Note that the Arboretum may be closed because of storm damage, in which case you'll have to start from Hardtimes Trailhead.

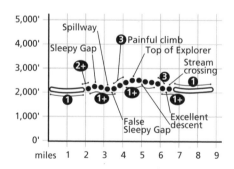

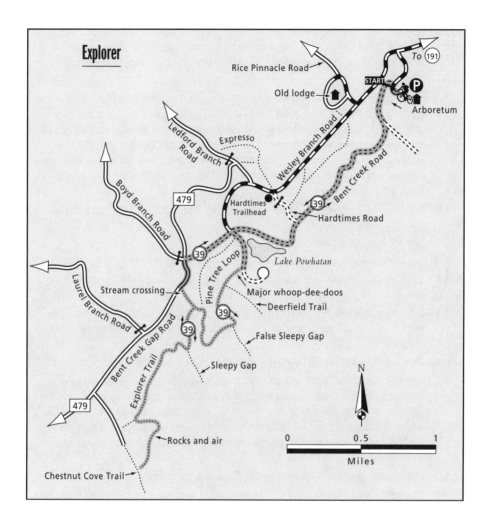

Miles and Directions

0.0 Head back out from the arboretum parking lot and look for a gravel path on the left (it's only 50 feet or so). Then hang another immediate left onto Wolf Branch Road, a gated gravel doubletrack.

0.2 Turn right onto Bent Creek Road (gated gravel doubletrack). Use small pedestrian door set beside large vehicle gate to get through the arboretum fence.

1.0 Bear left at the Y to continue on Bent Creek Road.

1.2 Continue straight on Bent Creek Road, past the water treatment plant, up over the curb, and past Lake Powhatan on your left.

1.6 Turn left onto paved campground road. Surface immediately changes to gravel, and you cross a small stone bridge. Just past bridge continue straight past the first entrance to Pine Tree Loop.

1.8 Now turn right onto the second Pine Tree Loop entrance, which is clearly signed. Trail starts off as a rocky tech 2+ singletrack and immediately begins climbing up over a long set of monster water bars (see Pine Tree Loop, Ride 40, for a chance to come down these puppies).

2.1 Go straight on Pine Tree, past the left for Deerfield Trail. Flat, easy contour climbing.

2.4 Continue straight past the sign for Sleepy Gap Trail (actually, another trail at the other end is signed Sleepy Gap as well, with no connection between the two). After the gap you'll roll into a fine buffed downhill old doubletrack that has faded to singletrack in most spots. It's fast and polished, with several smooth water bars that can convince even first-timers to reach for a little air. Pretty much a tech 1+ run with a few eroded spots in the middle.

3.0 Turn left onto the signed connector trail to Explorer. Trail wanders up through a gorgeous green meadow.

3.1 Turn left again as you intersect Explorer Loop Trail.

3.3 Trail crosses a concrete spillway. Yellow blazes on the trees.

3.5 Continue straight past another signed left for Sleepy Gap Trail. (See? What's up with that?)

4.1 Sharp turn left uphill to continue on Explorer Trail. Brutal, steep climb, lots of rocks and roots, tech 3. Track straight goes to unnamed gravel road leading to Bent Creek Gap Road.

4.4 Once the painful stuff stops, you get rewarded with some easy, tech 1+ contour climbing.

4.7 Here's the turnaround spot, as Explorer dead-ends into Chestnut Cove Trail (hiking only). The return run back down Explorer starts off building speed quickly and easily, until you suddenly realize you're just *cranking* through the woods. Then, just after your confidence settles in and you start to kick back, the bottom drops out and the rocks pop up, and you find yourself wrestling an angry, bucking bicycle down the trail. Just hang on and enjoy the ride.

5.9 Straight past the turn for Sleepy Gap Trail. Zip across the concrete causeway.

6.3 Hammer on past the connector trail. Now you gets lots of small but sweet root drops, a rhododendron tunnel, and some big mud.

6.6 Zoom through a wide tech 1+ stream crossing for an excellent cool-down as you catch your breath. Trail after stream forks with both choices leading up to Bent Creek Gap Road. One fork gradually climbs to a gate, and the other claws its way straight up the side of a big embankment to reach the road.

6.7 Turn right onto Bent Creek Gap Road (gravel; open to traffic).

7.1 Turn right, across from the gated entrance to Boyd Branch Road. Cross a few humps, and find yourself on smooth tech 1 doubletrack.

7.5 Cross Lake Powhatan Road (paved) and continue straight on dirt/gravel doubletrack past Lake Powhatan. Keep going straight, up over the curb, and down past the water treatment plant.

7.7 Bear right at the Y to continue on gravel doubletrack (Bent Creek Road).

8.5 Go through the door in the arboretum fence, then immediately turn left onto Wolf Branch Road.

8.7 Turn right onto the short gravel path that leads you back to the arboretum parking lot.

40 Pine Tree Loop

I'd consider this trail the perfect sampler for a novice rider who has bellied up to Pisgah's fat tire feast for the first time. Pine Tree offers up enough fun to get friends hooked on riding and enough scary stuff to keep them humble. It also makes a fine appetizer for advanced riders before moving on to the main course in the mountains above.

Pine Tree can be a bit two-faced. Ridden clockwise, the trail starts with a steep rocky climb that will have you out of the saddle one way or the other. Then, like a transformed ugly duckling, it melts into a long, swooping descent that runs over some gentle humps before returning to the flatter track below. Riding Pine Tree counterclockwise, though, shows a bit of its darker face. Although the climb to False Sleepy Gap is a piece of cake, the descent (particularly at speed) can get a bit ugly, with roots and rocks setting up unexpected ambushes. Directions are given for the counterclockwise trip only.

Location: Bent Creek Research Forest, twenty minutes south of Asheville.

Distance: 5.4-mile loop.

Approximate riding time: 30 minutes to 1 hour.

Difficulty rating: Tech 1+ if ridden clockwise and pushed up the climb. Tech 3 if ridden counterclockwise and bombed down the rocky descent and water bars. Several tech 3+ root moves scattered throughout will have novices and some intermediates wisely choosing to dismount.

Trail surface: 2 miles of singletrack; 3.4 miles of gravel Forest Service road.

Highlights: Excellent introductory or warm-up trail; fun swooping track through beautiful rhododendron tunnels; choice of fast and fun or fast and furious downhill.

Land status: Experimental forest, USDA.

Maps: USGS Dunsmore Mountain; USDA Forest Service Pisgah District Trail Map; National Geographic Trails Illustrated Pisgah Ranger District.

Finding the trailhead: From Asheville take Interstate 26 East (south) to North Carolina Highway 191 South. Go about 2 miles, then turn right at the light onto Bent Creek Ranch Road (from here you'll just follow the signs for Lake Powhatan). This road soon runs into a development and branches; bear left onto Wesley Branch Road. Go roughly 1 mile and look for the North Carolina Arboretum on your left. Enter the gates, hang an immediate right, and follow this paved road around to the greenhouse parking lot.

Miles and Directions

0.0 Heading back out from the arboretum parking lot, look for a gravel path on the left (it's only 50 feet or so). Then hang another immediate left onto Wolf Branch Road, a gated gravel road.

0.2 Turn right onto Bent Creek Road (gravel). Use small pedestrian door set beside large vehicle gate to get through the arboretum fence.

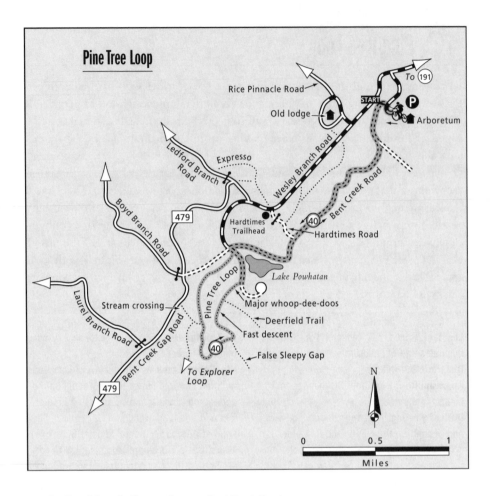

Pine Tree Loop

- Rice Pinnacle Road
- To 191
- START
- P
- Old lodge
- Arboretum
- Ledford Branch Road
- Expresso
- Wesley Branch Road
- Bent Creek Road
- Boyd Branch Road
- 479
- Hardtimes Trailhead
- 40
- Hardtimes Road
- Pine Tree Loop
- Lake Powhatan
- Laurel Branch Road
- Stream crossing
- Major whoop-dee-doos
- Deerfield Trail
- Fast descent
- 40
- False Sleepy Gap
- Bent Creek Gap Road
- To Explorer Loop
- 479

N

0   0.5   1
Miles

1.0   Bear left at the Y to continue on Bent Creek Road.

1.2   Continue straight on Bent Creek Road, past the water treatment and Lake Powhatan on left.

1.6   Turn left at the intersection with paved campground road. Surface changes to gravel and crosses a small stone bridge. Then make an immediate right onto Pine Tree Loop. The lower entrance is clearly signed.

2.0   Trail parallels the road; tight slipping and dipping through a beautiful rhododendron tunnel. Tunnel is laced with some difficult roots in spots with at least one tech 3 move along the way.

2.2   Tech 2+ stream crossing with roots lacing the far bank.

2.4   Pass through a small grassy meadow with a beautiful ribbon of singletrack snaking across it. Continue straight up Pine Tree Loop, and begin some easy climbing. Branch right is a connector trail that leads to Explorer Loop Trail.

2.8   Big sweeping climb up to left will leave even some intermediates pushing. Some more easier climbing, then the trail flattens out.

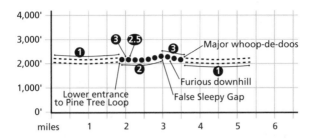

3.0 Continue straight past sign for Sleepy Gap. Following downhill is fast and treacherous, with small rooty drops, respectable rocks, washouts, and some big whoop-dee-doos. Call it a tech 3 descent. (**Note:** The Sleepy Gap sign is incorrect. The true Sleepy Gap Trail breaks off from Explorer Loop and continues up past South Ridge Road to the Blue Ridge Parkway. Locals call this trail False Sleepy Gap.)

3.3 Intersection with Deerfield Trail; continue straight on Pine Tree Loop. Beware of major whoop-dee-doos on steep return to the road.

3.6 Turn left as trail feeds out onto the same gravel road you came in on.

3.8 Pass the lower entrance to Pine Tree. As gravel turns into pavement, make an immediate right back onto Bent Creek Road (gravel).

4.2 Continue straight on Bent Creek Road, past the water treatment plant and Lake Powhatan.

4.4 Bear right at the Y to continue on Bent Creek Road.

5.2 Go through the door in the arboretum fence, then immediately turn left onto Wolf Branch Road.

5.4 Turn right onto the short gravel path that leads you back to the arboretum parking lot.

41 Lower Sidehill

Get ready for a preeminent ride with an easy singletrack warm-up, one big dose of pain on the way up, then nothing but fun for the rest of the ride. This is one of the most enjoyable descents in Bent Creek (if you like it rocky, that is) and certainly the most underridden. Seems like most riders don't want to venture up the road this far. Believe me, though, their loss is your gain. Once you get past the bone-breaking entrance climb, Lower Sidehill offers more than 2.5 miles of almost pure descending. It's sketchy, fast, and unpredictable, just like a good trail should be.

Location: Bent Creek Research Forest, twenty minutes south of Asheville.
Distance: 8.2-mile lariat.
Approximate riding time: 1 to 1.5 hours.
Difficulty rating: Tech 3 overall. The entry runs on Pine Tree and Explorer aren't too technical, but Lower Sidehill offers a tech 3+ climb and a long rock-spiked descent that rates a 4 for sheer pounding.
Trail surface: 5.1 miles of tasty singletrack; 2 miles of doubletrack; 1.1 miles of gravel road.

Highlights: Sweet contour running; crazy hairball descent; mud; lots of rocks; beautiful coves.
Land status: Research and demonstration forest.
Maps: USGS Dunsmore Mountain; USDA Forest Service Pisgah District Trail Map; National Geographic Trails Illustrated Pisgah Ranger District.

Finding the trailhead: From Asheville take Interstate 26 East (south) to North Carolina Highway 191 South. Go about 2 miles, then turn right at the light onto Bent Creek Ranch Road (from here you'll just follow the signs for Lake Powhatan). This road soon runs into a development and branches; bear left onto Wesley Branch Road. Go another 2 miles and look for the Hardtimes Trailhead sign on your left, along with a dirt parking area.

Miles and Directions

0.0 Start from Hardtimes Trailhead. Go past gate at bottom of parking area onto Hardtimes Road (doubletrack).

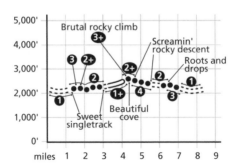

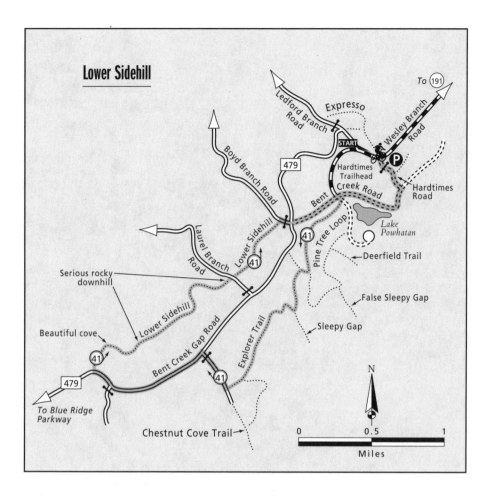

Lower Sidehill

0.2 Turn back right at the Y onto Bent Creek Road (gated doubletrack).

0.4 Continue straight on Bent Creek Road, past the water treatment plant and Lake Powhatan on left.

0.8 Intersection with paved campground road. Turn left; surface changes to gravel and crosses a small stone bridge. Take an immediate right onto Pine Tree Loop. This lower entrance is clearly signed.

1.2 Trail parallels the road; tight slipping and dipping through a beautiful rhododendron tunnel. Tunnel is laced with some difficult roots in spots with at least one tech 3 move along the way.

1.4 Tech 2+ stream crossing with roots lacing the far bank.

1.6 Pass through a small grassy meadow, then turn right onto the connector trail to Explorer Loop Trail.

1.7 Turn right again at T with Explorer Loop. Now you get lots of small but sweet root drops, a rhododendron tunnel, and some big mud.

Ned grinding up Lower Sidehill trail.

2.0 Zoom through a wide tech 1+ stream crossing. Immediately after, turn left up into the rhododendron thickets to follow the lower section of Explorer Loop. A painful tech 2+ climb awaits, then lots of smooth contouring.

3.0 Turn right as trail dead-ends into an unnamed gated gravel road.

3.1 Cross gated bridge (or take the stream option), then turn left onto Bent Creek Gap Road (gravel; open to traffic). Now for a bit of unpleasantness: a long gravel road climb that gets steeper as it goes.

4.1 Turn right onto the signed entrance for Lower Sidehill (notice the MOST DIFFICULT sign). Turn is just past a gated road on the left. Good news is you get to leave the road. Bad news: The climbing gets a whole lot uglier. Long, excruciating tech 3+ rocky climb. Not especially steep, but it's a killer all the same; just wait and see.

4.3 Turn right again out of the rocks by another sign for Lower Sidehill. Sweet, tech 2+ singletrack takes over for a bit.

4.5 Exceptionally cool track hangs along the side of a steep slope with log underpinnings beneath the curves. One of the most beautiful sections of singletrack you'll ever see anywhere. Track gradually picks up speed along some downhill contouring.

4.8 Now the Lower Sidehill shows you its ugly side. The bottom just drops out, and you're making a double black diamond run down through serious rocks and drops, often running along only 8 inches from a long drop off the side. Call it a tech 4 if you run it at warp speed.

5.7 Continue straight past unmarked connector trail (excellent side trip for anyone who loves big water bars).

5.8 Bust through a major set of mudholes, then turn right as trail Ts into Laurel Branch Road (gated; gravel). In fewer than 50 yards watch for sharp left back onto signed continuation of Lower Sidehill. Trail climbs a bit, tops out in a little meadow, then descends over a bone-jarring series of water bars and root drops into a tight, twisty rhododendron tunnel.

6.9 Turn right as Lower Sidehill dead-ends onto Boyd Branch Road (gated; gravel). Go straight past the big rocks and the gate at the end of Boyd Branch, cross Bent Creek Gap Road (gravel; open to traffic), and pick up dirt doubletrack (Bent Creek Road) on the other side.

7.4 Cross Lake Powhatan Road (paved), and continue straight on dirt/gravel doubletrack past Lake Powhatan and water treatment plant.

8.0 Turn left onto Hardtimes Road (doubletrack).

8.2 Pass gate and return to Hardtimes Trailhead.

42 Trace Ridge

Trace Ridge is one of the must-do classic descents in Pisgah National Forest. It's the kind of run that can shock you, rock you, melt your brakes, and leave you with scars to remember it by. The climb up to Spencer Gap is painful at times but well worth the payback. And the drop down Trace Ridge will take your breath away with scary amounts of speed over loose rocks, following tracks that twist, disappear, and skirt the edges of eroded, rocky disaster areas. Keep your eyes glued to the line, don't look at the nasty stuff, and just hang on. It's great fun—if you like your riding loose and crazy. Oh, and pay proper respect to the huge whoop-dee-doos at the end of Trace; they're known to exact a high toll in broken bones and shattered weekends from those who take them too lightly.

Location: Pisgah National Forest, Trace Ridge Trailhead area; twenty-five minutes south of Asheville.

Distance: 7.4-mile loop.

Approximate riding time: 1 to 2 hours.

Difficulty rating: Tech 3 overall. The gravel roads are tech 1, and Spencer Gap averages about tech 2+. The run back down Trace Ridge hits tech 3+ for most of the descent, with lots of loose baby heads and chicken heads and numerous eroded lines. Be aware that the extreme speed you'll experience dropping

Trace Ridge can push the technical requirements up a notch or two and means that busting will carry some severe penalties.

Trail surface: 4.7 miles of singletrack; 2.7 miles of gravel road.

Highlights: Screaming descent; beautiful contour running; huge whoop-dee-doos.

Land status: Pisgah National Forest.

Maps: USGS Dunsmore Mountain; USDA Forest Service Pisgah District Trail Map; National Geographic Trails Illustrated Pisgah Ranger District.

Finding the trailhead: From Asheville take Interstate 26 East (south) to North Carolina Highway 280 South. After about 5 miles turn right onto North Mills River Road. Just before the

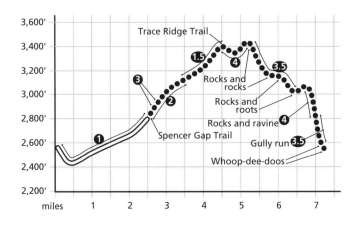

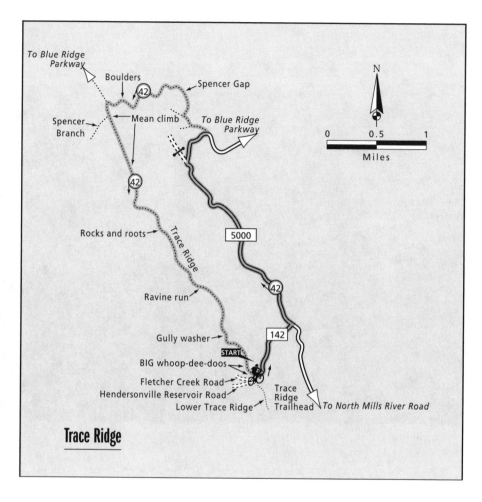

Trace Ridge

entrance to North Mills River Campground, turn right onto Forest Road 5000. After about 2 miles look for Forest Road 142 on the left; you'll know you're okay if you drive over a small concrete spillway. Trace Ridge Trailhead and parking area are at the end of the road.

Miles and Directions

0.0   From the Trace Ridge Trailhead, ride back down FR 142 and across the concrete causeway.

0.5   Turn left onto FR 5000, and start a long gradual climb. The road is narrow and windy, and the locals are known to blast down it, so keep an eye out and be ready to dive for the ditch.

2.3   Continue straight past a gated road down to the left. This is not the entrance to Spencer Gap, and if you take it, you'll be lost for days, believe me. FR 5000 starts to steepen, and you start to wonder if the descent will be worth it. It is, so just keep spinning.

Looking down onto Trace Ridge.

2.7 Turn left, just as the road makes an inside curve, onto Spencer Gap Trail (sign exists, but it's planted way back in there). First real trail payment in the form of a rocky, tech 2+ climb.

2.9 Turn right to follow the rocky singletrack. Old doubletrack continues straight into a grassy field.

3.0 Turn right again as trail runs up a steep rocky bank and into a small meadow. Track crosses meadow, then hits you with some tech 3 rocks and roots as you reenter the woods.

3.5 Flat tech 1+ contour running.

3.9 Wind your way through some huge boulders, and cross a small rocky stream as trail bends through an inside corner.

4.6 Turn left at this T onto Trace Ridge; trail is clearly signed. You get a short drop, pass the sign for Spencer Branch Trail 50 feet down on the right, then your final payment: a mean, heartbreaking, rock-filled climb that ranks a tech 4 to clean the whole mess.

4.9 Hit the top of the ridge, and now it's time for payback. Trail drops quickly, and before you're ready, you're sailing at speed down a treacherous rocky track. Some hops along the way, though the landing zones are very sketchy.

5.8 Trail flattens for a bit, rolling through a rhododendron thicket. Catch a quick breath, then dive back in for more warp speed running over more tech 3+ terrain, this time with some roots thrown into the mix. Remember that sometimes you've just got to ride over whatever's in front of you.

6.3 Short flat along a finger, then dropping again. Trail feeds into a shallow ravine, which may also be a stream depending on weather conditions. Dicey tech 4 run over loose, clattering rocks.

7.1 Short climb, then the last drop. Track skirts the edge of a steep gully. Hold the right line near the trees or face sliding into the gully's belly, which is a place you don't want to be.

7.4 At the end of Trace Ridge, like silent guardians, sit five massive whoop-dee-doos, ready to defend the trail's honor against any riders foolish enough not to be humbled. This spot is notorious for claiming victims, so pay proper respect or be able to handle 10 to 15 feet of air, five times over. Return to earth and slide back into the Trace Ridge Trailhead. Don't be ashamed of your wide eyes or shaking limbs—anyone down ahead of you will understand.

43 Wash Creek

This trail is a perfect warm-up—or cool-down—for any of the other trails off the Trace Ridge Trailhead. It's fun, frisky, and a good chance to stretch your legs a little to get the blood flowing. And most folks will tell you that this trail violates some law of physics, because it's a loop that's all downhill.

Location: Pisgah National Forest, Trace Ridge Trailhead area; twenty-five minutes south of Asheville.
Distance: 1.8-mile loop.
Approximate riding time: 10 to 20 minutes.
Difficulty rating: Tech 1+. Probably the easiest true singletrack that Pisgah has to offer. Very buff, though initial descent after turning onto Wash Creek may be a little scary for first-timers.

Trail surface: 1.4 miles of singletrack; 0.4 mile of gravel road.
Highlights: Roller-coaster contour running; forest tunnels; easy return.
Land status: Pisgah National Forest.
Maps: USGS Dunsmore Mountain; USDA Forest Service Pisgah District Trail Map; National Geographic Trails Illustrated Pisgah Ranger District.

Finding the trailhead: From Asheville take Interstate 26 East (south) to North Carolina Highway 280 South. After about 5 miles turn right onto North Mills River Road. Just before the entrance to North Mills River Campground, turn right onto Forest Road 5000. After about 2 miles look for Forest Road 142 on the left; you'll know you're okay if you drive over a small concrete spillway. Trace Ridge Trailhead and parking area are at end of the road.

Miles and Directions

0.0 Enter just to the left of the information station onto Lower Trace Ridge. Tread starts off as wide hardpacked clay and pine-needle surface—singletrack XXL.

0.2 Trail begins to narrow and drop, gaining speed and a certain zippy quality that will bring a smile to the face of any rider.

0.5 Take a sharp left back onto Wash Creek Trail. Brown Forest Service sign is broken off at knee height. Keep an eye out for this one, 'cause it's easy to miss, and you'll be sorry if you follow Lower Trace out. Wash Creek starts a little steep, but it's easy and fun and smooth as can be. Tech 1+, slight downhill contour cruising through the hemlocks.

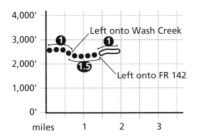

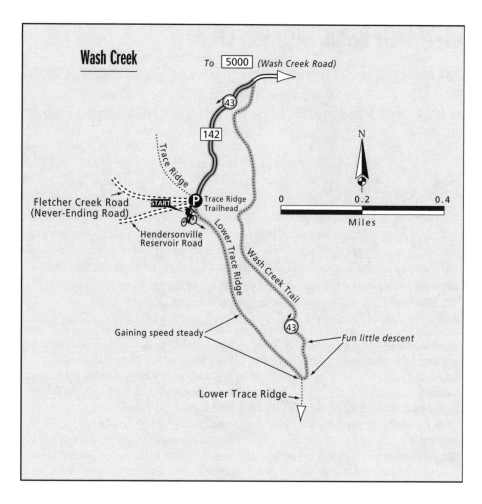

Wash Creek

To 5000 (Wash Creek Road)

43

142

Trace Ridge

N

0   0.2   0.4
Miles

Fletcher Creek Road
(Never-Ending Road)

START

P Trace Ridge
Trailhead

Hendersonville
Reservoir Road

Lower Trace Ridge

Wash Creek Trail

43

Gaining speed steady

Fun little descent

Lower Trace Ridge

0.8 Old road to left. Continue straight on Wash Creek.

1.1 Little ups, little downs, slipping through a dark forest.

1.4 Turn left onto FR 142 (gravel road). Watch for cars.

1.8 Return to Trace Ridge Trailhead.

44 Little Pisgah Ridge (Big Creek)

Dropping 1,800 feet in 2 miles insists that there'll be insane amounts of speed over some awfully scary terrain, regardless of your personal level of comfort. This is, quite simply, a downhill by which all others should be measured. After hiking 0.2 mile off the Blue Ridge Parkway to get to the bike-legal track, you'll find 2 miles of solid, sick, crazy speed over steep contour runs, lots of it incredibly buff with some extremely nice berms tossed in here and there. Washouts, off-camber turns laced with snaky roots, and short rocky patches generally come up too quickly to be scared about (which is probably the safest way to handle it). In some areas a 1-inch mistake is going to send you bouncing off trees down a sixty-degree drop for 100 feet, so be careful. A flatter, streamside track offers a chance to pedal for a change, rather than just hang on and pray, with lots of wood, stone, and water obstacles. There are some extremely hairy stream crossings for those emboldened to idiocy by the downhill. An ugly surprise drop at mile 4.5 requires total commitment and health insurance. The easy ride out gives you time to quit shaking before you get back to the car.

Location: Pisgah National Forest, Trace Ridge Trailhead area; twenty-five minutes south of Asheville.

Distance: 6.6 miles one way.

Approximate riding time: 45 minutes to 2 hours, depending on your level of speed or foolishness.

Difficulty rating: Tech 4 overall. The contour running is insanely fast. Several tech 4 switchbacks, rocks, and root crossings. High-speed, off-camber turns with little (sometimes no) margin for error. Stream crossings ranging from tech 3 to tech 5. If you could go really slow, this trail would drop back to a tech 2+ in many stretches, but it's just not an option.

Trail surface: 4.8 miles of primo, hardpacked forest singletrack; 1.8 miles of Forest Service road.

Highlights: Incredibly fast downhill singletrack; major rock/root moves; multiple stream crossings; logs; reservoir; serious adrenaline run.

Land status: Pisgah National Forest.

Maps: USGS Pisgah Forest; USDA Forest Service Pisgah District Trail Map; National Geographic Trails Illustrated Pisgah Ranger District.

Finding the trailhead: Because this is a one-way ride, you'll need to drop off a car at the Trace Ridge Trailhead or con some poor soul into ferrying you to the top and missing out on the ride of the day! Note that I do not recommend riding this trail alone because the chance of someone discovering your sorry mangled body 80 feet down in some cove before the raccoons start gnawing on you is pretty slim.

From Asheville take Interstate 26 East (south) to North Carolina Highway 280 South. After about 5 miles turn right onto North Mills River Road. Just before the entrance to North Mills River Campground, turn right onto Forest Road 5000. After about 2 miles look for Forest Road 142 on the left; you'll know you're okay if you drive over a small concrete spillway. Trace Ridge Trailhead and parking area are at the end of the road. Leave one vehicle here.

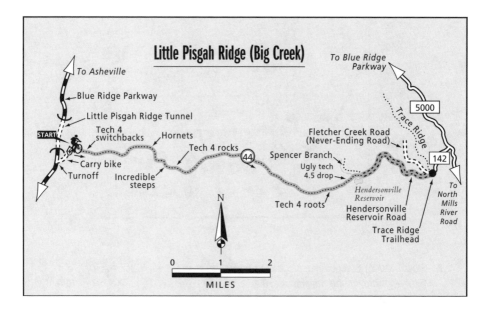

Little Pisgah Ridge (Big Creek)

From Trace Ridge Trailhead take FR 142 back out to FR 5000. Turn left onto FR 5000 and follow it all the way up to the Blue Ridge Parkway. Turn left (south) onto the Blue Ridge Parkway, go about 10 miles, and watch for the Little Pisgah Ridge Tunnel (*not* the Young Pisgah Ridge Tunnel). Go through the tunnel, then hang an immediate left onto a small, dirt service road that doubles back around the outside of the tunnel. Proceed to the end of a short road, park, and look for a faint trail through bushes, over rock piles, and up a 6-foot rooty embankment. *Carry* bikes approximately 0.2 mile along the trail to get off the Parkway property, through a twisty rhododendron tunnel and down stairs to the trail marker. From this point downward the trail is legal to ride. Please obey trail signs and carry to this point.

Miles and Directions

0.0 Start riding at sign for Big Creek Trail. Notice the "Most Difficult" rating, and keep it in mind when you start to get too cocky later. Remember to carry bikes from car to here; it's not far and will guarantee that the rest of the trail stays open to us.

0.3 Fairly smooth track, gradually faster and faster, much cleaner track than expected. Several tech 4 switchbacks.

0.5 Contour running gets fast, then faster, then insane. Hands and feet begin cramping at this point from high-speed pounding and instinctive desire to slow down. Some logs and fast rock sections.

0.7 Large downed tree crossing trail forces portage. **Caution:** The base of this tree is inhabited by big, fat, ill-tempered hornets, who *do not* grant the right-of-way. Give it a wide berth, or sneak underneath real quick and pray they go for your buddy behind you.

1.0 Beautiful contour running. Fast through the rhododendron thickets. Watch for unexpected water bars.

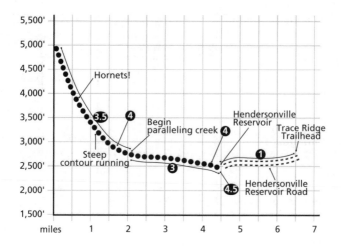

1.2 Steep! Steep! Steep! Fastest contour running you've ever seen, stuck somewhere between a dream and a nightmare. Big berms and extremely tight switchbacks. Here the world is just kick-ass fast, no way around it. Simply an amazing downhill run.

1.5 Serious tech 4 washout/rock crossing at speed. Sudden off-camber left turn filled with chicken heads and bordered by a respectable drop, for serious damage potential. Brakes could be the death of you here, causing a major slideout and a drop off the side. Either keep a heads-up and creep through it, or hold a tight inside line and pray the speed carries you through.

2.0 Trail flattens and starts to parallel Big Creek. Typical Pisgah streamside ride, always slightly downhill, allowing you to go as fast as you can pedal. Tech 3 overall. More frequent root and rock gardens. Multiple steep-sided stream crossings, some ridable, some not, with a few extremely dicey tech 4+ drops.

2.5 Nasty mudhole, deep and long, filled with old, rotten corduroy. Good place for a faceplant.

2.7 Stream crossing via a huge, 20-foot-long log. Long drop into the stream below. Not that tough of a move technically, but it carries an extremely high payment for failure.

3.2 Tasty rock garden, followed by a tech 3 stream crossing.

3.8 Long boulder head territory. Trail splits; bear uphill to left for a short hike-a-bike.

4.1 Nasty off-camber root crossing (tech 4) appears out of nowhere with a 25-foot drop on the side. Requires speed, belief, and a line on the high side to get you through. Anything less than total commitment here will leave you broken at the bottom. If you're not really sure about your skills (or aren't going way too fast to either stop or care), walk this one and save yourself a trip to the ER.

4.3 Beautiful rhododendron tunnel.

4.5 Very sudden, eroded, and rocky tech 4+ drop back to stream level. This spot is really mean, and it comes up really fast. Last opportunity for a serious bust before hitting the easy ride out.

Watch for the tunnel at Little Pisgah Ridge. David Tollerton photo

4.6 Climb up steps and cross old double-log bridge. Bear right at intersection with Spencer Branch Trail. Drop down a tough series of log steps to come out at the Old Hendersonville Reservoir. Beautiful old stone dam, nice and cool down below. Unfortunately, the lake itself looks pretty skanky and is definitely *not* inviting for a swim. From the dam turn right and follow Hendersonville Reservoir Road back up to the Trace Ridge Trailhead.

5.1 Nice double waterfall on left.

5.8 Begin your only bit of climbing.

6.6 Pass gate; return to Trace Ridge Trailhead and second vehicle.

45 Fletcher Creek

Fletcher Creek is a good ride for intermediates to hone their skills. The long spin out the Never-Ending Road warms you up plenty, then gets you ready for the drop back along the singletrack. Although the upper section of Fletcher Creek starts off running smooth and easy, don't get fooled, 'cause once you cross the creek, all hell breaks loose. A tough rocky climb leads into an adrenaline-inducing descent. If you like riding rocks—loose, sketchy rocks, at speed—do this trail. If you don't like rocks, bail out early off the Never-Ending Road onto Spencer Branch Trail instead, or you'll be really unhappy.

Location: Pisgah National Forest, Trace Ridge Trailhead area; twenty-five minutes south of Asheville.
Distance: 9.4-mile loop.
Approximate riding time: 1 to 2 hours.
Difficulty rating: Tech 1 (upper section) to tech 3+ (lower section). Upper section of Fletcher Creek Trail is buff to the point of being polished. Lower section more than makes up for it, though, with a long tech 3+ rocky descent that will have even experienced riders paying very close attention.

Trail surface: 2.4 miles of singletrack; 7 miles of gravel Forest Service road.
Highlights: Technical rocky descent; meadows; old homesite.
Land status: Pisgah National Forest.
Maps: USGS Dunsmore Mountain; USDA Forest Service Pisgah District Trail Map; National Geographic Trails Illustrated Pisgah Ranger District.

Finding the trailhead: From Asheville take Interstate 26 East (south) to North Carolina Highway 280 South. After about 5 miles turn right onto North Mills River Road. Just before the entrance to North Mills River Campground, turn right onto Forest Road 5000. After about 2 miles look for Forest Road 142 on the left; you'll know you're okay if you drive over a small concrete spillway. Trace Ridge Trailhead and parking area are at end of the road.

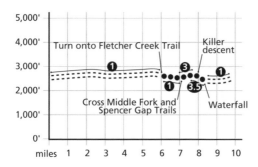

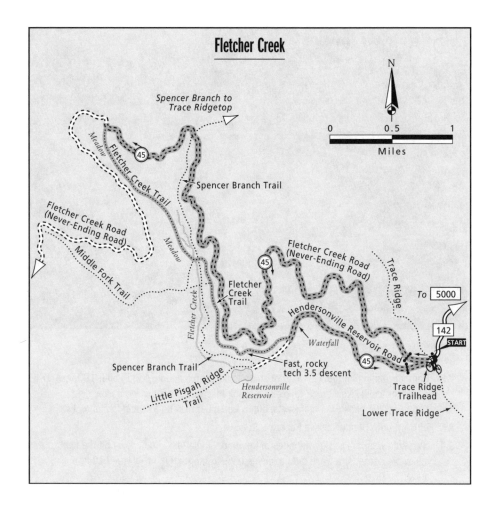

Fletcher Creek

Miles and Directions

0.0 Start at the Trace Ridge Trailhead. Enter past the right-most gate (the one next to the big humps of Trace Ridge) onto Never-Ending Road. This well-named gravel and dirt double-track winds on for a long, long way, and seems to go down as much as up.

2.7 The long, gradual climb on this section of the Never-Ending Road will have even sea-soned riders grousing. Blooming dogwoods or rhododendron and some long-range views will help to distract you from the pain.

4.7 Continue straight on Never-Ending Road, past the turn for Spencer Branch Trail.

5.7 Turn left onto Fletcher Creek Trail. Easy, smooth descent rolls past several meadows and an old homesite.

6.9 Middle Fork Trail branches off to the right, but continue straight. After about 50 yards, cross Spencer Branch Trail. Continue straight on Fletcher Creek Trail, which crosses its namesake creek and clearly picks up on the other side.

The Fletcher Creek Trail leads you past the Hendersonville Reservoir.

7.5 Contour running, mixed with a bit of steep rocky climbing, brings you about 100 feet up above the creek. Now brace yourself for a half mile of white-knuckled descending through switchbacks, laurel thickets, bunny hops, berms, and lots and lots of rocks.

8.1 Turn left onto Hendersonville Reservoir Road.

8.4 Nice little waterfall just on the edge of the road. Singletrack drops down off the right to follow creekside for a while before joining back to the road later—always better than gravel, in my book.

9.4 Finish one long grinder of a climb, pass the gate, and return to the trailhead.

46 Spencer Branch

This is a great ride for someone looking to do some spinning and have some technical fun without spending all day or working all that hard. It's also a perfect trail to give novice riders a chance to acclimate themselves to the wonders of singletrack. The Never-Ending Road is an easy up and down for a nice long warm-up, then Spencer Branch offers up a splendid lunch of buff, tech 1+ track sprinkled with some respectable technical challenges. The track can also be ridden as part of a loop linking the Fletcher Creek, Spencer Branch, and Middle Fork Trails.

Location: Pisgah National Forest, Trace Ridge Trailhead area; twenty-five minutes south of Asheville.
Distance: 8.2-mile loop.
Approximate riding time: 45 minutes to 1.5 hours.
Difficulty rating: Tech 1+ overall. Singletrack is generally quite buff with light roots and a scattering of rocks. Stream crossings can be tricky, as are some of the climbs.

Trail surface: 2 miles of singletrack; 6.2 miles of gravel Forest Service road.
Highlights: Reservoir; ridable log bridge; views; tough stream crossings; sweet cruising.
Land status: Pisgah National Forest.
Maps: USGS Dunsmore Mountain; USDA Forest Service Pisgah District Trail Map; National Geographic Trails Illustrated Pisgah Ranger District.

Finding the trailhead: From Asheville take Interstate 26 East (south) to North Carolina Highway 280 South. After about 5 miles turn right onto North Mills River Road. Just before the entrance to North Mills River Campground, turn right onto Forest Road 5000. After about 2 miles look for Forest Road 142 on the left; you'll know you're okay if you drive over a small concrete spillway. Trace Ridge Trailhead and parking area are at end of road.

Miles and Directions

0.0 Start at the Trace Ridge Trailhead. Enter past the rightmost gate (the one next to the big humps of Trace Ridge) onto the Never-Ending Road. This well-named gravel and dirt doubletrack winds on for a long, long way and seems to go down as much as up.

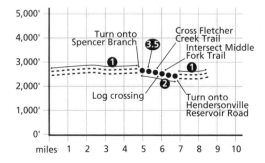

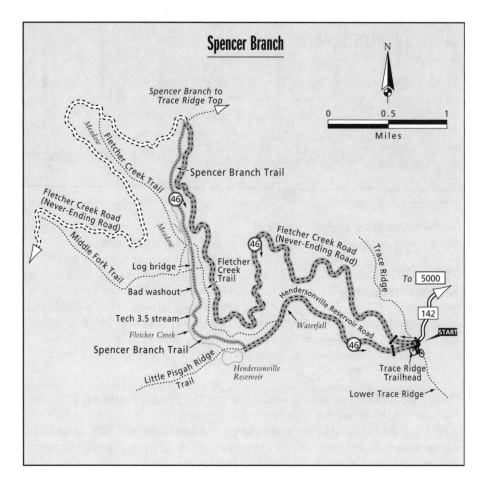

Spencer Branch

Spencer Branch to Trace Ridge Top

Meadow

Fletcher Creek Trail

Spencer Branch Trail

46

Fletcher Creek Road (Never-Ending Road)

Meadow

Middle Fork Trail

Log bridge

Fletcher Creek Trail

46

Fletcher Creek Road (Never-Ending Road)

Trace Ridge

To 5000

Bad washout

Hendersonville Reservoir Road

142

Tech 3.5 stream

Waterfall

START

Fletcher Creek

Spencer Branch Trail

Little Pisgah Ridge Trail

Hendersonville Reservoir

Trace Ridge Trailhead

Lower Trace Ridge

N

0   0.5   1
Miles

2.7 The long, gradual climb on this section of Never-Ending Road will have even seasoned riders grousing. Blooming dogwoods or rhododendron and some long-range views will help to distract you from the pain.

4.7 Turn left onto Spencer Branch Trail. Brown wooden sign points the way to some prime tech 2 Pisgah singletrack: smooth, twisty, and turny with enough roots, rocks, logs, and mudholes to make it interesting.

5.1 Tech 3+ stream crossing with a tough rock/root combo on the far bank. This move earns you a bit of a break afterward with a long stretch of tech 1 singletrack cruising.

5.6 Intersection with Fletcher Creek Trail. Continue straight on Spencer Branch.

5.7 Trail turns right to cross feeder stream over a 12-inch-wide, 12-foot-long log bridge. This move is only about a tech 2, but the drop to the stream looks really scary. Just after the log, a signed shortcut to Middle Fork Trail peels off to the right. Continue straight on Spencer Branch, up a funky tech 3 climb, then into some fun contour running through the rhododendron.

Keep your wheels straight on this bridge at Spencer Branch.

6.2 Challenging tech 3+ section with multiple stream crossings, quick ups and downs, and snaky playgrounds of roots and rocks. Log bridge requires walking.

6.5 Big Creek Trail joins in from the right. Continue straight on Spencer Branch.

6.7 Trail splits. Spencer Branch continues up to the left for a gradual return to Hendersonville Reservoir Road. Big Creek Trail drops down to the right over a series of steep water bars, bringing you out at the old Hendersonville Reservoir. Note that these eight to ten steps combine for a tech 4+ maneuver, one that will slam you down hard and maybe toss you in the drink if you get too cocky or sloppy about it (believe me; it's not deep, but it's damned embarrassing). If you're not really sure, best to walk this one. (If you end up taking Spencer Branch to the end, just double back down the gravel road to get to the reservoir. I highly recommend the visit to the bottom of the dam: It's really gorgeous, and the spray is just the ticket after a hot ride. Once you've cooled off enough, start up Hendersonville Reservoir Road for the return trip to the trailhead.)

6.9 Pass the signed entrance to Spencer Branch Trail back to the left. Pass Fletcher Creek Trail marker shortly afterward. Continue straight up Hendersonville Reservoir Road.

7.2 Nice little waterfall just on the edge of the road. Singletrack drops down off the right to follow creekside for a while before joining back to the road later—always better than gravel, in my book.

8.2 Finish one long grinder of a climb, pass the gate, and return to your vehicle for those cold drinks you remembered to pack.

47 Middle Fork

If you like a long warm-up, then want to spice up things a bit, this is a good trail for you. Never-Ending Road gives you plenty of time to work the kinks out. A quick descent over small rocks and roots down Middle Fork starts to wake you up. Then the descent out on Lower Fletcher Creek will have you either walking or working all the body English you've got just to stay upright and intact.

Location: Pisgah National Forest, Trace Ridge Trailhead area; twenty-five minutes south of Asheville.

Distance: 12.1-mile loop.

Approximate riding time: 1.5 to 2.5 hours.

Difficulty rating: Tech 2 overall. Middle Fork is generally a smooth track, though a good bit steeper and rootier than the other drops off the Never-Ending Road. Lower section of Fletcher Creek is full of loose melon-sized rocks, running rampant over several fast eroded downhill sections.

Trail surface: 2.6 miles of singletrack; 9.5 miles of gravel doubletrack.

Highlights: Long warm-up ride; fast tight singletrack; nice stream views; stream crossings; rocky downhill.

Land status: Pisgah National Forest.

Maps: USGS Dunsmore Mountain; USDA Forest Service Pisgah District Trail Map; National Geographic Trails Illustrated Pisgah Ranger District.

Finding the trailhead: From Asheville take Interstate 26 East (south) to North Carolina Highway 280 South. After about 5 miles turn right onto North Mills River Road. Just before the entrance to North Mills River Campground, turn right onto Forest Road 5000. After about 2 miles look for Forest Road 142 on the left; you'll know you're okay if you drive over a small concrete spillway. Trace Ridge Trailhead and parking area are at end of road.

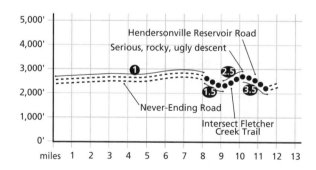

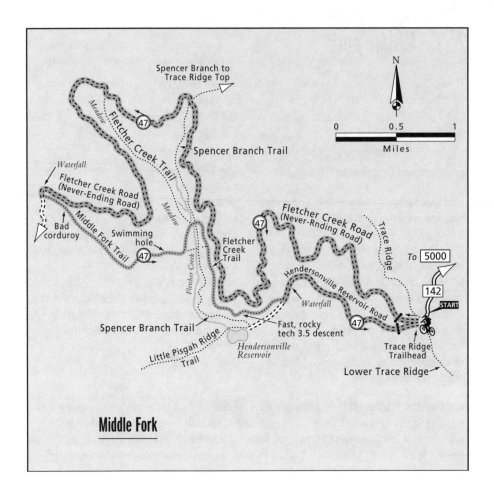

Middle Fork

Miles and Directions

0.0 Start at the Trace Ridge Trailhead. Enter past the rightmost gate (the one next to the big humps of Trace Ridge) onto Never-Ending Road. This well-named gravel and dirt double-track winds on for a long, long way and seems to go down as much as up.

4.7 Continue on Never-Ending Road. Spencer Branch Trail breaks off left and right.

5.7 Continue on Never-Ending Road. Fletcher Creek Trail breaks off down to the left.

7.9 Pretty, 6-foot waterfall on inside corner of road. Good place to cool your head.

8.2 Turn left onto Middle Fork Trail. Sweet tech 1+ trail zips along a wide little valley, dancing over lots of small root drops just perfect for hopping. Beautiful creekside running with some tech 2+ rocks and a few easy stream crossings.

9.3 Nice swimming hole in the stream down beside the trail.

9.5 Sign for shortcut down right to Spencer Branch Trail. Continue straight on Middle Fork Trail.

9.6 Turn right onto Fletcher Creek Trail and cross the creek.

10.2 Contour running, mixed with a bit of steep, rocky climbing. After topping, get ready for a frightening, or exhilarating, descent (tech 3+) over lots of loose rocks and wicked water bars.

10.8 Turn left onto Hendersonville Reservoir Road.

11.1 Nice little waterfall just on the edge of the road. Singletrack drops down off the right to follow creekside for a while before joining back to the road later—always better than gravel, in my book.

12.1 Finish one long grinder of a climb, pass the gate, and return to the trailhead.

48 South Mills River

We affectionately call this loop the Bataan Death Ride; it's not especially fun, but it will test your mettle. Once fooled into believing it was a three-hour cruise (yeah, I know, us and Gilligan), a crew of us spent the next seven hours trying to escape from the forest's clutches. This is the kind of trail that can crush your will to live, so bring plenty of water and food, and most importantly, a good attitude. Smooth sections running along the river can lull you into an easy cruising frame of mind, then slap you down with some nasty rock/mudhole combinations. Then, after you're already worn down, you get a brutally steep climb and a descent that's just plain hateful. Plan to get very wet, as you've got to ford, ride, wade, or swim across the South Mills River no fewer than fourteen times. Start the ride early or take a chance on spending a cold, wet night in the woods.

Location: Pisgah National Forest, South Mills River area; thirty minutes south of Asheville.
Distance: 19.2-mile lariat.
Approximate riding time: 4 to 7 hours.
Difficulty rating: Tech 1 to tech 4. Initial doubletrack is an easy tech 1. Later riverside running is a tech 2, with tough river crossings and mudholes. Horse's Gap and Cantrell Creek run from tech 3 to tech 4.

Trail surface: 9.8 miles of singletrack; 9.4 miles of doubletrack.
Highlights: River crossings; rhododendron tunnels; cliff faces; beautiful fern gardens; long, treacherous descent; lots of mud.
Land status: Pisgah National Forest.
Maps: USGS Pisgah Forest; USDA Forest Service Pisgah District Trail Map; National Geographic Trails Illustrated Pisgah Ranger District.

Finding the trailhead: From Asheville take Interstate 26 East (south) to North Carolina Highway 280 South and follow it for about 8 or 9 miles. Just past the sign for Etowah, watch carefully for Turkey Pen Gap Road on the right. Follow this rough, single-lane gravel road all the way to the end to the Turkey Pen Gap Trailhead.

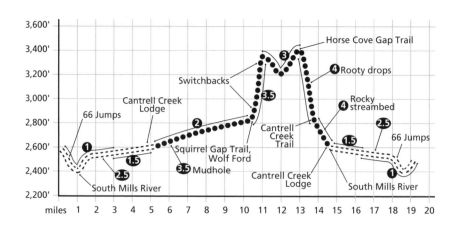

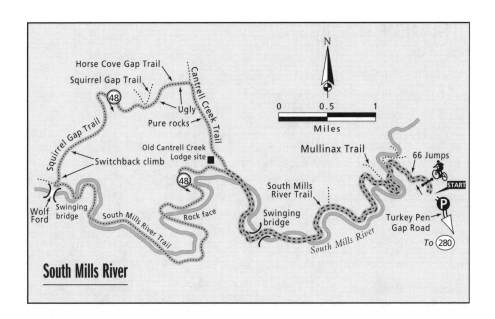

South Mills River

Miles and Directions

0.0 From the Turkey Pen Gap Trailhead, go straight past the gate at the end of the parking area and onto 66 Jumps, a long, dirt and gravel doubletrack. You open the trail with a smile as you launch yourself over one perfect water bar after another, all the way to the bottom. Enjoy this trip down, because you'll be dragging by the time you come back this way. Control your speed, particularly over those bars located in corners or covered with new gravel, and watch for hikers, anglers, horses, and other riders grinding their way back up.

1.0 Cross the South Mills River and continue straight onto the South Mills River (SMR) Trail on the other side. Tread is still gravel doubletrack with white blazes.

1.4 Bear left and down at this Y to stay on SMR and continue following white blazes. The track straight ahead is the bottom of Mullinax Trail.

1.5 Continue on SMR past a turnoff to the river. Tread gradually changes to hardpacked dirt doubletrack, tech 1+.

2.4 Pass several gorgeous campsites as trail wanders along this heavily wooded river bottom. Just continue following the white blazes, ignoring any turnoffs. Hit a respectable tech 2+ rock garden for your first taste of things to come.

2.6 Continue straight on SMR past the turn for Pounding Mill Trail (hiking only) on the right.

3.6 Trail turns left and crosses the river on a cool swinging bridge that's great fun to wobble across. Turn right after you cross the bridge and pick up SMR and the white blazes again.

4.3 Turn right just before an old washed-out bridge, and cross the river again. This one's generally ridable, but you'll still get wet.

Daniel table-tops in 66 Jumps on the South Mills River Trail.

4.7 Cross a pair of streams and enter a clearing with the remains of the old Cantrell Creek Lodge. Only the chimney of the lodge still survives; the rest (built in 1890) was moved to the Cradle of Forestry. Continue straight at the split after the lodge, staying on SMR as it changes to more of a wide singletrack. Cantrell Creek Trail cuts off to the right and is your return leg of the loop.

5.0 Bear left to continue on SMR and follow the white blazes.

5.4 Cross the river again, and fight your way up the steep-sided ravine on the other side. Anyone seriously *not* enjoying themselves by this point in the ride should turn back now, 'cause it only gets worse, and dragging some waterlogged whiner another 14 miles could be grounds for a spontaneous human sacrifice.

5.5 Nasty corduroy-filled mudhole. Excellent faceplant opportunity.

5.7 Cross the river again. This crossing is deep, with big slick rocks, and can be a bit daunting to the uninitiated. No one rides across this spot without the use of pontoons.

6.0 Super mudhole, steamy, skanky, and full of hidden rocks. Keep churning and keep the front wheel light, and you'll be the only one without shoes full of goo.

6.3 Cross the river three times in very short order. Tech 3 rock sections begin to appear with more frequency.

7.7 Trail turns sharply down right and crosses the river yet again. There's a deep hole in the middle of the river, so keep an eye out for each other—you don't want to miss an opportunity to help your buddies or at least laugh at them as they go under.

8.3 Cross the river again and begin to silently curse whoever decided on this trail.

8.8 Cross the river just as the trail bends around the base of a big rock face. Ride some more, then cross the river another two or three times (we've all lost count by now; just resign yourself to it).

10.1 Bear left at this unmarked fork, crossing a small creek and following the white blazes to stay on SMR.

10.3 Enter a clearing by another swinging bridge; this spot is known as Wolf Ford. Don't cross the bridge; instead turn right onto the (signed) entrance for Squirrel Gap Trail. Fortunately, you get to finally leave the river. Unfortunately, you now have to start some heinous climbing with a whole mess of tight, steep switchbacks.

12.1 Cross a small creek surrounded by huge spruce trees with blue blazes. Sign for Wolf Ford points back the way you came.

12.7 Grind your way up a last ridge and come face to face with a choice of three trails. Bear right, following the sign for Horse Cove Gap. Note that Horse Cove Gap is not especially bike-friendly, being filled with extremely steep, mud-filled rooty drops. It's a tech 3+ descent with several tech 4 moves along the way. Everyone in our crew of seven took at least one endo, even the ones who walked it.

13.5 Turn right at the T, heading down on Cantrell Creek Trail. The "trail" part seems to have been thrown in as an afterthought, because it's pretty much just a dry creekbed, a continuous tech 4 assault that will pound your legs, arms, and spine into mush. Busting along here somewhere is almost a certainty.

14.1 Follow the trail as it bears up and to the left, out of the creekbed.

14.5 Return to the clearing by the old Cantrell Creek Lodge site, and turn left back onto the SMR Trail. This is a good spot to share that last bit of power food you've been hoarding because you've still got nearly 5 miles, a couple of river crossings, and a mile-long climb before you get back to the trailhead.

15.6 Turn left to cross the swinging bridge again, then right to continue on SMR. Ignore any turnoffs and slog through the river when necessary to follow the trail.

17.8 Continue straight on SMR past the turn for Mullinax. Not that you'll have the energy for such foolishness at this point, but there's twenty or more beautiful water bars between here and the river that you could sail off, had you the notion.

18.2 Cross the South Mills River one last time. Continue straight across and start the long grind back up 66 Jumps.

19.2 Drag yourself back into the Turkey Pen Gap parking area. Wait to make sure that all of your crew manages to escape as well—unless you're the ride leader, in which case start worrying about a possible lynching.

49 Mullinax

Do you love to jump your bike and sail through the air off smooth, rounded water bars? Do you cherish those fleeting airborne moments when gravity no longer pins you to the earth? If you answered Yes!, then you absolutely, positively must ride Mullinax. In 6 miles you'll hit more than one hundred smooth-lipped, knee-high water bars, most of which provide excellent opportunities for some supreme air. Of course, those riders more fond of gravity's embrace can simply roll over them for the finest roller-coaster action this side of Six Flags. But don't think this is some kiddy ride—the upper section of Mullinax is a mine field of tech 4 and 4.5 root drops and erosion gullies that can chew up even the most experienced rider.

In the midst of a scorching Carolina summer, the best part of the ride may just be zooming into the South Mills River at the end of the ride.

Location: Pisgah National Forest, South Mills River area; thirty minutes south of Asheville.
Distance: 6-mile lariat.
Approximate riding time: 1.5 to 2 hours.
Difficulty rating: Tech 3 overall. 66 Jumps is a wide-open tech 1 run, though it's full of smooth, 2- to 3-foot water bars, as the name implies. Pea Gap is a painful tech 3+ climb, full of loose rocks and water bars. Mullinax itself is a tech 4 descent with a few deadly tech 4 and 4.5 rooty sections and another slew of jump-ready water bars. The South Mills River Trail drops it down to tech 1+ with twenty or so more water bars.

Trail surface: 3.7 miles of singletrack; 2.3 miles of doubletrack.
Highlights: A hopper's paradise with more than one hundred water bar–induced soaring opportunities; river crossings; technical descent; mud runs; typical Pisgah rocks and roots.
Land status: Pisgah National Forest.
Maps: USGS Pisgah Forest, USDA Forest Service Pisgah District Trail Map; National Geographic Trails Illustrated Pisgah Ranger District.

Finding the trailhead: From Asheville take Interstate 26 East (south) to North Carolina Highway 280 South and follow it for about 8 or 9 miles. Just past the sign for Etowah, watch carefully for Turkey Pen Gap Road on the right. Follow this rough, single-lane gravel road all the way to the end to the Turkey Pen Gap Trailhead.

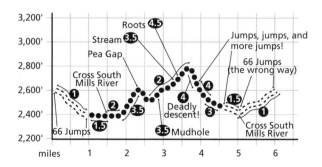

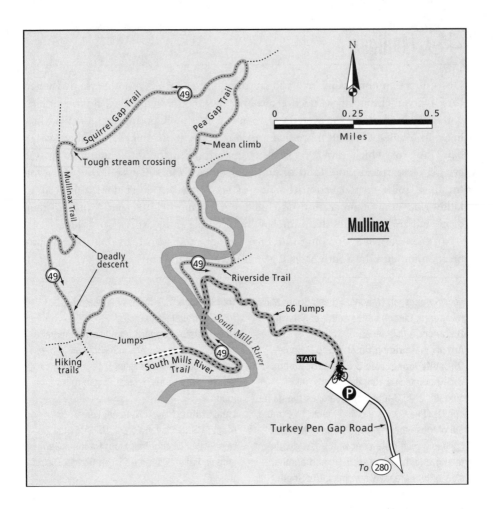

Miles and Directions

0.0 From the Turkey Pen Gap Trailhead, go straight past the gate at the end of the parking area and onto 66 Jumps. Brace yourself for some nonstop water bar action for the next mile, with perfectly sculpted launching pads every 15 or 20 feet on a wide, hardpacked, gravel and dirt doubletrack. Watch for hikers, anglers, horses, and other riders grinding their way back up.

1.0 Turn right *before* the river onto Riverside Trail. Tread changes to tech 1+ sandy hardpack with some tech 2 rocks and occasional mudholes.

1.4 At your first opportunity bear left, and cross the South Mills River. Crossing may be ridable depending on recent rains and your waterdog status. Riverside Trail picks up on the other side with red blazes, rockier track, and some serious mudholes. Don't miss this turn, or you're going to be hopelessly lost.

Paying for Mullinax.

1.8 Bear left onto Pea Gap Trail, and start climbing up away from the river. There's no sign, but it's a very clear split. You'll know you're on the right course if you're hating life within the first 100 yards; it's a mean tech 3+ climb over water bars and lots of loose baby heads.

2.3 Cross over Pea Gap and past a small campsite. Trail immediately begins to descend afterward over some steep water bars.

2.5 Cross a stream (Pea Branch), and turn left at the T onto Squirrel Gap Trail. Track is fairly flat, tech 1+ with blue blazes.

2.7 Tech 3+ rock-filled mudhole, then a ridable—but scary—log bridge crossing.

3.2 Tech 3+ steep-sided stream crossing with some tech 4 root lace on the far side. Just after stream turn left at the T onto Mullinax Trail. Squirrel Gap Trail continues to the right.

3.5 Mullinax abruptly changes from easy toodling to life-threatening. Starts off with a long twisty section of heinous tech 4+ roots, then a bunch of old log water bars with steep washouts on their back sides. A short rooty climb is your only rest, then you dive back in for some more mean water bars. This is a tech 4 descent that will leave you quivering at the bottom and thankful to have survived unscathed.

4.1 Cut sharply back left at this four-way intersection to stay on Mullinax and follow the yellow blazes (straight and right are hiking-only trails). As a reward for riding that heinous upper section, Mullinax now dishes out twenty or so smooth water bars of the dirt-hump variety. It's a quick descent and a little dicey at times, with some loose chicken heads scattered about, but it pegs the fun meter.

4.6 Continue straight as Mullinax merges with the South Mills River Trail. Trail flattens and changes to hardpacked doubletrack, but the water bar action continues with at least another twenty-five smooth-topped beauties just waiting to launch you as high as you care to fly. Watch for gravel on some of the bars, along with other trail traffic.

5.0 Splash straight into the South Mills River. You get an official River MacDaddy patch if you make it across without dabbing. In warm weather you'll probably want to stop and roll around in the river awhile before continuing. In cold weather you'll be hustling your freezing carcass back to the car as fast as your little legs will carry you.

6.0 Climbing back up 66 Jumps isn't especially fun, but it'll give you a chance to appreciate just how big some of those puppies are that you were sailing off of on the way down. Return to the parking area, and decide if you have enough juice left for one more trip down to the bottom of 66 Jumps and back.

50 Big Avery Loop

In some parts the trail is a smooth dirt highway; in other parts it's frame-buckling, rocky madness and wheel-wide cliff ledges. There are climbs that an alpaca would struggle with and descents that will plaster a rictus of thrill and terror across your face. An imposing ride, this thing will humble you, thrill you, kiss you, maybe kill you. Pay the insurance premium, then go enjoy yourself.

"I ain't too proud to call for m' granny." —Author
"No, Timm, there is no top." —David T, victim of Satan's Staircase

Location: Pisgah National Forest, Davidson River Campground area; forty-five minutes south of Asheville.

Distance: 12.9-mile loop.

Approximate riding time: 3 to 5 hours. However long it takes, you'll have nothing left at the end of it.

Difficulty rating: Tech 4 overall. Brutally steep rocky climbs and long, pounding rock gardens that go on for miles. If you don't like rocks, stay away.

Trail surface: 11.6 miles of butt-stomping Pisgah singletrack; 1.3 miles of gravel road.

Highlights: Incredible rocky descents; water bars (both up and down); ascent up Satan's Staircase; rhododendron tunnels; tons of stream crossings; long-range views of Looking Glass Rock.

Land status: Pisgah National Forest.

Maps: USGS Pisgah Forest; USDA Forest Service Pisgah District Trail Map; National Geographic Trails Illustrated Pisgah Ranger District.

Finding the trailhead: From Asheville take Interstate 26 East (actually south) to North Carolina Highway 280 South. Follow NC 280 for about 15 miles to the town of Brevard. Turn right onto U.S. Highway 276, which leads up into the heart of Pisgah National Forest. Go about 5 or 6 miles and watch for the Coontree Gap Picnic Area on the left. Park here; the trail begins just down the road.

Miles and Directions

0.0 From the Coontree Gap Picnic Area, turn right and head down US 276 just 20 or 30 yards. The entrance for Coontree Mountain Trail is clearly marked on the left. Track immediately hits you with a climb up loose rocks and respectable log water bars, tech 2+.

0.5 Cross a log bridge, then bear right at the Y (hiking-only trail to the left). Cross another bridge, then hunker down for a tougher climb, up and over no less than eight major water bars. Plenty of time to admire the beautiful stream and magnificent trees along the trail, as you'll probably be pushing somewhere along the way.

1.0 Double log, then a knee-high single. Trail starts to look and feel like a seasonal streambed, steep and full of tech 3+ moves.

1.2 Massive 3-foot water bars that are just about undoable on the way up (but a heck of a lot of fun on the way down). Long, painful climb follows, a rooty assault that requires a

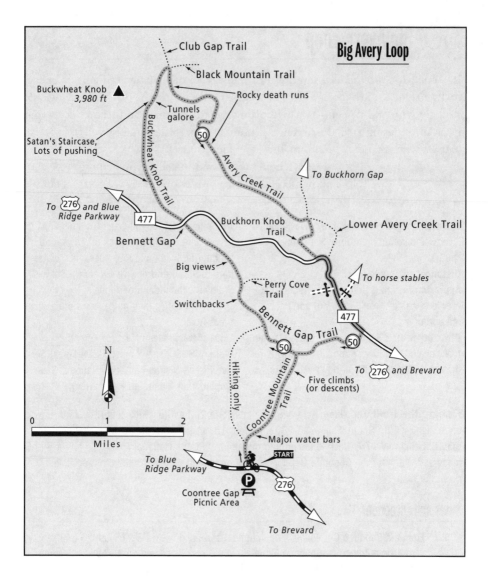

Big Avery Loop

Club Gap Trail

Black Mountain Trail

Buckwheat Knob ▲
3,980 ft

Rocky death runs

Tunnels galore

Satan's Staircase,
Lots of pushing

Buckwheat Knob Trail

50

Avery Creek Trail

To Buckhorn Gap

To 276 and Blue
Ridge Parkway

477

Buckhorn Knob
Trail

Lower Avery Creek Trail

Bennett Gap

Big views

Perry Cove
Trail

To horse stables

Switchbacks

477

N

Bennett Gap Trail

50

50

To 276 and Brevard

0   1   2

Miles

Hiking only

Coontree Mountain Trail

Five climbs
(or descents)

Major water bars

To Blue
Ridge Parkway

START

P

276

Coontree Gap
Picnic Area

To Brevard

lot of spinning and a lot of pain to conquer. Four more climbs follow, like the most foul-tempered quintuplets in Mother Earth's nursery. All five are steep, rooty, rocky, washed out, and most other uncomplimentary adjectives.

2.0 Bear left as you intersect Bennett Gap Trail.

2.4 Top Coontree Mountain and commence contour running fast and narrow, like an evil car-nival ride. Zip through a dark rhododendron tunnel, pop out onto track only as wide as your tire, no margin for error, with a 50- to 80-foot drop off the side. Toss in one of those chest-to-seat switchback turns, and you've got some white-knuckle stuff. Tech 4 descent, pegging the adrenometer.

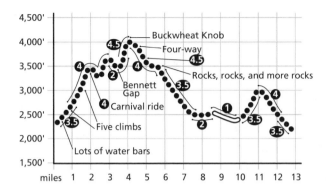

2.6 Continue straight, past Perry Cove Trail down to the right. And now face the first step in Satan's Staircase: huge rock stairs that laugh at puny mortals who attempt to surmount them. These monsters continue now and again, mixed in with some hellish steeps, all the way to Buckwheat Knob. Just think about what it'd be like to come down it.

2.7 In the midst of a raging rock garden, check out the phenomenal view of Looking Glass Rock, off to the left. After the appropriate amount of appreciation, get ready for more of Satan's Staircase.

3.2 Pass through a beautiful mountaintop meadow, then on to a campsite with a gorgeous view. Afterward you get a chance to hit warp speed as you dash down a long clear track into Bennett Gap.

3.5 Hit Forest Road 477 (gravel road). Jag left just for a bit, then pick up Buckwheat Knob Trail on the other side. Now for the last of Satan's Staircase: long, rooty climbs, one after another after another. It's a tech 4+ slice of trail hell.

4.2 Finally crest Buckwheat Knob, just below 4,000 feet. Take note as to how you feel after 1,600 feet of climbing. As you drop off the upper side of the knob, you get a chance to work the kinks out as you soar along buff tech 2 track through dark, silent rhododendron tunnels.

5.0 Drop down into Club Gap and a four-way intersection. Turn right onto Avery Creek Trail. (Note the name: Avery Creek Trail. Called this perhaps because for some of its length, it *is* Avery Creek. Imagine a continual, tech 4 barrage of rocks and deep holes. Picking the right line here is essential for survival.)

5.2 Hug trail left; sudden washout on right could swallow bike and rider alike.

5.3 Steep staircase of rocks 10 to 15 feet long, a tech 4+ move requiring total commitment. Trail pounds through a rocky stream that follows, then cruises through a deep emerald cove with a high-banked berm in the corner.

6.0 Cross a Forest Service road and zip past a 5-foot double waterfall. Track is rocky and loose, ugly through and through, but not quite as bad as up top, more like a tech 3+.

6.6 Long, fast downhill with a bad drop off the right side of the trail. Root drops start to appear in the trail at an alarming rate, growing from respectable 12-inchers to wide-eyed, 3-foot hungry beasts ready to make you or break you.

7.2 Track smoothes out to a tech 2, granting you a breezing brakes-free section down through a couple of streams and over a string of easy root drops.

7.6 Bear right just after the HORSE FORD, PEOPLE FORD sign onto Buckwheat Knob Trail. For some mysterious reason, this trail is inaccurately signed UPPER AVERY CREEK TRAIL at this point, which makes little sense 'cause you just came down Avery Creek Trail. Whatever you call it, follow this trail and it will take you back to the road. Smooth tech 2 cruising, some of the smoothest stuff you'll find anywhere in Pisgah.

8.5 Turn left as you pop out onto FR 477. Watch for cars.

9.2 Keep rolling as you pass the gated road on your right for Perry Cove.

9.8 Turn right at the sign for Bennett Gap Trail. Brace yourself for some more pain in the form of a brutal steep climb studded with big old water bars every 50 feet or so. And this goes on for a long time.

10.8 Turn left onto Coontree Mountain Trail. Now, remember those five brutal climbs at the beginning of the ride? Well, you get to salvage your ego a bit and take a shot at trouncing them on the way back down. They're tech 4 descents, and any one of them will be happy to blood-type you if you're not careful. But it's a hoot, make no mistake.

12.8 Drop back down onto US 276 and turn right to return to the Coontree Gap Picnic Area.

12.9 Return to the picnic area.

51 Laurel Mountain

Though I generally don't like out-and-backs, this one rates up there as a great ride. It's a straightforward ride, with no turns to worry about, and a relatively easy climb— for 1,400-foot elevation gain, that is. Even determined beginners can make it up to Good Enough Gap, and the run back down is like a dirt-faced roller coaster that pegs the fun meter. You'll come back down the mountain like your ass is on fire and you like the heat. Just watch for the off-camber rocks and rattlesnakes.

Location: Pisgah National Forest, 8 miles west of North Mills River Campground; about forty-five minutes south of Asheville.
Distance: 12.4 miles out-and-back.
Approximate riding time: 1.5 to 2.5 hours.
Difficulty rating: Tech 2 with a number of tough, off-camber tech 3 and 3.5 rock moves. The tech 4+ move at the cave is a bike (or rider) breaker, so use caution.
Trail surface: 12.4 miles of pure, prime Pisgah singletrack.

Highlights: Roller-coaster descent; smooth track; rhododendron tunnels; wildlife (that you'd just as soon miss).
Land status: Pisgah National Forest.
Maps: USGS Dunsmore Mountain; USDA Forest Service Pisgah District Trail Map; National Geographic Trails Illustrated Pisgah Ranger District.

Finding the trailhead: From Asheville take Interstate 26 East (south) to North Carolina Highway 280 South. Drive about 6 miles, pass the airport and the fairgrounds, then turn right onto North Mills River Road. After passing the North Mills River Campground, the road turns from pavement to gravel, becoming Forest Road 1206 or Yellow Gap Road. Go another 3.5 miles, and look for a small parking area on the left in the middle of an inside curve, just past a gated road. Trail sign is on the right.

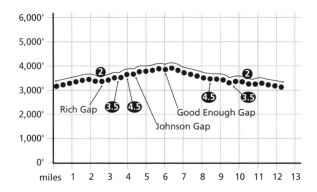

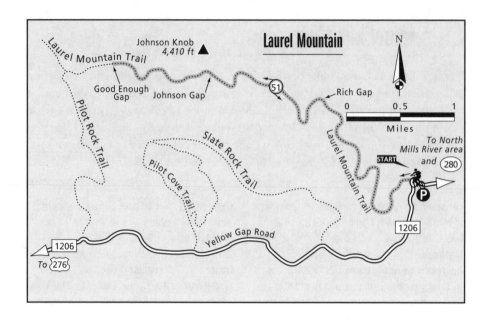

Miles and Directions

0.0   From the parking area at Yellow Gap, follow the brown trail sign across the road to begin climbing up Laurel Mountain. Trail begins with easy tech 2 track with occasional tech 3 rock moves.

1.0   Cool, beautiful rhododendron tunnel. Track begins to narrow with often only a 2-inch margin for error on the side.

2.8   Cross Rich Gap. Small campsite on the right.

3.0   Tech 3+ rock move. Last time through, we found a timber rattler sunning itself here, so be careful.

3.5   Big rocky overhang, almost a cave. Tech 4+ rock move or a wise carry.

4.7   Drop into Johnson Gap. Use caution as you drop through the saddles, as some of the off-camber curves could send you tumbling for a long, long way.

5.8   Small campsite to right. Trail curves left uphill (of course) for the nastiest climb yet up a steep, eroded rock-strewn slope. This is one of those climbs where you just take off your helmet, take a nice big drink, then start pushing. Take note of the beautiful huge oak trees (maybe 5 feet in diameter) as you trudge by.

6.2   Short descent into Good Enough Gap. Now's the time to rest and laugh away the pain. Then turn around and brace yourself for a wild, high-speed descent down narrow track and through tight rhododendron thickets.

6.6   Watch it on this descent, as the rocks are loose and hungry for human flesh.

8.9   Pass the cave again. Don't be emboldened to foolishness by the descent-induced adrenaline rush. Walk your bike over this tech 4+ rock move, unless you cleaned it on the way up.

12.4   Return to the parking area and consider doing it all over again. It's that much fun.

52 Pilot Rock Loop

This ride contains what may be the most technically challenging descent in the entire forest. Dropping more than 1,400 feet in just a little more than 2 miles is the easy part. You feel like you're riding on the bones of the mountain as you descend over huge rock slabs and pick your way through tight, 180-degree switchbacks that are simply solid boulders and chicken heads. Sometimes the tight rhododendron thickets on either side are all that keep you from flying off into space. And if the rocks up top weren't bad enough, the lower part of the descent is just one knee-high water bar after another, like some sick suspension torture test. I recommend this ride only for advanced riders and really game intermediates.

Location: Pisgah National Forest, 8 miles west of North Mills River Campground; about forty-five minutes south of Asheville.
Distance: 14.5-mile loop.
Approximate riding time: 3 to 5 hours.
Difficulty rating: Climb, tech 2; descent, tech 4+. The trip up Laurel Mountain is fairly smooth (except for the last climb), with only a handful of tech 3 rock moves and one tech 4+. The descent down Pilot Rock is extremely challenging, with incredibly tight switchbacks,

huge rock slabs, big erosion gullies, and dozens and dozens of water bars.
Trail surface: 9.4 miles of singletrack; 5.1 miles of gravel road.
Highlights: 1,400-foot descent; long-range views; rocky switchbacks; rhododendron tunnels; water bars; wildlife.
Land status: Pisgah National Forest.
Maps: USGS Dunsmore Mountain; USDA Forest Service Pisgah District Trail Map; National Geographic Trails Illustrated Pisgah Ranger District.

Finding the trailhead: From Asheville take Interstate 26 East (south) to North Carolina Highway 280 South. Drive about 6 miles, pass the airport and the fairgrounds, then turn right onto North Mills River Road. After passing the North Mills River Campground, the road turns from pavement to gravel, becoming Forest Road 1206 or Yellow Gap Road. Go another 3.5 miles, and look for a small parking area on the left in the middle of an inside curve, just past a gated road. Trail sign is on the right.

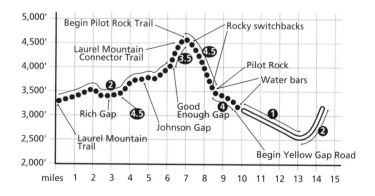

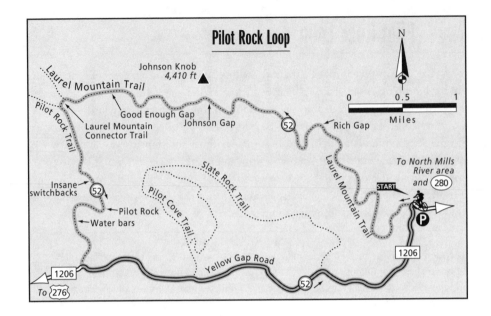

Miles and Directions

0.0 From the parking area at Yellow Gap, follow the brown trail sign across the road to begin climbing up Laurel Mountain. Trail begins with easy tech 2 track with occasional tech 3 rock moves.

1.0 Cool, beautiful rhododendron tunnel. Track begins to narrow with often only a 2-inch margin for error on the side.

2.8 Cross Rich Gap. Small campsite on the right.

3.0 Tech 3+ rock move. Last time through, we found a 5-foot timber rattler sunning itself here, so be careful.

3.5 Big rocky overhang, almost a cave. Tech 4+ rock move or a wise carry.

4.7 Drop into Johnson Gap. Use caution as you drop through the saddles, as some of the off-camber curves could send you tumbling for a long, long way.

5.8 Small campsite to right. Trail curves left uphill (of course) for the nastiest climb yet up a steep, eroded rock-strewn slope. This is one of those climbs where you just take off your helmet, take a nice big drink, then start pushing. Take note of the beautiful huge oak trees (maybe 5 feet in diameter) as you trudge by.

6.2 Short descent into Good Enough Gap.

6.5 Watch carefully for a trail split here as it's not marked and is easy to miss; a landmark is another small campsite. Turn sharply uphill left onto the Laurel Mountain Connector Trail, which will take you up to Pilot Rock Trail. This is an extremely steep and painful climb.

6.8 Final climb leads you up to Pilot Rock Trail. Turn left at this clearly marked intersection, but not before checking that all of your crew made the connector trail. Check your brakes, lower your seat, tighten up your suspension, and cough up some courage

What a line! DAVID TOLLERTON PHOTO

because here begins one hair-raising descent. Starts off with a fairly level ridge run. Then begins the nastiest switchbacks you've ever seen: These things are filled with solid rocks, and it feels like you're coming down a cliff face, which basically you are. Call it a continuous tech 4+ nightmare.

8.0 Trail turns back into some semblance of hardpack, then drops into a big erosion gully. You'll probably curse the tight thicket, until you realize it's protecting you from the 600-foot drop on your left.

8.4 When you notice nothing but air to the left, you'll know you're at Pilot Rock. Stop for a break and some pictures, as this 180-degree view is not to be missed. Valley floor lies 800 feet below.

8.5 Now that the rocks have stopped, the water bars take over: Some you can slalom around, but most you just need to either jump or eat.

9.2 Old road to the left. Do *not* make the mistake of thinking this is a shortcut; you'll regret it, believe me.

9.4 Finally, just as the last drop of oil leaks from your shocks and your hands fall useless by your sides, you return to Yellow Gap Road. Turn left, and begin the long haul back to the start. If you were really smart, you left a shuttle vehicle here, 'cause the last mile of the return leg is a bitch.

14.5 Return to the Laurel Mountain Trailhead at Yellow Gap.

53 Slate Rock–Pilot Cove Loop

The view—ohmygod, the view! Slate Rock perches 500 feet or so above the cove floor, with a breathtaking 180-degree view of the cove and an incredible profile of Pilot Rock across the way. Certainly one of the top three views in Pisgah Forest, with a hawk drifting on the thermals 100 yards out in front of you if you're as lucky as I was. About 80 percent of this trail runs through rhododendron thickets and tunnels, with brutal, heartbreaking climbs up a number of false tops, a descent down through Pilot Cove that screams for the first mile, and several challenging technical moves tossed in throughout the return leg.

Location: Pisgah National Forest, 8 miles west of North Mills River Campground; about forty-five minutes south of Asheville.

Distance: 3.9-mile fat lariat (that feels like 12 miles).

Approximate riding time: 45 minutes to 3 hours. No kidding. If you're a fresh, strong rider, you'll grind up the switchback climbs then fly back to the start. If you're already gassed or out to just take in the scenery, you'll probably push (and cuss) up the climbs, then hang out at the overlook until your camera is empty.

Difficulty rating: Tech 2+ overall but with some big spikes. The switchbacks are agonizingly tight and numerous but ridable. Downhill begins with some serious speed over roots, rocks, and water bars, mixed well for a knuckle-clenching tech 4 descent. Two large tech 3+ rock slabs spice up the return trip along the creek.

Trail surface: 100 percent Carolina single-track.

Highlights: Lots of mud, roots, twists and turns, and short surprising climbs.

Land status: Pisgah National Forest.

Maps: USGS Dunsmore Mountain; USDA Forest Service Pisgah District Trail Map; National Geographic Trails Illustrated Pisgah Ranger District.

Finding the trailhead: From Asheville take Interstate 26 East (south) to North Carolina Highway 280 South. Drive about 6 miles, pass the airport and the fairgrounds, then turn right onto North Mills River Road. After passing the North Mills River Campground, the road turns from pavement to gravel becoming Forest Road 1206 or Yellow Gap Road. Go another 3.5 miles, and look for a small parking area on the left in the middle of an inside curve. Trail sign is on the right.

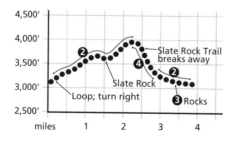

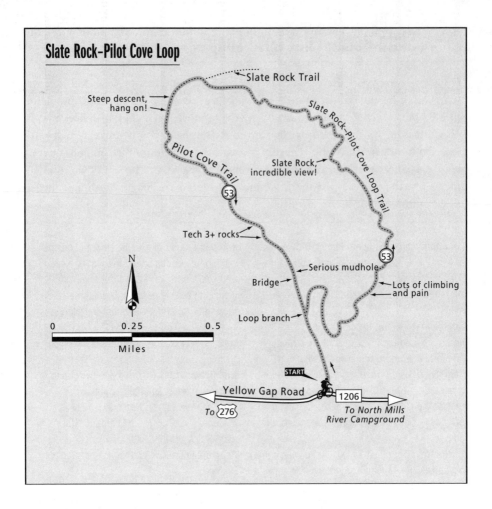

Slate Rock-Pilot Cove Loop

Slate Rock Trail

Steep descent, hang on!

Slate Rock-Pilot Cove Loop Trail

Pilot Cove Trail

Slate Rock, incredible view!

53

Tech 3+ rocks

53

N

Serious mudhole

Bridge

Lots of climbing and pain

Loop branch

0   0.25   0.5
Miles

START

Yellow Gap Road

1206

To 276

To North Mills River Campground

Miles and Directions

0.0 Start at sign for Pilot Cove-Slate Rock Loop. Nice, easy tech 1 riding along stream through gorgeous rhododendron tunnels.

0.2 Trail splits to begin loop. Turn right uphill over set of rock/log steps. If you get to a narrow log bridge, you missed the turn.

0.3 Trail gets rockier. First tough climb is only a mild annoyance, compared with the pain ahead.

0.4 Ugly root crossing. First set of tough switchbacks; ridable but by no means easy.

0.7 Topping first climb. Don't get excited—it's only a finger, and the real top is still way above you.

0.9 Steep switchbacks, climbing to top of actual knob. Heavy rhododendron thickets.

1.0 Nice view off to right. Sweet little descent through saddle, slipping and dipping with no effort but lots of smiles.

Timm shows the only way to fly on Sliding Rock Falls near the Slate Rock Loop.

1.2   Saddle ends too quickly; begin climbing again.

1.4   Tough climbs that always seem just about to top out, but only flatten out on a finger for a short while before throwing some more at you.

1.5   Trail breaks out of the brush and dumps you right on top of Slate Rock for one of the most spectacular views on these trails. Though it's early in the ride, no one will complain about stopping here for a break. Turn right as soon as you come out on Slate Rock to pick up the trail again. Incredible rhododendron tunnel just after leaving the rock. **Warning:** Do not ride straight out onto rock, as it curves away off into space. Also beware of walking too close to edge wearing cleated shoes, unless you have a desire to test out a new theory on unpowered human flight.

1.7   After drop through saddle, pump up a long, steep climb only to meet five (count 'em, five) steep-ass switchbacks in a row. Any one or two is doable, but five in a row is a righteous challenge. Tech 3 move on toughness alone.

1.9   Top another false peak, then drop through saddle past large rock outcropping and well-used campsite.

2.2   Top last peak, then a quick, steep descent off back of knob. Seems to drop for a long time, and you'll be grinning the whole way. Watch for water bars and super bunny hop potential.

2.4   Sign marks intersection of Slate Rock and Pilot Cove Trails. Turn left to follow Pilot Cove Trail back to starting point. This begins a very steep and rocky tech 4 downhill assault.

Lots of high water bars and tight sections through some nasty rocks that must be maneuvered at speed. It's easy to gain dangerous amounts of speed through here. Beware that forearms may suddenly burst into flames from braking.

2.8 Tech 3+ move up and over ugly 2.5-foot rock ledge.

3.0 Tech 3 move over large rock slabs crossing stream. Looks intimidating but just loft the front wheel and keep pedaling.

3.3 Tough though short technical climb. Incredibly sweet twisting singletrack follows, slipping through the rhododendron.

3.5 Narrow path branches left, leading to large campsite. Stay straight on main trail.

3.6 Monster mudhole with tight heavy brush on either side. You'll get sloppy whether you walk it or ride it, so you may as well give it a shot!

3.7 Trail crosses stream on narrow log bridge. Unridable by mortal men (but probably doable by some gutsy gals). Track rejoins entry trail 100 feet farther along with beginning of loop branching back to left. Stay straight to return to trailhead.

3.9 Supremely easy, relaxing (and slightly downhill) return trip alongside stream brings you back to the trailhead.

54 Buckwheat Knob Loop

Some of this trail is just simply insane. We rode up a waterfall; we rode down several small cliff faces. Sometimes you'll be afraid to continue, and sometimes you'll be too terrified to stop. The descent down from Buckwheat Knob is brutal and pounding, with several ridable but life-threatening tech 5 moves along the way. This ride will test every limit you've got: endurance, technical skills, courage, fortitude, and strength. If you pride yourself on riding the hairy stuff, come to Buckwheat Knob, and come prepared to be humbled. This is the stuff that legends are made of.

Location: Pisgah National Forest, Davidson River Campground area; forty-five minutes south of Asheville.

Distance: 11.3-mile loop.

Approximate riding time: 4 to 6 hours. This is an epic, all-day ride; plan accordingly for food and water.

Difficulty rating: Tech 4. This trail is a supreme technical challenge. Long, continuous tech 3 and tech 4 sections. Many tech 4+ moves, with the first one within the first half

mile of trail. And at least three sick tech 5 rock moves that will leave you broken and bleeding if you blow it.

Trail surface: 9.3 miles of phenomenal Pisgah singletrack; 2 miles of gravel road.

Highlights: Water bars; rhodo tunnels; tough climbs; insane technical descents.

Land status: Pisgah National Forest.

Maps: USGS Pisgah Forest; USDA Forest Service Pisgah District Trail Map; National Geographic Trails Illustrated Pisgah Ranger District.

Finding the trailhead: From Asheville take Interstate 26 East (actually south) to North Carolina Highway 280 South. Follow NC 280 for about 15 miles to the town of Brevard. Turn right onto U.S. Highway 276, which leads up into the heart of Pisgah National Forest. About 2 miles in, pass the Pisgah Ranger Station and turn right onto Forest Road 477 (gravel road), following the sign for the Pisgah Horse Stables. Go about another 2 miles, pass the gated road for the horse stables on your right, then look for another gated road immediately to your left. I like to park here because it's the return leg for the loop. If this spot is taken, drive a little farther and park in the pullout at the Buckhorn Gap Trailhead (you can take Buckhorn Gap to the intersection at mile point 0.9, and the trail mileage will be just about the same).

Miles and Directions

0.0 Turn left and head up FR 477, the gravel road you came in on.

0.1 Turn right onto the signed lower entrance to Avery Creek Trail. It's a fast, slippery descent with a half dozen mean water bars. Trail is mostly tech 1+ with some tech 2+ rocks and roots.

0.2 Bear left at the T, following the blue blazes. Trail right to Clawhammer Cove is hiking only.

0.5 Small but pretty waterfall to the left.

0.6 First major technical move, and it's a doozy: a tech 4+ stream crossing, with steep sides and some incredibly ugly roots on the back side. Of course, you could use the nearby log bridge, but where's the fun in that?

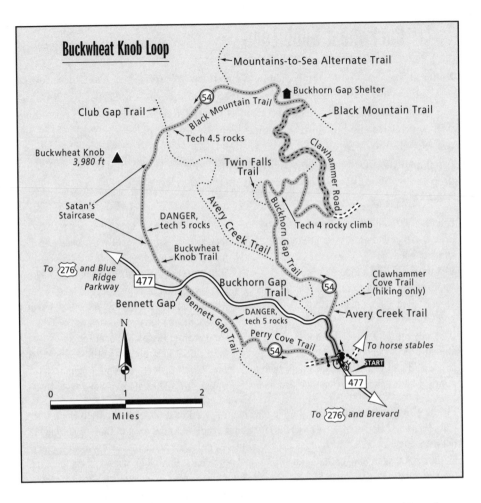

Buckwheat Knob Loop

Mountains-to-Sea Alternate Trail

Buckhorn Gap Shelter

Club Gap Trail

Black Mountain Trail

Black Mountain Trail

Tech 4.5 rocks

Clawhammer Road

Buckwheat Knob
3,980 ft

Twin Falls
Trail

Satan's
Staircase

Avery Creek Trail

DANGER,
tech 5 rocks

Buckhorn Gap Trail

Tech 4 rocky climb

Buckwheat
Knob Trail

To 276 and Blue
Ridge
Parkway

477

Buckhorn Gap
Trail

54

Clawhammer
Cove Trail
(hiking only)

Bennett Gap

Bennett Gap Trail

DANGER,
tech 5 rocks

Avery Creek Trail

N

Perry Cove Trail

54

To horse stables

START

477

0   1   2

Miles

To 276 and Brevard

0.9 Bear right at this intersection toward the sign that says HORSE FORD, PEOPLE FORD. Ignore the UPPER/LOWER AVERY CREEK signs, as they really don't make any sense. Trail back left is the beginning of Buckhorn Gap Trail and leads up to FR 477 and the alternate parking area.

1.0 Forty feet of continuous tech 4+ roots. If this is too ugly for you, turn around now and find an easier trail to ride, because you won't enjoy the next 10 miles.

1.1 Buckhorn Gap Trail turns right and crosses a creek over a log bridge, following orange blazes. Trail straight is the continuation of Avery Creek Trail.

1.4 Several tech 3+ stream crossings and some walking log bridges bring you to a miserable tech 4 rock garden and some unridable stairsteps and water bars. Trail hint: A puddle that's small isn't necessarily shallow.

1.8 Turn sharply right and look for the orange blazes to continue on Buckhorn Gap Trail. Blue trail straight is the Twin Falls Trail (hiking only). These falls are very beautiful and definitely worth seeing, but please either stash your bike in the bushes (yeah, right!), carry it the quarter mile to the falls, or come back later with your hiking boots and a camera.

2.0 Long, continuous tech 4 rocky section. If the stream up top gets diverted, like it was for us, you'll find yourself floundering up a rushing stream and a small waterfall for a unique riding experience.

2.3 Turn right, following blue blazes, as trail mellows to a tech 1+ (albeit uphill still). Track straight is clearly marked shortcut for hikers only (or cyclically challenged, as we call them).

3.2 A long, grinding tech 2 climb finally brings you to Clawhammer Road (gated gravel Forest Service road). Turn left onto the aptly named Clawhammer, which will tease you with a cool descent, then proceed to claw your lungs apart and hammer your body for the next mile or so.

5.1 Turn left at this five-way intersection onto Black Mountain Trail, which starts with a hideous tech 5 root-riddled staircase. Look carefully for the sign, because your mind may simply choose to ignore what your eyes say is an unridable goat path. Blue and white blazes.

5.3 Pass through an enchanted mountain laurel forest; the Buckhorn Gap Shelter appears on the right like something from a Grimm's fairy tale. Trail along here is an easy tech 1+ cruise.

5.7 Nasty, tech 4 corduroy, with excellent faceplant opportunity. Shortly after you'll hit a tech 4+ log that's cut out, with a steep drop off the back side, then a long series of tech 3 and 3.5 rock and root moves every 30 feet or so. Easy flat cruising through a saddle lulls you into a false sense of security. Sudden appearance of some hungry tech 3+ dragons-teeth and a big log drop remind you where you are.

6.3 Bear left to continue on Black Mountain Trail. Track right is the Mountains-to-Sea Alternate Trail (hiking only).

6.8 Pass over a knob and begin a mere sample of the heinous descents to follow. A fast, rocky tech 3 run leads you into some even nastier tech 4+ rocks.

7.2 Continue straight onto Buckwheat Knob Trail at this four-way intersection. Black Mountain Trail turns right to head up to Club Gap, and the upper end of Avery Creek peels down to the left (your last chance to bail out before the real nastiness begins).

7.8 Top Buckwheat Knob, and the technical trial of your riding life begins. Descent begins fast and swooping over some respectable logs and water bars and through some very tight rhododendron tunnels.

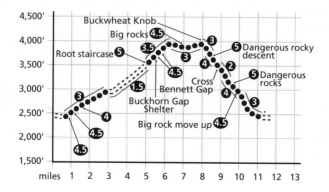

"This is the way up Buckwheat Knob? You must be kidding."

8.4 Satan's Staircase begins. This is a good place to say a prayer, strap on any body armor you may be carrying, and leave all caution behind. Starts out steep and fast, over tech 3+ rock gardens with jumps in the midst of it all. **Warning:** Watch for the first tech 5 move, a 6-foot staircase of boulders and rock slabs. Do not even attempt this move if you're alone, as it could easily be your ticket to the ER.

9.0 Trail regains some measure of sanity and crosses Bennett Gap Road (gated; gravel). Jag left onto the road, then take an immediate right to pick up Bennett Gap Trail on the other side. Short tech 2+ climb awaits.

9.1 Pass a beautiful high-alpine meadow and an ugly campsite with about 10,000 beer cans. Easy tech 1 grassy track.

9.5 Drop and climb through several small saddles, then run along a sharp ridgeline. Nice view of Looking Glass Rock to the right.

9.6 The nightmare continues with a number of tech 4 and tech 4+ rock slabs, leading you into another tech 5 move: a big rock garden staircase that requires two ninety-degree turns in the middle. Big, big bust potential. Follow it up with a tech 4, 2-foot ledge drop that seems almost tame in comparison.

9.7 Satan's Staircase's final offering: a tech 4+ move *up* a 4-foot-high pile of rocks. Then a long continual barrage of tech 4 and 4.5 boulders and rock slabs. Get your butt so far back it's buzzing the rear tire, let go of the brakes, and scream like a kid on his first trip to the carnival.

9.9 Sharp left turn back onto Perry Cove Trail, just after the insane rock garden above (it's easy to miss, so keep an eye out). Trail signs rate this trail as MOST DIFFICULT, which is bull after what you've just been through. Tech 2 run at the most, though it's fast and off-camber in spots with lots of switchbacks.

10.6 Cross a ridable log bridge, and pass through a gorgeous fern garden. Then drop through some wickedly fast swooping turns with some great smooth water bar jumps.

11.2 Turn left as Perry Cove dumps you onto gravel doubletrack.

11.3 Pass the gate and you're back at your vehicle. Say a prayer of thanks to the protective divinity of your choice, and celebrate your survival. Now you can honestly tell folks you're a mountain biker.

55 Thrift Cove Loop

Think of this trail as Black Mountain Extra, Extra Light. It's got a respectable (if smooth-surfaced) climb up Thrift Cove, then returns along the lower section of Black Mountain. The descent back down is either a lazy roller coaster (with a few surprise rock gardens) or a scorching, teeth-chattering run, depending on your choice of speed. It's a good alternative if anyone in your group isn't up to the challenge of a full assault on Black Mountain.

Location: Pisgah National Forest, Davidson River Campground area; forty-five minutes south of Asheville.

Distance: 3.7-mile loop.

Approximate riding time: 30 minutes to 1 hour.

Difficulty rating: Tech 1+. Some of the rock gardens on the return down Black Mountain rate a tech 3 and 3.5, but most of the track is wide, smooth, and fast. One avalanche jumble of rocks and trees across the trail throws up a tech 4+ for a serious challenge. Know that some riders make this move (though not me, not yet).

Trail surface: 3.3 miles of singletrack; 0.4 mile of gravel Forest Service road.

Highlights: Relatively easy climb; zippy return; big berms; fun run for little cost.

Land status: Pisgah National Forest.

Maps: USGS Pisgah Forest; USDA Forest Service Pisgah District Trail Map; National Geographic Trails Illustrated Pisgah Ranger District.

Finding the trailhead: From Asheville take Interstate 26 East (actually south) to North Carolina Highway 280 South. Follow NC 280 for about 15 miles to the town of Brevard. Turn right onto U.S. Highway 276, which leads up into the heart of Pisgah National Forest. Just a mile or so in, watch for the brown ART LOEB TRAIL sign on the right. Just after the sign turn right into a service area parking lot by a big metal power line tower. If you get to the ranger station, you've gone too far. Gated gravel road at back of lot is the beginning of Black Mountain.

Miles and Directions

0.0 Start in on old gravel doubletrack at back of parking lot. Sign for Black Mountain points the way.

0.2 Turn right at sign onto Thrift Cove Trail. This way up gives your legs a good warm-up before the real climbing begins.

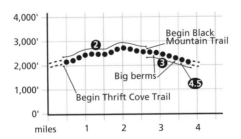

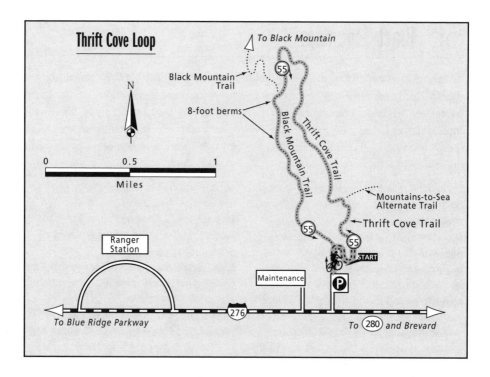

0.4 Continue straight past a group campsite, as the gravel gives way to XXL dirt singletrack. The Mountains-to-Sea Alternate Trail breaks off to the right.

0.5 Thrift Cove turns up to the left, following red blazes, and starts making some serious elevation gain. An unmarked gravel road (Grassy Road Trail) breaks off to the right.

2.5 Continue straight at intersection onto the lower section of Black Mountain for the return. Track starts to drop right away, and you can easily gain scary amounts of speed. Two high inside corners offer 8-foot-tall berms or runaway ramps. Watch for sudden rock gardens and a huge tech 4+ log/rock obstacle.

3.5 Turn right as Black Mountain spills you out onto the gravel entrance road. Four or five nice rounded water bars to jump on the way out.

3.7 Return to parking lot.

56 Black Mountain

Simply put, this is one of the top three descents in the entire forest. It should be on the "A" list for any rider who requires enormous doses of heartbreak, challenge, and adrenaline. Make no bones about it: This descent is rough and treacherous, filled with high water bars and hungry rocks. Never mind what any of the signs or maps say: This is an advanced trail for advanced riders. I can't recall a more pounding descent.

Location: Pisgah National Forest, Davidson River Campground area; forty-five minutes south of Asheville.

Distance: 9.9-mile lariat.

Approximate riding time: 2.5 to 4.5 hours, depending on how slow you push and how quickly you hammer back down.

Difficulty rating: Tech 4. Uncountable slippery water bars set at bad angles; big, loose rocks; serious drops—at speed—into even more serious rock gardens. With this kind of trail, you just point the bike downhill, say a quick prayer, and try to hang on. A constant barrage

of trail chaos will leave you battered and respectful at the bottom.

Trail surface: 9.5 miles of rough-and-ready Pisgah singletrack; 0.4 mile of gravel Forest Service road.

Highlights: Killer climbs; long-range views; no-holds-barred descent; insane bunny hops; wild irises along trailside.

Land status: Pisgah National Forest.

Maps: USGS Pisgah Forest; USDA Forest Service Pisgah District Trail Map; National Geographic Trails Illustrated Pisgah Ranger District.

Finding the trailhead: From Asheville take Interstate 26 East (actually south) to North Carolina Highway 280 South. Follow NC 280 for about 15 miles to the town of Brevard. Turn right onto U.S. Highway 276, which leads up into the heart of Pisgah National Forest. Just a mile or so in, watch for the brown ART LOEB TRAIL sign on the right. Just after the sign turn right into a service area parking lot by a big metal power line tower. If you get to the ranger station, you've gone too far. Gated gravel road at back of lot is the signed beginning of Black Mountain.

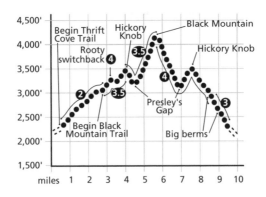

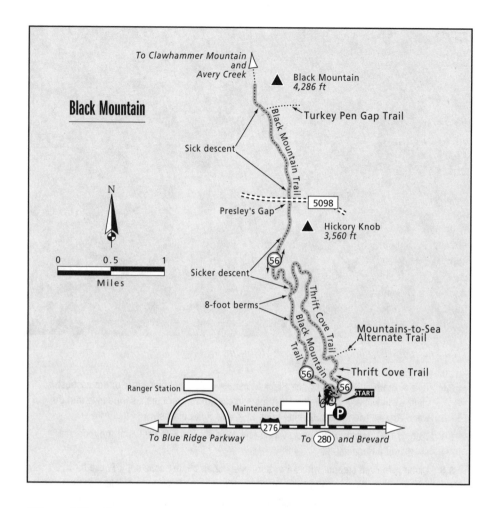

Miles and Directions

0.0 Start in on old gravel doubletrack at back of parking lot. Sign for Black Mountain points the way.

0.2 Turn right onto Thrift Cove Trail. This way up gives your legs a good warm-up before the real climbing begins. You can go straight up Black Mountain, but you'll catch it on the way back down, and the surprise will be worth it.

0.4 Continue straight past a group campsite, as the gravel gives way to XXL dirt singletrack. The Mountains-to-Sea Alternate Trail breaks off to the right.

0.5 Thrift Cove turns up to the left, following red blazes, and starts making some serious elevation gain. An unmarked gravel road (Grassy Road Trail) breaks off to the right.

1.3 Trail smoothes out and flattens into an easy tech 1+ cruise. Don't be fooled—this is Mother Nature's idea of a joke.

Curt finds the yellow brick road to Black Mountain.

2.5 Take a sharp right turn onto the Black Mountain Trail. Now begins one of the nastiest climbs you will ever experience. Just roots, rocks, and water bars disappearing into the woods above you for a long, long time. Blue and white blazes.

3.1 Tech 4, 180-degree switchback, with a choice of either the log stairs or the root-encrusted embankment.

3.6 Climb gets even steeper with water bars pitching up almost constantly. Pause for a moment to think about what the return down this slope is going to be like. Yep, that bad.

3.9 Top out on Hickory Knob at 3,560 feet. You just rode/pushed/crawled over 1,400 feet vertical, so rest a bit and enjoy the view. You even get a fun—if somewhat scary—downhill when you leave. Bad news though: It climbs another 1,000 feet from there. Watch for the racing turkeys.

4.3 Enter intersection at Presley's Gap. Continue straight on Black Mountain Trail. Forest Road 5098 heads left and right, and an unmarked grassy doubletrack cuts back to the right as well. March on, intrepid soul, for the climbing begins again here.

4.9 Old unmarked logging road left and right. Continue straight on Black Mountain.

5.3 Continue straight on Black Mountain. Turkey Pen Gap Trail breaks off to the right and links up with trails in the South Mills River area.

5.6 Top out on Black Mountain, elevation 4,286 feet, and turn around. Rest well, because the trip back down will test all your limits. It's fast and steep, covered with slippery water bars, loose baby heads, and dragonsteeth. You can get big bunny hops and bypass some of the real nasty stuff, but the landings are sketchy at best.

5.9 You never saw it, but Turkey Pen Gap Trail peeled back off to your left.

6.9 Straight through intersection at Presley's Gap. Here's a good place to check the health of your traveling companions and share a bit of hysterical laughter as you ride or push up a short stretch to Hickory Knob.

7.3 Top out on Hickory Knob. Believe it or not, this next descent is even worse than the top section. It's very steep, with nothing even vaguely resembling a clean line.

8.7 Return to intersection with Thrift Cove. This time, turn right to follow Black Mountain back to the bottom. Trail changes to fairly wide, flat tech 2, then starts to gain the kind of speed that can melt the brakes right off your wheels. Two high inside corners offer 8-foot-tall berms or runaway ramps. Watch for sudden rock gardens and a huge tech 4+ log/rock obstacle.

9.7 Turn right as Black Mountain spills you out onto the gravel entrance road. Four or five nice rounded water bars to jump on the way out—if you don't have the shakes too bad, that is.

9.9 Return to parking lot.

57 Daniel Ridge Loop

The cove of Daniel Ridge Creek may just be the most peaceful, beautiful place you have ever seen. Words cannot do justice to the wonder of this place, where the air, the stream, the rocks, and the trees all sparkle as if freshly made by the Creator's hands. It touched me that strongly. Be sure to bring your camera, as the 60-foot waterfall at the beginning is only a prelude to the beauty of this place.

But be forewarned that this sylvan paradise is guarded by one of the meanest descents around. After leaving Farlow Gap, the next mile is nothing but rocks, more rocks, and gaping holes where the rocks used to be. In spots the trail narrows to 6 inches wide, running along an almost sheer fall line. This trail would scare most people to simply walk it in some places. Riding it seemed like insanity. I loved it.

Location: Pisgah National Forest, near fish hatchery; about 35 miles south of Asheville.
Distance: 4.8-mile loop.
Approximate riding time: 1 to 2 hours, depending on time spent just admiring the beauty.
Difficulty rating: Tech 1+ for the climb and the lower descent. Tech 4 for the upper descent from Farlow Gap; it's a continual rock field.

Trail surface: 3.8 miles of singletrack; 1 mile of Forest Service road.
Highlights: Spectacular waterfall and cascades; extremely technical descent.
Land status: Pisgah National Forest.
Maps: USGS Shining Rock; USDA Forest Service Pisgah District Trail Map; National Geographic Trails Illustrated Pisgah Ranger District.

Finding the trailhead: From Asheville take Interstate 26 East (actually south) to North Carolina Highway 280 South. Follow NC 280 about 15 miles to the town of Brevard. Turn right onto U.S. Highway 276, which leads up into the heart of Pisgah National Forest. Follow US 276 for roughly 4 miles, then turn left onto Forest Road 475 (paved at this point), which leads to the fish hatchery. About 1.5 miles past the fish hatchery, watch for the second gated road on the right. Trail entrance is signed.

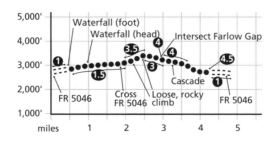

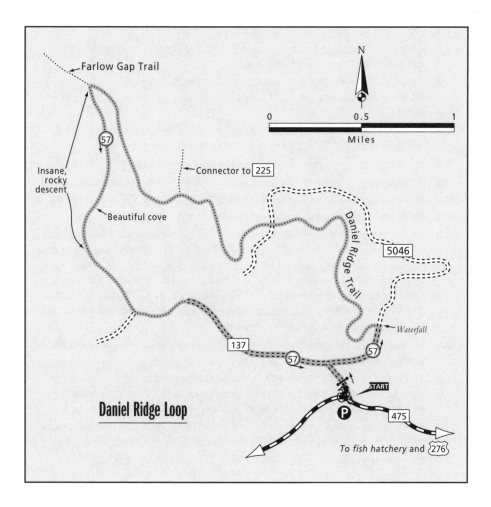

Daniel Ridge Loop

Miles and Directions

0.0   Enter past the gate onto Forest Road 5046.

0.1   Cross a wide concrete bridge, and continue straight. Return leg of the trail enters from the left.

0.4   Turn left onto Daniel Ridge Trail. Trail starts out as tech 2 leafy hardpack, gaining some easy elevation as it climbs through a mountain laurel thicket. You can't miss the trailhead, because it starts at the foot of a gorgeous 60-foot waterfall.

0.7   Steep rocky switchback, tech 2+.

0.9   Trail swings by the very top of the waterfall. You can't see much, but it sounds really cool. Don't be stupid enough to walk out onto it; the rocks are really slick, and it's a long way down. Cross a short wooden bridge just after the falls, then bear up to the right.

1.2   Four more wooden bridges in a row. Trail is pristine along here; just a clean dirt ribbon through the green.

1.3 Stream and log crossing, then edge along a small meadow.

1.5 Another wooden bridge, then a nasty tech 3 climb that's steep and rocky and littered with water bars. This one is probably a pusher.

1.7 Cross FR 5046 again. This is the same gated road you started the ride on. Trail picks up straight across with red blazes on the trees. Unfortunately, the climbing picks up again as well.

1.8 Nice long-range view to left. Track is extremely loose and rocky, which makes for one bitch of a climb.

2.0 Trail turns suspiciously smooth (tech 1+) and begins contour running.

2.3 Continue straight. Unmarked singletrack breaks off uphill to the right, eventually leading to Forest Road 225. Cross over saddle and begin some fast downhill contour running.

2.6 Pair of super-tight switchbacks, followed by some tech 3+ corduroy.

2.9 Turn left at intersection with Farlow Gap, down some nasty-looking stairs (tech 4). The gorgeous stream below is Daniel Ridge Creek, and it is truly a thing of beauty. The following descent is filled with peril in the form of big loose rocks and big rock-shaped holes. It's pounding and unrelenting and a good place for a bad bust. There are also two spots where the trail narrows to about 6 inches wide with a seventy-five-degree fall line dropping 50 or 60 feet down the side. Don't even think about blowing your move there. I'd rate the next half mile a solid tech 4 descent.

3.5 Trail drops down alongside the creek. You'll find an awe-inspiring cascade here by the sound of its laughter.

3.6 Pass an old stone bridge to the right. Trail begins to run along an old roadbed, Forest Road 137. Not doubletrack but maybe XXL singletrack. Smooth cruising in some places, sketchy running over loose chicken heads in others. Red blazes still on the trees.

4.2 Go straight, as another old road breaks to the right. Trail leads down a ferocious drainage ditch/stairs combination, tech 4+. Track afterward turns into true Forest Service road.

4.7 Track dumps you back onto FR 5046. Turn right to return to the parking area.

4.8 Pass the gate and return to your car.

58 Caney Bottom

This may well be the most purely fun trail available in all of Pisgah National Forest. The climb is relatively mild, the waterfall is spectacular, and the descent will have you waking up the next morning with a grin still stretched across your face. Novices will be spoiled by the sheer beauty and exhilaration of this ride. More advanced riders can take what's offered, add several healthy dollops of speed, then holler themselves hoarse over one massive jump, two waist-high berms that belong on a NASCAR track, and enough bunny hops to make you think your bike sprouted wings.

Location: Pisgah National Forest, near fish hatchery; about fifty minutes south of Asheville.

Distance: 5.2 miles out-and-back.

Approximate riding time: 45 minutes to 1 hour, depending on time at the waterfall.

Difficulty rating: Tech 2 overall. Most of this trail is smooth and well groomed. However, a number of tech 3 and 4 root maneuvers lurk along the way, and the unending root drops on the way back down can get you pogo-ing with amazing regularity and astounding results. Ridable and enjoyable by bikers of all ability levels.

Trail surface: 4.4 miles of primo Pisgah singletrack; 0.8 mile of Forest Service road.

Highlights: Spectacular waterfall; easy climb; gravity-defying berms; an amazing number of little root drops; and a 4-foot-high jump at the bottom of the extension for those who need a little more altitude in their lives.

Land status: Pisgah National Forest. **Note:** This trail is only open seasonally to bike riders, from October 15 to March 15.

Maps: USGS Shining Rock; USDA Forest Service Pisgah District Trail Map; National Geographic Trails Illustrated Pisgah Ranger District.

Finding the trailhead: From Asheville take Interstate 26 East (actually south) to North Carolina Highway 280 South. Follow NC 280 about 15 miles to the town of Brevard. Turn right onto U.S. Highway 276, which leads up into the heart of Pisgah National Forest. Follow US 276 for roughly 4 miles, then turn left onto Forest Road 475 (paved at this point), which leads to the fish hatchery. Roughly 1 mile past the fish hatchery, look for gated road and sign on right for Cove Creek Group Campground area. Parking area is across the road on the left.

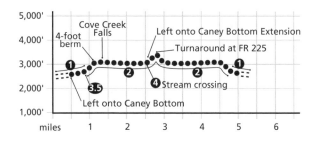

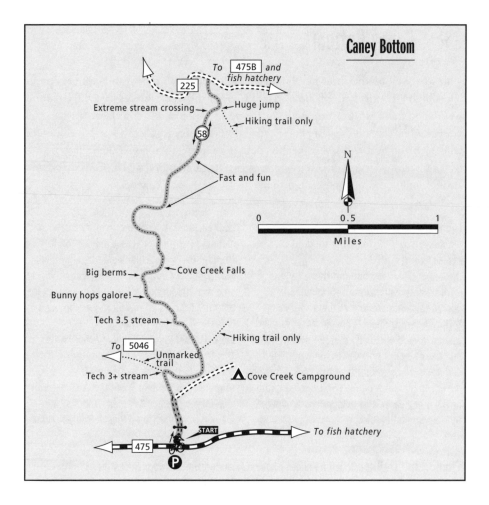

Miles and Directions

0.0 Start at parking area across from gated road to the Cove Creek Group Campground area (on the road from the fish hatchery). Go around gate and up gravel road.

0.1 Cove Creek Road goes through a wide but doable creek crossing. Path to right ducks into a pretty rhodo tunnel, crosses a creek on short wooden bridge, then returns to the road.

0.4 Turn left at trail entrance. Trail marker (Caney Bottom Loop) planted 20 feet in. Also brown sign: GROUP CAMPING BY RESERVATION ONLY.

0.5 Turn right across steep, rocky tech 3+ stream crossing. Blue arrow mounted on tree. Trail straight is an ugly climb up to an uncharted fire road. Campground down to right.

0.6 Turn left uphill, following blue blazes. Right is shortcut back down to road. About 2 miles of easy climbing starts now.

0.8 Turn left (straight) to continue on bike trail. Hiking-only trail turns off to the right. Tech 3+ rocky stream crossing, followed shortly by a serious portage over a log bridge, then more climbing.

1.0 Three respectable root drop/water bars in a row, followed by beautifully carved 4-foot-high berm. Remember this spot for the trip back down; with a little speed, it pegs the fun meter.

1.2 Stop. Listen for the sound of rushing water and look for faint trail to the right. A very tough little track leads you through the rhododendron and right to the top of Cove Creek Falls, an incredible waterfall that rivals anything in Pisgah. Do *not* be a fool and attempt to walk or ride across the stone at the top; it'd either be your best move ever or your last. Look for branch trail that leads down to the bottom. The falls are 20 to 25 feet wide and drop 50 to 60 feet; easily as beautiful as Looking Glass Falls.

2.3 Nasty tech 4 descent through rocks and roots down to bridge with more roots on the climb up the other side. Definitely one of those all-or-nothing spots; do it right or walk it.

2.5 Turn left onto Caney Bottom Extension Trail (yellow blazes). Blue trail to right is beginning of hiking-only leg. Climb up and over a sinister 4-foot-high erosion bar, which will be waiting patiently for your return.

2.6 Hit Forest Road 225 (gravel road). Turn around, rest, drink lots of water, and prepare yourself for what may just be the largest shot of straight fun this side of New Orleans. Very fast descent leads you back to that mammoth jump at the bottom of the extension. Even relatively sane levels of speed can send you soaring 6 feet or more, so either slow down and enjoy the ride or hit it hard, hang on, and pray for a safe landing.

2.7 Turn right at bottom of jump to stay on bike trail; straight is hiking only.

3.3 Track from here gets sweet and swoopy, with lots of long buff sections, fast curves, and short carpets of tech 3+ roots laid down in some of the corners. Oh, and those two magnificent berms lie somewhere along here for an opportunity to get horizontal with your bike without eating any dirt.

4.2 Unridable log across trail forces portage. Afterward watch for series of three good-sized root drops in a row that will have you doing more flying than rolling; I score this section a 9.5 for fun alone.

4.6 Bear right to stay on trail. Curve to left is shortcut back to Cove Creek Road.

4.7 Turn left after steep-sided tech 3+ stream crossing.

4.8 Turn right to put you back on Cove Creek Road for the return trip to the parking area.

5.1 Excellent cool-down opportunity crossing wide stream.

5.2 Return to parking area.

59 Pink Beds

The Pink Beds is just about as easy a trail as you'll find in Pisgah. It doesn't drop more than 40 feet in elevation along its entire length. And yet, it's still Pisgah, with enough roots, rocks, and logs to keep you grinning. You used to be able to loop this trail with Forest Road 1206, but some industrious beaver families have claimed the bottom for themselves and thrown up a formidable moat around their mile-high property. So until our fat-tailed brothers decide to move on, this trail is an out-and-back ride or a swim, take your pick.

Location: Pisgah National Forest, near the Cradle of Forestry; about fifty minutes south of Asheville.

Distance: 5.4 miles out-and-back.

Approximate riding time: 45 minutes to 1.5 hours.

Difficulty rating: Tech 1+ overall. Most of this trail is wide-open XXL singletrack with minimal roots and rocks. There are a few respectable logs to cross, a long washed-out section to navigate, and a tech 3+ rock garden along the way.

Trail surface: 4.6 miles of singletrack; 0.8 mile of gravel road.

Highlights: Long rhodo tunnel; easy cruising; logs; bridges; beaver dam.

Land status: Pisgah National Forest. Trail open to bikes October 1 through March 31.

Maps: USGS Shining Rock; USDA Forest Service Pisgah District Trail Map; National Geographic Trails Illustrated Pisgah Ranger District.

Finding the trailhead: From Asheville take Interstate 26 East (actually south) to North Carolina Highway 280 South. Follow NC 280 for about 15 miles toward Brevard. At the first Brevard stoplight, turn right onto U.S. Highway 276. Follow US 276 for 10 or 12 miles, nearly to the Blue Ridge Parkway. Turn right at the sign for the Pink Beds Picnic Area, just past the Forest Discovery Center. Park in the lot. Trail picks up on the far side of the picnic area.

Miles and Directions

0.0 From the parking lot head toward the back of the picnic area by a gate that's signed ROAD CLOSED.

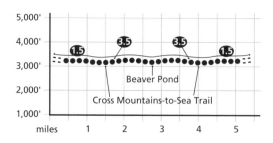

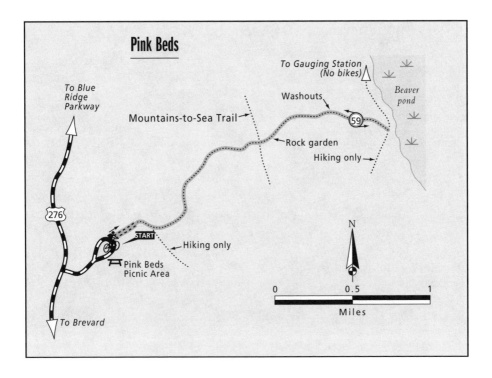

Pink Beds

To Blue Ridge Parkway

To Gauging Station (No bikes)

Washouts

Beaver pond

Mountains-to-Sea Trail

Rock garden

Hiking only

276

START

Hiking only

Pink Beds Picnic Area

N

0   0.5   1

Miles

To Brevard

0.1 Turn left at the Y to stay on the bike portion of the trail. Track starts out down an easy gravel doubletrack and crosses a wide but shallow stream. The stream is more than ankle deep and very cold, I can attest. Nearby bridge provides easy bypass.

0.4 Tread changes to dirt singletrack, tech 1+. Nice descent through the woods and along the edges of several small meadows.

0.7 Cross two wooden foot bridges. Some twisting through the trees, then a swooping descent.

1.0 Ridable stream with accompanying footbridge. Trail then drops into a long rhodo tunnel so tight you can touch the ceiling. Orange blazes on the trees.

1.5 Pass between the cut halves of a huge fallen cedar tree. Continue straight as Pink Beds Trail crosses the Mountains-to-Sea Trail.

1.6 Tech 3+ rock garden covering both sides of a small ravine. Ridable, except for the fallen tree in the bottom.

2.2 Trail becomes very washed out and eroded. Enormous number of downed trees, some of which cross the trail for hopping opportunities.

2.5 Turn right at the T, following the orange blazes. Nice 18-inch log hop waiting around the corner.

2.7 Turn around when you reach a wide, unbridged stream and a four-way intersection. Trail used to continue straight, but the beavers decided against it. Even if you wade across, the beaver pond has flooded the trail on the other side as well. Trail left is signed TO

Tony, Butchie, and Tom show us what "young at heart" really means.

GAUGING STATION—NO BIKES AT ALL. Trail right is the other end of the hiking loop, which is also flooded. So, it's time to either turn around or start swimming.

2.9 Turn left, following the orange blazes.

3.2 Washed-out section again.

3.8 Return to the rock garden. Big jumble of rocks stacked at odd angles with a bit of a stream running down the middle. Some of this may rate a tech 4 if you get the line wrong. Remember the downed tree at the bottom.

3.9 Cross the Mountains-to-Sea Trail. Several creeks and footbridges follow.

5.3 Tread changes back to gravel, crosses the wide stream, and drops you back at the picnic area.

5.4 Return to parking lot.

60 Long Branch Loop

There are only two words for this trail: water bars. They're big, they're ugly, and there's an entire army of them waiting along Long Branch Loop to test your suspension and your mettle. Sometimes you can slalom around them, sometimes you can set up a rhythm and just start pogo-ing from one to the next. And sometimes you hit one wrong or blow the line, and your bike starts bucking like a bee-stung bronco. The views of Cedar Rock and John's Rock are impressive, and the old McCall cemetery holds a sense of quiet respect for earlier times.

"Awesome! Just freakin' awesome!" —Curt Atkinson, crew member
"It's the best ride I know out here." —John Grout, local trail hound

Location: Pisgah National Forest, near fish hatchery; about fifty minutes south of Asheville.

Distance: 8-mile loop.

Approximate riding time: 1 to 2 hours.

Difficulty rating: Tech 3+ overall. Nearly every water bar on this trail rates at least a tech 3, and there are dozens of them along the way. Toss in an ill-tempered climb, a couple of tough stream crossings, and a mean tech 4 rooty drop. Be prepared to either fly well or land badly.

Trail surface: 4.3 miles of prime singletrack; 3.7 miles of gravel road.

Highlights: Water bars; views of John's Rock and Cedar Rock; stream crossings; extremely tight rhodo tunnels; more water bars; fast slalom downhill; old cemetery; still more water bars.

Land status: Pisgah National Forest.

Maps: USGS Shining Rock; USDA Forest Service Pisgah District Trail Map; National Geographic Trails Illustrated Pisgah Ranger District.

Finding the trailhead: From Asheville take Interstate 26 East (actually south) to North Carolina Highway 280 South. Follow NC 280 for about 15 miles to the town of Brevard. At the first Brevard stoplight, turn right onto U.S. Highway 276, which leads up into the heart of Pisgah National Forest. Follow US 276 for roughly 4 miles, then turn left onto Forest Road 475 (paved at this point), which leads to the fish hatchery. Park in the hatchery visitor's lot.

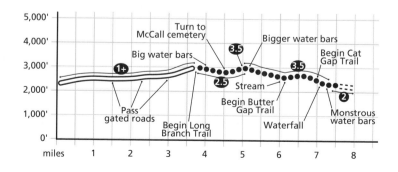

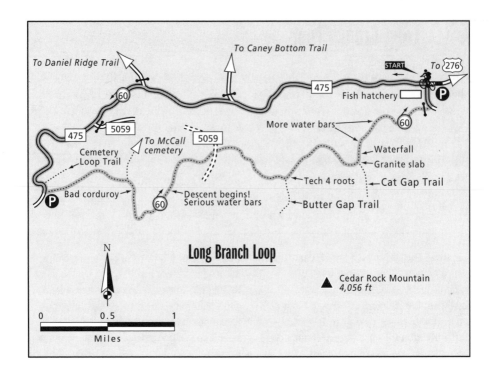

Long Branch Loop

Miles and Directions

0.0 Start from the fish hatchery parking lot. Leave the lot and turn left onto FR 475, which immediately turns to gravel.

1.4 Pass gated road to right, which leads to Cove Creek Group Campground and Caney Bottom Trail.

2.1 Pass gated road to right, which leads to Daniel Ridge Loop Trail.

2.7 Pass gated road (Forest Road 5059) on left.

3.4 Pass trailhead for Cemetery Loop on left.

3.5 Turn left at dirt parking area and onto trailhead for Long Branch. Look for standard brown Forest Service trail sign. Trail starts fairly flat, though water bars grow wherever possible. Cool rhodo tunnels and hemlock groves to ride through. Watch for megamudholes if wet.

4.5 Turn right just before stream to stay on Long Branch Trail (orange blazes). Trail straight leads to McCall cemetery with tombstones from the mid-1800s. It's a beautiful, peaceful place; be respectful. To check it out, cross the stream, turn right at the T, and you're there.

4.6 Long Branch Trail runs straight through a small meadow. Keep an eye out for 30 feet of nasty corduroy shortly after.

5.1 Tough tech 3+ move up and over a big rock. Trail tops out, with an excellent view of Cedar Rock off to the right. Hitch up your britches and tighten your shoelaces here folks, because the following descent leads into the Land of the Wild Water Bars. **Caution:** You'll pick up speed really quickly, and most of the bars drop at least 2 feet off the back side. The bars are generally too tall to ease over, so either slalom around them or keep the faith and just sail off the edge.

5.5 Good view of John's Rock off to right. Water bars up the ante even more, with some 3-footers in quick succession through incredibly dark rhodo tunnels. Watch for logs hidden in the depths of a large mudhole.

6.1 Cross Searcy Creek (tech 2+). Left side of the stream is deceptively deep—stay right. Follows up with a tough short climb and a tech 3+ off-camber rock/log combination.

6.4 Steep descent drops down to intersection with Butter Gap Trail (blue blazes). Turn left. Watch for extremely nasty tech 4 root drop shortly after with a cool slalom section to follow.

6.9 Challenging tech 3 climb with a dozen or so tough root sections in a row. No one is undoable, but the difficulty seems to multiply exponentially when there's this many of them. Large clearing afterward.

7.0 Turn left onto Cat Gap Trail just as you ride over a huge slab of granite. You'll soon hear the sounds of a nice waterfall down to the right.

7.3 Really crazy through here. The water bar/root/rock combos will shake the fillings out of your head. *Big* bunny hop potential in the middle of the descent.

7.5 Hit a gravel service road. Continue straight over the wooden bridge signed TO FISH HATCHERY PARKING LOT. Tough rooty climb and rocky, tech 2+ stream crossing.

7.8 Hit another gravel road. Immediate left across gated bridge takes you back into the fish hatchery parking lot.

8.0 Return to your vehicle in the parking lot.

Nantahala National Forest

N antahala National Forest is the home of the famous Tsali trails. Tsali is the Autobahn of singletrack. Imagine 45 miles of smooth, undulating track that snakes along, high above the edge of Lake Fontana, flaring out into huge carved berms in the corners. First-timers can ride Tsali and become enraptured by the sport. Hammerheads can just smoke through it all day long and still have enough left for a night ride. It's the closest thing to flying available on two wheels.

Nearby Fontana Village and the Nantahala Outdoor Center offer all the logistical support you'll need for outings in the area: lodging, rentals, repairs, supplies, and guided tours. Fontana has continued to expand its trail network and now boasts more than 20 miles of prime Pisgah-style singletrack, available year-round for free.

61 Tsali—Left Loop

If you like some spice in your cruising, then Left Loop is the ride for you. It's just as fast as the other loops in Tsali, but it twists back and forth a good deal more with some excellent 4-foot berms laid in many of the inside corners. Outside corners often hide tricky off-camber rock sections just on the other side that can cost you big if you're not paying attention. The descent down from the overlook is fast and treacherous with a nasty switchback at the bottom over big rock slabs.

Location: 12 miles west of Bryson City, about 1.5 hours from Asheville.

Distance: 12.2-mile loop.

Approximate riding time: 1.5 to 2.5 hours.

Difficulty rating: Tech 2 overall. Left Loop is probably the most technically challenging ride in Tsali, though most riders can still cruise through it. The trail is much more twisty than the other loops, with some tough stream crossings and a number of off-camber tech 3 and 3.5 rock moves that can slap you down in a hurry.

Trail surface: 9.2 miles of singletrack; 3 miles of old gravel road.

Highlights: Big berms; stream crossings; fast twisty track; long-range view from overlook.

Land status: Nantahala National Forest and gameland. Entrance fee: $2.00 per rider per day. The Left and Right Loops are available to mountain bikers on Monday, Wednesday, Friday, and Sunday only.

Maps: USGS Noland Creek; *Tsali Mountain Bike Trails* by WMC Publishing, available at local outdoor centers.

Finding the trailhead: From Asheville take Interstate 40 West and exit onto U.S. Highway 74 West to Dillsboro. Just after crossing a high bridge over the Little Tennessee River, turn right onto North Carolina Highway 28. Follow NC 28 for five minutes or so, and watch for right turn at brown sign: TSALI RECREATION AREA. Follow this gravel road to the bottom and park in the parking area.

Miles and Directions

0.0 Ride out the entrance to the parking lot, and hang an immediate right onto the gravel road heading up to the horse stables, a small parking circle, and the end of County Line Road.

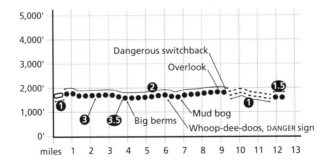

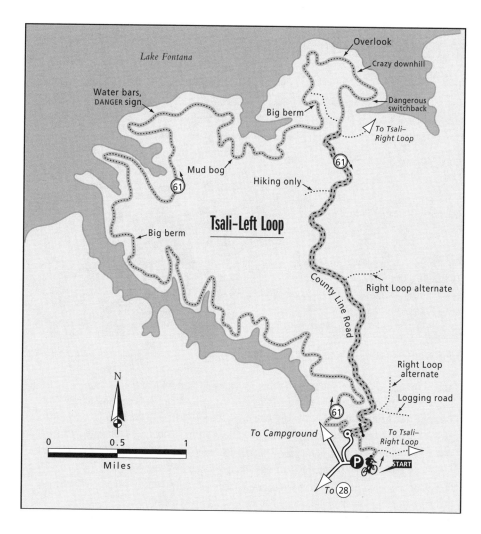

0.5 Turn left onto the Left Loop singletrack, following signs TO STABLES AND LEFT LOOP. Trail starts with some big sweeping turns downhill and sweet contour running.

1.0 Trail wanders all the way down to the lake's edge. Wooden sign: MILE MARKER 1.0.

2.4 Tech 3 stream crossing with some big rocks to avoid and a steep exit.

3.6 Tech 3+ off-camber rock move comes up with no warning around outside corner. Serious injury potential.

6.3 Short, brakes-free descent leads you into a painful climb. DANGER sign lets you know there's some great whoop-dee-doos on the back side.

6.9 Major mud bog and a goopy stream crossing.

8.0 Sweet 4-foot berm, polished like a dirt roller coaster.

8.2 Continue straight for overlook. Trail back right is a shortcut to County Line Road.

Three down in Tsali.

8.7 Overlook. Gorgeous views and a prime resting spot. Descent afterward is loose and fast. When you hit some big rock slabs, drop speed quickly for a sharp switchback right. Missing this turn would be a really bad option, as it's a long drop to the lake.

9.4 Four-way intersection. Continue straight up County Line Road for the return trip.

9.8 Turn left at T, following sign TO TRAILHEAD. Careful, 'cause you'll pick up speed easily on the ride back from here, and the gravel can be both fickle and unforgiving.

10.6 Continue straight. Alternate trail peels in back to left. You're probably really rolling by this point, so be careful of the whoop-dee-doos and the high-speed turns.

11.5 Pass by gate and roll into a small parking area. Turn left onto unmarked singletrack for a fun ride back to the trailhead. If you're too tired, you can follow the gravel road out, which drops you back at the parking lot entrance.

12.2 Intersect beginning of Right Loop. Hang a right, pass the bike wash station, and return to the parking area.

62 Tsali–Right Loop

The Right Loop is an excellent aerobic trail, where you can just cruise. It is also an aerialist's paradise, with lots of dips for small bunny hops and mondo water bars on the downhills for major air. Use caution or land well. Contour running is fast and furious (or slow and reflective, if that's your preferred flavor), but use caution, because a 60-foot drop off a sudden off-camber turn is never a good thing.

Location: 12 miles west of Bryson City, about 1.5 hours from Asheville.

Distance: 12.6-mile loop.

Approximate riding time: 1 to 2.5 hours.

Difficulty rating: Tech 1+. Typical flat high-speed, Tsali cruising. Some of the climbs are loose and eroded. The tech 3+ off-camber rock move on the way out to the overlook is doable, but the long drop off the side lends some serious consequences to failure.

Trail surface: 9.6 miles of singletrack; 3 miles of old gravel road.

Highlights: Prime cruising terrain; multiple water bars for big, big air; waist-high berms; nice views.

Land status: Nantahala National Forest and gameland. Entrance fee: $2.00 per rider per day. The Right and Left Loops are open to mountain bikers on Monday, Wednesday, Friday, and Sunday only.

Maps: USGS Noland Creek; *Tsali Mountain Bike Trails* by WMC Publishing, available at local outdoor centers.

Finding the trailhead: From Asheville take Interstate 40 West and exit onto U.S. Highway 74 West to Dillsboro. Just after crossing a high bridge over the Little Tennessee River, turn right onto North Carolina Highway 28. Follow NC 28 for five minutes or so, and watch for right turn at brown sign: TSALI RECREATION AREA. Follow this gravel road to the bottom and park in the parking area.

Miles and Directions

0.0 From the Tsali parking lot, enter in past the information board and the bike washing station. Follow track straight in, ignoring turn back to the left. Sign: RIGHT LOOP.

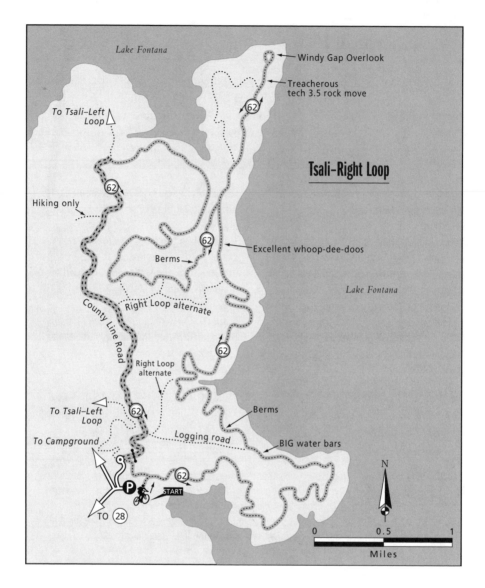

Tsali–Right Loop

1.0 Exceptional cruising along super-smooth tech 1 hardpack, averaging 12 miles per hour. Big inside berms are a joy, though watch for off-camber outside turns.

2.0 Mile marker 2, followed by a tough climb up some big water bars.

2.3 Sign at top of climb: WHOOP-DEE-DOOS. DANGER. STAY IN CONTROL. Good advice. You've got six or seven serious water bars waiting on the downhill ahead, every one of which could launch the space shuttle. Enjoy.

2.6 Turn right to follow Right Loop; trail straight is hiking only. Now Tsali really starts to shine, with a high-speed mix of dips, twists and humps, little drops and huge water bars, big berms, rhodo tunnels, and long stretches where you can just flat out get it!

View from the Right Loop Overlook. DEBRA MOYLAN PHOTO

3.6 Continue straight on main trail. Right Loop alternate turns back left for a quick return to County Line Road for those who feel that they've bitten off more than they can chew.

4.5 Old logging road back to left. Continue straight (and follow sign) for Right Loop.

5.6 Intersection with Right Loop Overlook Trail. Go straight to overlook (my recommendation), or turn left to follow the main track and miss out on the view.

5.8 Continue straight to the overlook. Alternate loop out to the overlook peels off here to the left and eventually brings you back to the overlook trail. It's very hard to spot but worth the effort if you like tight high-speed carving.

6.2 Be prepared for the tech 3+ rock move along overlook trail. Although not too tough of a move, blowing this can result in a 60-foot fall off the side, so be *really* sure of your skills or walk it.

6.3 Windy Gap Overlook. Impressive view of lake and mountains. Excellent photo op. Once you're ready to ride again, saddle up and head back the way you came. Ignore any side trails.

7.1 Back at overlook intersection. Turn right to continue on Right Loop. Following descent is eroded and a bit shaky in spots. Leads into some more excellent cruising and big berms.

7.8 Continue straight. Alternate trail back to left for quicker return.

8.1 Continue straight. Second alternate trail back; this one leads over some huge water bars that occasionally hide small ponds behind them.

8.5 Enter an old clearcut area. Watch for snakes here, as it's a prime sunning spot.

9.8   Turn left onto County Line Road and begin a long, grinding climb. Sorry, but most of the fun ends here. This gravel track eventually leads back to the trailhead. Tracks straight and left are two legs of the Left Loop Overlook Trail.

10.2   Turn left at T, following sign TO TRAILHEAD. Careful, 'cause you'll pick up speed easily on the ride back from here, and the gravel can be both fickle and unforgiving.

11.0   Continue straight. Alternate trail peels in back to left. You're probably really rolling by this point, so be careful of the whoop-dee-doos and the high-speed turns.

12.1   Pass by gate and roll into a small parking area. Turn left onto unmarked singletrack for a fun ride back to the trailhead. If you're too tired, you can follow the gravel road out, which drops you back at the parking lot entrance.

12.6   Intersect beginning of Right Loop. Hang a right, pass the bike wash station, and return to the parking area.

63 Tsali–Mouse Branch Loop

Many riders call this their favorite Tsali trail. It's an excellent intro into what Tsali has to offer. For most of its length, Mouse Branch is a buffed dirt highway that slips and dips along the lake's edge. Completely ridable by novices, but the whoop-dee-doos on the downhills might throw a scare into them. The Mouse Branch Overlook is arguably the finest view from any of the trails.

Location: 12 miles west of Bryson City, about 1.5 hours from Asheville.
Distance: 9.1-mile loop.
Approximate riding time: 1 to 2 hours.
Difficulty rating: Tech 1+. Several tough switchback climbs; otherwise, smooth and buff singletrack all the way.
Trail surface: 7.6 miles of singletrack; 1.5 miles of gravel road.

Highlights: Fast contour runs; perfect hardpack track; incredible views; blackberries in season.
Land status: Nantahala National Forest and gameland. Entrance fee: $2.00 per rider per day. Mouse Branch is open to mountain bikers on Tuesday, Thursday, and Saturday only.
Maps: USGS Noland Creek; *Tsali Mountain Bike Trails* by WMC Publishing, available at local outdoor centers.

Finding the trailhead: From Asheville take Interstate 40 West and exit onto U.S. Highway 74 West to Dillsboro. Just after crossing a high bridge over the Little Tennessee River, turn right onto North Carolina Highway 28. Follow NC 28 for five minutes or so, and watch for right turn at brown sign: TSALI RECREATION AREA. Follow this gravel road to the bottom and park in the parking area.

Miles and Directions

0.0 Start from Tsali parking lot. Pay your fee first, then head back out of the parking lot entrance. As you leave the lot, the gated gravel road straight ahead is the entrance for both Mouse Branch and Thompson Loop. Follow it.

0.7 Turn right onto the signed entrance for Mouse Branch Loop. This is one of the finest opening sequences of any trail: big dips, fast contour running, perfect hardpack, and rhodo tunnels. Just the thing to get your morning started, together with that espresso.

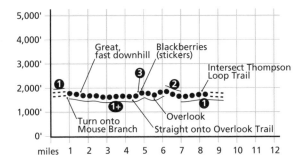

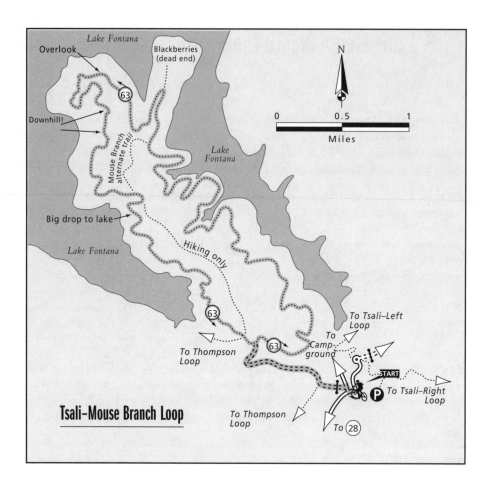

Tsali–Mouse Branch Loop

1.3 Mile marker 0.6. The signmakers must have started their mileage from the turnoff above. All tech 1 track with lots of downhill action for seemingly little cost.

4.3 Tech 2 rock move. Tough outside climb. Ignore the unmarked trail to the left.

4.5 Go straight for Mouse Branch Overlook Trail (highly recommended). Gorgeous long-range views of mountains and lake frame several long swooping downhills. The Mouse Branch alternate cuts back to the left and provides a bailout for anyone who really needs to shave 2 miles off the ride. You'll really miss out, though.

4.7 Sharp turn back to left to follow Mouse Branch Overlook Trail. Watch for this turn; it's not well signed, and judging from the tire tracks, a lot of folks miss it. False trail heads straight into a blackberry thicket, which is a wonderful thing only in July when the berries are ripe (and the bears are absent).

5.3 The Mouse Branch Overlook provides a simply spectacular view: gorgeous long-range mountain vistas, islands dotting the lake, occasional beavers, and other critters swimming far below.

Mouse Branch Loop rewards you with this view of Lake Fontana.

5.7 Trail turns fast, hard, and rutty after leaving overlook. Turn left at the T. Track fades from singletrack to old doubletrack for a high-speed descent. Make your own line, but watch for obstacles hidden in the deep grass. Getting air is just about a required course for this section.

6.7 Turn right to rejoin main trail.

6.9 Turn down to the right to continue on Mouse Branch; trail straight is hiking only. While you're enjoying the following contour running, try to ignore the 100-foot drop on your right.

8.3 Intersection with Thompson Loop and hiking trail. Follow track straight past arrowed sign: TO TRAILHEAD. This puts you back on the gravel entrance road.

9.1 Back at Tsali parking lot.

64 Tsali–Thompson Loop

A bit more twisty than its longer cousins, Thompson Loop offers up what is probably the finest and fastest descent in Tsali. The singletrack starts off with sweet downhill cruising through the rhododendron. The maps show that you start climbing from
there, but you'll swear that you're going down more than up. Then you'll want to
check your brakes (particularly you Clydesdales!) before you climb onto the luge run
back down to the road. This mile-long downhill puts any roller coaster to shame and
will have you screaming with delight for the entire length.

Location: Almond, Nantahala National Forest;
1.5 hours west of Asheville.
Distance: 7.6-mile loop.
Approximate riding time: 1 to 2 hours.
Difficulty rating: Tech 2. Rootier than the
other loops but still mostly just wide-open
cruising.
Trail surface: 6.6 miles of singletrack; 1 mile
of gated Forest Service road.

Highlights: Slippery contour running; big
berms; lots of bunny hops; one kick-ass
downhill!
Land status: Nantahala National Forest and
gameland. Entrance fee: $2.00 per rider per
day. Thompson Loop is open to mountain bikers on Tuesday, Thursday, and Saturday only.
Maps: USGS Noland Creek; *Tsali Mountain
Bike Trails* by WMC Publishing, available at
local outdoor centers.

Finding the trailhead: From Asheville take Interstate 40 West and exit onto U.S. Highway 74
West to Dillsboro. Just after crossing a high bridge over the Little Tennessee River, turn right onto
North Carolina Highway 28. Follow NC 28 for five minutes or so, and watch for right turn at
brown sign: TSALI RECREATION AREA. Follow this gravel road to the bottom and park in the parking
area.

Miles and Directions

0.0 Start from Tsali parking lot. Pay your fee first, then head back out the parking lot
entrance. As you leave the lot, the gated gravel road straight ahead is the entrance for
both Thompson and Mouse Branch Loop. Follow it.

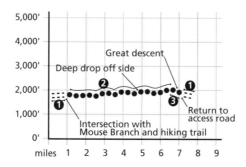

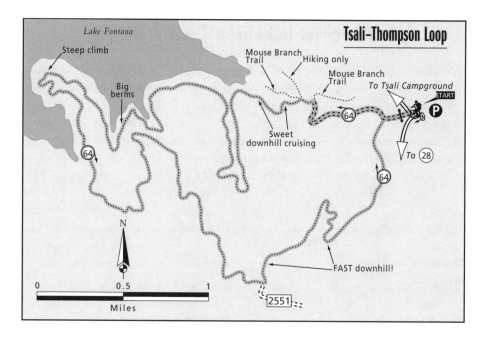

0.7 Pass entrance to Mouse Branch Loop on right.

0.8 Three-way intersection: turn left to follow THOMPSON LOOP sign; straight is the return for Mouse Branch; right is a hiking-only trail. Trail leads into some sweet downhill running, with quick corners and well-angled hops.

1.5 Mile marker 1.5. Fabulous tunnel running, particularly during late spring. More stream crossings and some treacherous sinkholes. Sweet, sweet descents.

2.7 Trail snakes through several of the glassy-smooth berms for which Tsali is so revered.

3.0 Mile marker 3. Climbing starts to get a little more serious, but never gets too bad. Still the most fun you ever had going uphill.

5.0 As you round an outside corner and zip smartly along the buff Tsali singletrack, you may notice that 2 feet or so to the left of your front tire, the ground abruptly drops away into an emerald-cloaked canyon, 80 feet deep. It is a marvelous sight.

6.2 Turn left to follow Thompson Loop (right is Forest Road 2551). Here begins a descent, brothers and sisters, that at times may be considered transcendent. Huge waist-high berms, creekbed running, serious switchbacks, and big, big air if you want it.

7.3 Trail suddenly spits you back out on the entrance road—pointing the wrong way. Turn around, and bear right to return to the trailhead.

7.6 Return to parking lot.

65 Fontana–Elmer Hollow/First Blood/Whiting

If you've only got time for one ride at Fontana, this is the one to make, a gift from both the Forestmaker and the trailmakers—blessed be they! Elmer actually drops in elevation as it runs through rock gardens up into the cove, then you get swoopy descents back along Whiting (with a few tricky spots tossed in). And if you've got the nerve, the fortitude, and the brake pads for it, you can visit First Blood, a trail with enough altitude and attitude for any rider.

"Once I tucked my shirt in, it was easy."—Mud Pie, the Rock Garden Goddess

"It wasn't easy at all! It was scary down through there!"—Timm the (humbled) Trailrat

"That was *crazy!* Slippery rocks, rooty, boulder, stream-crossing nastiness! Yeah!"— Adrenaline-saturated author

Location: Fontana Village, two hours west of Asheville.
Distance: 5.2-mile loop.
Approximate riding time: 1 to 2.5 hours.
Difficulty rating: Ranges from tech 1 to tech 4. Whiting is mostly a wide-open rail trail, but it can get ugly in places. Elmer offers up some challenging rock gardens, and you'll find that First Blood is aptly named.
Trail surface: 4.2 miles of singletrack; 0.2 mile of doubletrack; 0.8 mile of pavement.

Highlights: Cool, swooping descents; sick, tilted boulder field; rock gardens; crazy streambed that runs both up and down; easy bypass around First Blood and the worst climbs.
Land status: Private land (Fontana Village) and Nantahala National Forest.
Maps: USGS Fontana Dam; trail map of entire system available at the Fontana Village Adventure Center.

Finding the trailhead: From Asheville take Interstate 40 West to exit 27, U.S. Highway 74 West (Great Smoky Mountain Expressway). Follow US 74 past Cherokee and Bryson City, then turn right onto North Carolina Highway 28 just as the road narrows from four lanes to two. Take NC 28 past Tsali, then drive another thirty-five minutes out to Fontana Dam. When NC 28 hits a stop sign and a T, turn left, then left again into Fontana Village. All trail directions start from the Adventure Center.

Miles and Directions

0.0 From the front of the Adventure Center, turn right onto Welch Road. Follow the bike stencils straight through two stop signs, past the dual slalom course, and on to the end of the road.

0.4 As the pavement ends, follow the track between some big rocks out to the side of NC 28. Trailhead signs on right for Lewellyn and Whiting Trails. Faced with three choices up, pick the path on the right. It's another short but steep rocky climb, tech 2, that quickly gives way to some gradual contour climbing.

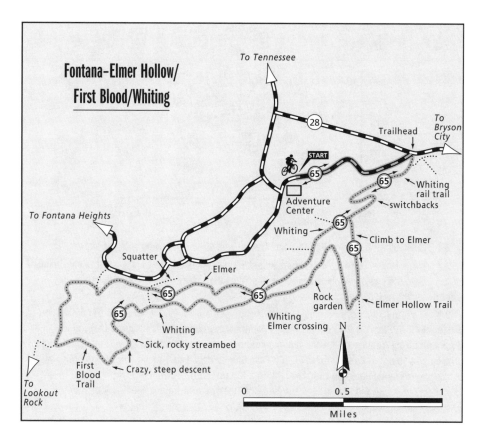

Fontana–Elmer Hollow/ First Blood/Whiting

0.7 Pair of big switchbacks up, then a cool swoopy downhill and a muddy stream crossing.

1.0 Turn left as you start to cross an old rocky roadbed. This climb up to Elmer Hollow is mean, steep, and slick; even Granny 1 may not be enough to help you clean this one. If you passed the substation on Whiting, you missed your turn.

1.1 Turn right onto a clear singletrack for the start of Elmer (brown and yellow arrow sign), which drops you down over an old bridge. If the road you were climbing suddenly gets twice as ugly as it was, you probably missed the turn.

1.5 Singletrack contouring, tech 2, with lots of roots brings you to the first of several tech 3 rock gardens. If you look down to your right, you'll see both Whiting and Squatter Trails lower down along the ridge.

1.6 Cross over Whiting Trail (wide, rocky roadbed). Either cut straight across on a faint track down Elmer, or jag right and left to pick it back up.

1.7 Elmer and Whiting run within 10 feet of each other, with both trails outlined by lines of rocks. Stay on the lower track to follow Elmer, up through a tech 3 mossy rock pile. It's a little tricky, so stay on your toes or on your head for this one.

2.0 Stream crossing carries you into a set of tech 3.5 rock slabs, known as the Lunchbox. Check out the giant grape vines as you wind your way through.

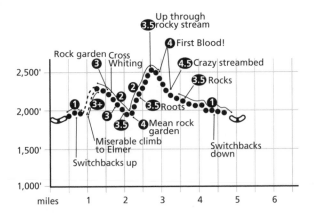

2.1 Cross old trail running left and right. Faded sign tells you to keep going straight.

2.2 Elmer Hollow joins up with Squatter Trail. Turn left, cross a short bridge by a hiking/biking sign, then get ready for a serious technical challenge: a twisty line up through a slick, tech 4 rock garden.

2.4 A sharp switchback up brings you to a choice of trails (signed). Turn right to continue on to First Blood. A mean, rooty tech 3 climb awaits, one that'll sadistically fool you into thinking it's finished several times before the end. **Note:** If you've been really challenged to this point, then it's best to skip First Blood, 'cause that place can be a nightmare for the uninitiated. In that case, hang a left onto Whiting instead, follow it for a mile or so to where the end of First Blood feeds back in, and wait to see if any of your buddies survive it.

2.5 Trail finally (and gratefully) spits you out onto an old road, the beginning of the Lookout Rock trail. Turn left to continue onto First Blood, up past the ropes course and the starting gate for the downhill races.

2.7 If you're feeling lost 'cause the trail disappeared into a stream, just keep paddling onward, and know that it'll eventually reappear. As you're pushing up through here, think about the local folks who can *ride* up through this stuff. Those people should be tested for extraterrestrial DNA.

2.8 Turn left at the T, and cross a rocky tech 3.5 streambed. Sign for First Blood then directs you up another stream for a bit, past a small waterfall. The Lookout Rock trail peels off right and heads up the side of the mountain.

2.9 Top of First Blood. Note the SLOW–DANGER sign: best to drop your seat now, and maybe go take a look first. First Blood starts with a rooty, twisting descent along a finger. Then you switchback and drop into a severely rock-strewn pitch. This section requires some real finesse to survive, so either lock the brakes up and slide down, or let 'em go and try to carve through the rocks at warp speed, just to see if your guardian angel is paying attention.

3.1 *Crazy* tech 4 streambed run. Insane mountain biking at its best.

3.3 Bear right as First Blood feeds into Whiting. This is where the folks who weren't up for First Blood should be waiting. And no, they'll never really be able to appreciate what you just ran until they do it themselves.

3.4 Just so you don't get too comfortable, Whiting suddenly turns into a rocky tech 3 minefield, carrying a bunch of speed. Near the bottom you'll pass straight through the intersection with Elmer again.

4.0 Continue straight on Whiting, past a cut down to Squatter. Then take a big bermed right turn up, along the outside edge of one of Squatter's downhill switchbacks, and then past another shortcut down to Squatter. This section gives you an idea of what a maze of trails this place is. Be sure to explore them all.

4.2 Run past the substation, then cut straight across an old rocky roadbed to continue on Whiting. Up that old road is the hellacious climb you suffered at the beginning of Elmer. You can always loop back for a second run if you've still got the gas and the gumption!

4.4 Sweet 180-degree switchbacks left and right, with a swoopy downhill in between. Shortly after, follow the tracks up right as an old road cuts off down to the left.

4.8 Quick rocky descent, with a switch left at the bottom, puts you back out at the trailhead on NC 28. *Watch for cars!* Turn left to follow the track between the boulders. Then follow straight back on the pavement into the village.

5.2 Return to the Adventure Center.

66 Fontana–Brooks Cove/Turkey Chute

Once you finish the lung-busting climb up Turkey Chute, then the heart-busting climb up Piney Ridge, the rest isn't so bad. Brooks Cove was still freshly made at the time of this writing—and was still fun to ride. That tells you that as the trail gets ridden, it'll get faster and smoother and just cook in places. The drop back down Turkey Chute will satisfy the worst adrenaline junkies in your crowd.

Location: Fontana Village, 2 hours west of Asheville.

Distance: 5.3-mile figure-eight.

Approximate riding time: 1 to 2 hours.

Difficulty rating: Tech 2, but the switchbacks can be intimidating.

Trail surface: 3.1 miles of singletrack; 0.8 mile of doubletrack; 0.1 mile of gravel; 1.3 miles of pavement.

Highlights: Long swooping descents; ridge run; bonsai downhill; humbling climbs; great aerobic route.

Land status: Private land (Fontana Village) and Nantahala National Forest.

Maps: USGS Fontana Dam; trail map of entire system available at the Fontana Village Adventure Center.

Finding the trailhead: From Asheville take Interstate 40 West to exit 27, U.S. Highway 74 West (Great Smoky Mountain Expressway). Follow US 74 past Cherokee and Bryson City, then turn right onto North Carolina Highway 28 just as the road narrows from four lanes to two. Take NC 28 past Tsali, then drive another thirty-five minutes out to Fontana Dam. When NC 28 hits a stop sign and a T, turn left, then left again into Fontana Village. All trail directions start from the Adventure Center.

Miles and Directions

0.0 Starting from the Adventure Center, turn left, go to the end of the parking lot, then turn right and ride down by the softball field. Just past the round house, turn left onto Welch Road.

0.2 The shortcut up to Turkey Chute goes into the trees on the right, just past the banquet hall.

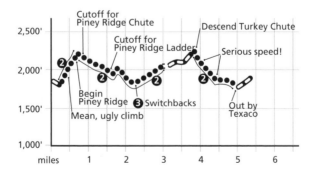

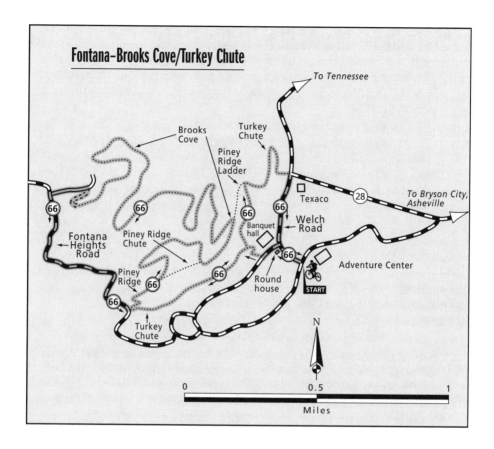

Fontana–Brooks Cove/Turkey Chute

0.3 Turn left as the shortcut Ts into Turkey Chute. What follows is one mean, miserable climb.

0.4 Continue straight up Turkey Chute. Piney Ridge drops out of the rhododendron and joins in from the right.

0.5 Continue straight on Turkey Chute. Whiting peels off down to the left.

0.6 Right when you start to wonder if this hell will ever end, it does, and you pop out onto Fontana Heights Road (paved) at the apex of the cove that Fontana Village occupies. After a long breather, make a U-turn, and you'll see signs for Turkey Chute down to the right and Piney Ridge up to the left. Now, if you think you can really climb your bike, if you think you've got moves on a billy goat, then take a running start at Piney Ridge— and be prepared to lose. It's steep for a long way, and it sucks to even push it. No one should feel bad for walking this one.

0.7 Finally gain the top, and get a cool knife-edge ridge ride in return, with the village far down to the right.

0.8 Continue straight on Brooks Cove, past the cutoff to the right. Following track is a sweet, swoopy run down through the rhododendron, with a wide tech 2 track, some great water bars, and a steep switchback along the way. (**Note:** The cutoff is for the Piney Ridge

Chute. It's an *incredibly* steep, tech 4+ descent, a straight-down-through-a-tunnel-in-the-rhododendron, brakes-locked, surfing-through-the-rhodo-leaves, chest-on-your-seat, laughing-like-a-loon kind of ride. It can be a little freaky the first time, but it's not that fast, and you just bounce off the walls and keep going 'til it joins back up with Brooks Cove farther along. You really need to check it out some other time, 'cause it is a serious hoot.)

1.3 Continue straight past an old cutoff down to Turkey Chute.

1.5 At the Y take the sharp switchback left to stay on Brooks Cove. Wide tech 1+ track with some speed, rounded water bars, fast contouring, rootballs, and great swoopiness follows. (**Note:** If you take the right instead and stay on Piney Ridge, you'll wind out to the end of the ridge, then drop down the Piney Ridge *Ladder.* The Chute is straight down and crazy, but the Ladder is switchbacked and demented. Steep, narrow, sharp switchbacks, sliding on the rhodo leaves through solid tunnels. It's a tech 4+ to clean the whole thing, a righteous test of anyone's bike-handling skills. And yet you're sliding so slow, if you dab there's little penalty to pay. Definitely another one to add to your list.)

2.3 Pair of tight tech 3 switchbacks drops you down into the bottom of the cove. Cross a pair of new bridges, and get settled in for the climb out.

3.1 Turn left as the trail drops you onto an old Forest Service road.

3.2 Turn left as you turn into Fontana Heights Road (paved) again.

3.9 Return to the Turkey Chute/Piney Ridge trailhead. This time, pick Turkey Chute down on the right, and be prepared for some awfully high-speed singletracking. This tech 2 run is fast and loose, with quick turns, steep sudden drops, and some serious berms on the inside corners. Pay attention to what you're doing on this one; otherwise, as both Justin and I can attest, the Turkey can take a big bite out of your hiney.

4.4 Keep straight on Turkey Chute. Down right is the shortcut you came in on by the banquet hall.

4.7 At the Y head up to the left if you want a few more challenges before you're done. Otherwise, the cut down to the right takes you straight to the bridge at the end of the trail.

4.8 Big steep switchback right, then a cool vertical switchback. A bit of tight contouring leads you into one last chance for a bust; a switchback covered with root lace.

4.9 Cross the bridge (sometimes slippery), and pop out by the Texaco station. Turn right onto Welch Road and head back up past the ballfield. Go through the four-way stop, then turn left into the parking lot.

5.3 Return to the Adventure Center.

67 Fontana–Lewellyn Cove/Gold Branch/Hoor Hollow

Lewellyn offers new riders, or riders new to Fontana's trails, a chance to check things out one stage at a time. A cruise up Upper Lewellyn and the connector trail and back gives newbies a chance to just ride in the gorgeous woods and not worry too much about keeping themselves intact. The more adventurous can keep going and give Gold Branch's whoops and switchbacks a go. And those who are still feeling stout after that can try dropping some speed into Lower Lewellyn and testing out that old "sticks and stones" theory.

> "That was no beginner ride." —Mud Pie, the Tired and Doubtful

Location: Fontana Village, two hours west of Asheville.

Distance: 8 miles.

Approximate riding time: 1- to 3-hour loop.

Difficulty rating: Tech 1 to tech 3. Upper Lewellyn is mostly flat and smooth, whereas the lower section is anything but.

Trail surface: 4.7 miles of singletrack; 1.9 miles of doubletrack; 0.6 mile of gravel; 0.8 mile of pavement.

Highlights: Beautiful, primeval creekbeds; swooping contour runs; high-speed rock garden navigational opportunities; view of dam; initial section offers easy out-and-back for beginners.

Land status: Private land (Fontana Village) and Nantahala National Forest.

Maps: USGS Fontana Dam; trail map of entire system available at the Fontana Village Adventure Center.

Finding the trailhead: From Asheville take Interstate 40 West to exit 27, U.S. Highway 74 West (Great Smoky Mountain Expressway). Follow US 74 past Cherokee and Bryson City, then turn right onto North Carolina Highway 28 just as the road narrows from four lanes to two. Take NC 28 past Tsali, then drive another thirty-five minutes out to Fontana Dam. When NC 28 hits a stop sign and a T, turn left, then left again into Fontana Village. All trail directions start from the Adventure Center.

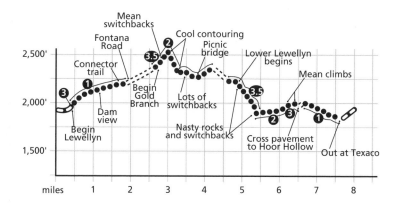

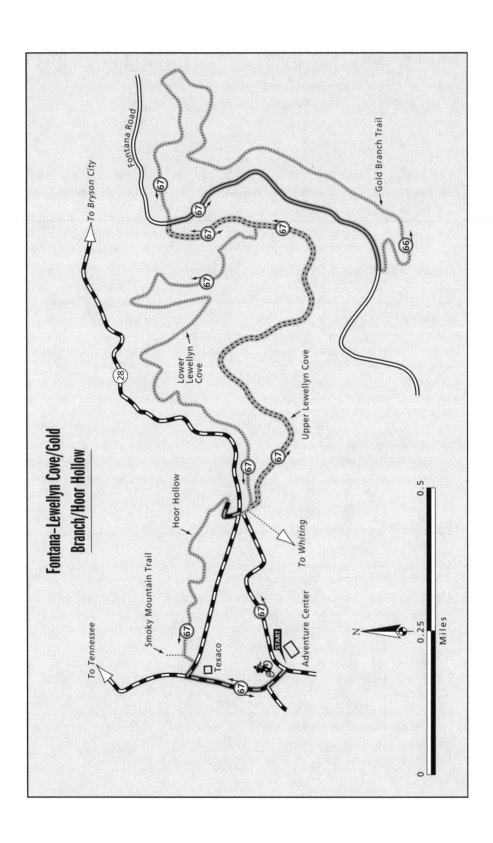

Fontana–Lewellyn Cove/Gold Branch/Hoor Hollow

To Bryson City

Fontana Road

Gold Branch Trail

To Tennessee

Smoky Mountain Trail

Hoor Hollow

Lower Lewellyn Cove

Upper Lewellyn Cove

To Whiting

Texaco

START

Adventure Center

N

Miles

0   0.25   0.5

Miles and Directions

0.0 From the front of the Fontana Village Adventure Center, turn right onto Welch Road. Follow the bike stencils straight past two stop signs, past the dual slalom course, and on to the end of the road.

0.4 As the pavement ends, follow the track between some big rocks out to the side of NC 28. Trailhead signs on right for Lewellyn and Whiting. Faced with three choices up, pick the middle path. It's a short but steep and rocky climb that'll have some folks walking and wondering if they'd made a mistake. But trust that it flattens out up ahead into an easy tech 1 climb.

1.3 Nice view of Fontana Dam off to the left. Some tech 2 rocks along the way.

1.6 Cross over a gorgeous, laughing, mossy creek. You can't help but smile at such beauty, and you'll find cascades like these meandering all over this forest. Enjoy.

1.7 Continue straight onto the connector trail, past the sign pointing left to Lower Lewellyn. You'll make this turn on the way back down.

2.0 Turn right at four-way intersection with Fontana Road (gravel) to continue. Anyone struggling or really tired at this point should consider turning back here. It's an easy return trip straight back the way you came, and you can coast for three-fourths of it. Just watch it, 'cause you can easily gain a lot of speed, and the inside corners can get really squirrelly.

2.6 As the road beds right, watch for a sharp singletrack cut back left, the entrance to Gold Branch. You probably want a running start if you want to make that first climb.

2.8 Mean mother of a switchback up, tech 3.5. Then another one soon after, for a second slap. Then a little twisty speed and some sailable water bars to sweeten things up.

3.4 Follow main trail up right, past an old road cutoff to the left. Climb up through the saddle, then some easy hardpack contouring.

3.5 Pair of steep switchbacks down, with a long drop off the side as incentive to get it right.

3.7 Follow bermed switchback right to stay on Gold Branch. (**Note:** As an alternative, the adrenaline junkies in your crew can go straight up over the berm to follow Gold *Rush* instead, a fast, water bar–laden shortcut down to the road.)

3.8 Excellent bridge/rest area, built up over a beautiful, mossy creek. Fine place to stop for a snack and a photo.

4.6 A great speed run through the trees and water bars drops you back onto Fontana Road. Cut straight across, and hook left onto the connector trail you came up on.

4.9 Watch for the signed right to Lower Lewellyn that you passed on the way up. Here's another point of no return for beginners. Lewellyn ups the ante here, with a steep, fast drop that sends you hammering right into some tech 3.5 rocks and drops. Game beginners should take it real slow or risk some real pain. For the rest, I say get your butt back and let it go!

5.2 A mess of sharp switchbacks, slapped in the middle of some fast contouring, decorated liberally with tech 3.5 rock gardens.

6.2 Tough, steep, rooty climb, tech 3—and about an 8 on the pain scale. Congratulate yourself if you clean this one, or the next.

6.4 Round an outside corner, cut up through a tricky, narrow set of rocks, then down over a bridge. Then comes a last chance for some humbling: another steep, slippery climb.

6.5 Drop back out at the trailhead, by the edge of NC 28. (**Note:** If you just ain't had enough yet, then cut straight across the highway and up the old paved road, past the old burned-down cabins, to follow Hoor Hollow. If instead you're ready for a swim or a nap, cut back between the big rocks, and follow the paved road straight back to the Adventure Center.)

6.7 Pavement turns into tech 1 doubletrack, climbs a little, then gives you a fast, smooth drop down through the trees.

6.9 Pop out onto an old paved road by an orange metal gate. Turn left to pick up clear singletrack across the road. You get some cool swoopy drops, then a fast descent into a big sweeping right for a screaming good time.

7.4 Very sweet, very well-bermed 180-degree switchback left, then a drop and a hop, and another switch right. If you ain't grinning at this point, you must've died in the saddle somewhere along the way.

7.5 Bear down left at Y, signed TO VILLAGE. Quick drop over a couple of sharp water bars, then drop out onto NC 28, across from the Texaco station. *Watch for cars!*

7.6 Cross road, cut through the Texaco lot, and head up Welch Road back into the village, past the ballfield. Go through the four-way stop, then turn left into the Grill's parking lot.

8.0 Return to the Adventure Center.

The Art of Mountain Biking

Within the following pages, you will find everything you need to know about off-road bicycling in North Carolina. This section begins by exploring the fascinating history of the mountain bike itself, then goes on to discuss everything from the health benefits of off-road cycling to tips and techniques for bicycling over logs and up hills. Also included are essential equipment ideas to keep your rides smooth and trouble-free, and descriptions of off-road terrain to prepare you for the kinds of bumps and bounces you can expect to encounter.

The mountain bike, with its knobby tread and reinforced frame, takes cyclists to places once unheard of—down rugged mountain trails, through streams of rushing water, across the frozen Alaskan tundra, and even to work in the city. There seem to be few limits on what this fat-tired beast can do and where it can take us. Few obstacles stand in its way, few boundaries slow its progress. Except for one—its own success. If trail closure means little to you now, read on and discover how a trail can be here today and gone tomorrow. With so many new off-road cyclists taking to the trails each year, it's no wonder trail access hinges precariously between universal acceptance and complete termination. But a little work on your part can go a long way to preserving trail access for future use. Nothing is more crucial to the survival of mountain biking itself than to read the examples set forth in the following pages and practice their message.

Without open trails, the maps in this book are virtually useless. Cyclists must learn to be responsible for the trails they use and to share these trails with others. This section addresses such issues as why trail use has become so controversial, what can be done to improve the image of mountain biking, how to have fun and ride responsibly, on-the-spot trail repair techniques, and some general mountain biking guidelines.

Mountain Bike Beginnings

It seems the mountain bike, originally designed for lunatic adventurists bored with straight lines, clean clothes, and smooth tires, has become globally popular in as short a time as it would take to race down a mountain trail.

Like many things of a revolutionary nature, the mountain bike was born on the West Coast. But unlike Rollerblades, purple hair, and the peace sign, the concept of the off-road bike cannot be credited solely to the imaginative Californians—they were just the first to make waves.

The design of the first off-road-specific bike was based on the geometry of the old Schwinn Excelsior, a one-speed, camelback cruiser with balloon tires. Joe Breeze was the creator behind it, and in 1977 he built ten of these "Breezers" for himself and his Marin County, California, friends at $750 apiece—a bargain.

Breeze was a serious competitor in bicycle racing, placing thirteenth in the 1977 U.S. Road Racing National Championships. After races, he and friends would scour local bike shops hoping to find old bikes they could then restore.

It was the 1941 Schwinn Excelsior, for which Breeze paid just five dollars, that began to shape and change bicycling history forever. After taking the bike home, removing the fenders, oiling the chain, and pumping up the tires, Breeze hit the dirt. He loved it.

His inspiration, while forerunning, was not altogether unique. On the opposite end of the country, nearly 2,500 miles from Marin County, East Coast bike bums were also growing restless. More and more old, beat-up clunkers were being restored and modified. These behemoths often weighed as much as eighty pounds and were so reinforced they seemed virtually indestructible. But rides that take just forty minutes on today's twenty-five-pound featherweights took the steel-toed-boot-and-blue-jean-clad bikers of the late 1970s and early 1980s nearly four hours to complete.

Not until 1981 was it possible to purchase a production mountain bike, but local retailers found these ungainly bicycles difficult to sell and rarely kept them in stock. By 1983, however, mountain bikes were no longer such a fringe item, and large bike manufacturers quickly jumped into the action, producing their own versions of the off-road bike. By the 1990s the mountain bike had firmly established its place with bicyclists of nearly all ages and abilities, and it now commands nearly 90 percent of the U.S. bike market.

There are many reasons for the mountain bike's success in becoming the hottest two-wheeled vehicle in the nation. They are much friendlier to the cyclist than traditional road bikes because of their comfortable upright position and shock-absorbing fat tires. And because of the health-conscious, environmentalist movement of the late 1980s and 1990s, people are more activity minded and seek nature on a closer front than paved roads can allow. The mountain bike gives you these things and takes you far away from the daily grind—even if you're only minutes from the city.

Mountain Biking into Shape

If your objective is to get in shape and lose weight, then you're on the right track, because mountain biking is one of the best ways to get started.

One way many of us have lost weight in this sport is the crash-and-burn-it-off method. Picture this: You're speeding uncontrollably down a vertical drop that you realize you shouldn't be on—only after it is too late. Your front wheel lodges into a rut and launches you through endless weeds, trees, and pointy rocks before coming to an abrupt halt in a puddle of thick mud. Surveying the damage, you discover, with the layers of skin, body parts, and lost confidence littering the trail above, that those unwanted pounds have been shed—permanently. Instant weight loss.

There is, of course, a more conventional (and quite a bit less painful) approach to losing weight and gaining fitness on a mountain bike. It's called the workout, and bicycles provide an ideal way to get physical. Take a look at some of the benefits associated with cycling.

Cycling helps you shed pounds without gimmicky diet fads or weight-loss programs. You can explore the countryside and burn as much as 10 to 16 calories per minute or close to 600 to 1,000 calories per hour. Moreover, it's a great way to spend an afternoon.

No less significant than the external and cosmetic changes of your body from riding are the internal changes taking place. Over time, cycling regularly will strengthen your heart as your body grows vast networks of new capillaries to carry blood to all those working muscles. This will, in turn, give your skin a healthier glow. The capacity of your lungs may increase up to 20 percent, and your resting heart rate will drop significantly. The Stanford University School of Medicine reports to the American Heart Association that people can reduce their risk of heart attack by nearly 64 percent if they can burn up to 2,000 calories per week. This is only two to three hours of bike riding!

Recommended for insomnia, hypertension, indigestion, anxiety, and even for recuperation from major heart attacks, bicycling can be an excellent cure-all as well as a great preventive. Cycling just a few hours per week can improve your figure and sleeping habits, give you greater resistance to illness, increase your energy levels, and provide feelings of accomplishment and heightened self-esteem.

Be Safe on the Road

Occasionally, even the hard-core off-road cyclists will find they have no choice but to ride the pavement. When you are forced to hit the road, it's important for you to keep safety in mind.

Outlined below are a few common sense rules.

- Avoid urban freeways.
- Follow the same driving rules as motorists. Be sure to obey all road signs and traffic lights.
- Wear a helmet and bright clothing so you are more visible to motorists. Bright colors such as orange and lime green are also highly visible at night.
- Wear a CPSC (Consumer Product Safety Commission)-approved helmet.

- Equip your bike with lights and wear reflective clothing if you plan on riding at night. When riding at night the bicycle or rider should have a white light visible at least 500 feet to the front and a red light or reflector visible at least 600 feet to the rear.
- Pass motorists on the left and not the right. Motorists are not expecting you to pass on the right and they may not see you.
- Ride single file on busy roads so motorists can pass you safely.
- Stop off the roadway.
- Use hand signals to alert motorists to what you plan on doing next.
- Ride with the traffic and not against it.
- Follow painted lane markings.
- Make eye contact with drivers. Assume they don't see you until you are sure they do.
- Ride in the middle of the lane at busy intersections and whenever you are moving at the same speed as traffic.
- Don't ride out to the curb between parked cars unless they are far apart. Motorists may not see you when you try to move back into traffic
- Turn left by looking back, signaling, getting into the left lane, and turning. In urban situations, continue straight to the crosswalk and walk your bike across the crosswalk when the pedestrian walk sign is illuminated.
- Never ride while under the influence of alcohol or drugs. DUI laws apply in many states when you're riding a bicycle.
- Avoid riding in extreme foggy, rainy, or windy conditions.
- Watch out for parallel-slat sewer grates, slippery manhole covers, oily pavement, gravel, wet leaves, and ice.
- Cross railroad tracks as perpendicular as possible. Be especially careful when it's wet out. For better control as you move across bumps and other hazards, stand up on your pedals.
- Don't ride too close to parked cars—a person opening the car door may hit you.
- Avoid riding on sidewalks. Instead, walk your bike. Pedestrians have the right-of-way on walkways. Give pedestrians an audible warning when you pass. Use a bike bell or announce clearly, "On your left/right."
- Slow down at street crossings and driveways.

The Mountain Bike Controversy

Are Off-Road Bicyclists Environmental Outlaws? Do We Have the Right to Use Public Trails?

Mountain bikers have long endured the animosity of folks in the backcountry who complain about the consequences of off-road bicycling. Many people believe that the fat tires and knobby tread do unacceptable environmental damage and that our uncontrollable riding habits are a danger to animals and other trail users. To the contrary, mountain bikes have no more environmental impact than hiking boots or horseshoes. This does not mean, however, that mountain bikes leave no imprint at all. Wherever man treads, there is an impact. By riding responsibly, though, it is possible to leave only a minimal impact—something we all must take care to achieve.

Unfortunately, it is often people of great influence who view the mountain bike as the environment's worst enemy. Consequently, we mountain bike riders and environmentally concerned citizens must be educators, impressing upon others that we also deserve the right to use these trails. Our responsibilities as bicyclists are no more and no less than those of any other trail user. We must all take the soft-cycling approach and show that mountain bicyclists are not environmental outlaws.

Etiquette of Mountain Biking

When discussing mountain biking etiquette, we are in essence discussing the soft-cycling approach. This term, as mentioned previously, describes the art of minimum-impact bicycling and should apply to both the physical and social dimensions of the sport. But make no mistake—it is possible to ride fast and furiously while maintaining the balance of soft-cycling. Here first are a few ways to minimize the physical impact of mountain bike riding.

- **Stay on the trail.** Don't ride around fallen trees or mudholes that block your path. Stop and cross over them. When you come to a vista overlooking a deep valley, don't ride off the trail for a better vantage point. Instead, leave the bike and walk to see the view. Riding off the trail may seem inconsequential when done only once, but soon someone else will follow, then others, and the cumulative results can be catastrophic. Each time you wander from the trail you begin creating a new path, adding one more scar to the earth's surface.

- **Do not disturb the soil.** Follow a line within the trail that will not disturb or damage the soil.

- **Do not ride over soft or wet trails.** After a rain shower or during the thawing season, trails will often resemble muddy, oozing swampland. The best thing to do is stay off the trails altogether. Realistically, however, we're all going to come across some muddy trails we cannot anticipate. Instead of blasting through each section of mud, which may seem both easier and more fun, lift the bike and walk past. Each time a cyclist rides through a soft or muddy section of trail, that part of the trail is permanently damaged. Regardless of the trail's conditions, though, remember always to go over the obstacles across the path, not around them. Stay on the trail.

- **Avoid trails that are considered impassable and impossible.** Don't take a leap of faith down a kamikaze descent on which you will be forced to lock your brakes and skid to the bottom, ripping the ground apart as you go.

Soft-cycling should apply to the social dimensions of the sport as well, since mountain bikers are not the only folks who use the trails. Hikers, equestrians, cross-country skiers, and other outdoors people use many of the same trails and can be easily spooked by a marauding mountain biker tearing through the trees. Be friendly in the forest and give ample warning of your approach.

- **Take out what you bring in.** Don't leave broken bike pieces and banana peels scattered along the trail.
- **Be aware of your surroundings.** Don't use popular hiking trails for race training.
- **Slow down!** Rocketing around blind corners is a sure way to ruin an unsuspecting hiker's day. Consider this: If you fly down a quick singletrack descent at 20 mph, then hit the brakes and slow down to only 6 mph to pass someone, you're still moving twice as fast as they are!

Like the trails we ride on, the social dimension of mountain biking is very fragile and must be cared for responsibly. We should not want to destroy another person's enjoyment of the outdoors. By riding in the backcountry with caution, control, and responsibility, our presence should be felt positively by other trail users. By adhering to these rules, trail riding—a privilege that can quickly be taken away—will continue to be ours to share.

Trail Maintenance

Unfortunately, despite all of the preventive measures taken to avoid trail damage, we're still going to run into many trails requiring attention. Simply put, a lot of hikers, equestrians, and cyclists use the same trails—some wear and tear is unavoidable. But like your bike, if you want to use these trails for a long time to come, you must also maintain them.

Trail maintenance and restoration can be accomplished in a variety of ways. One way is for mountain bike clubs to combine efforts with other trail users (i.e., hikers and equestrians) and work closely with land managers to cut new trails or repair existing ones. This not only reinforces to others the commitment cyclists have in caring for and maintaining the land, but also breaks the ice that often separates cyclists from their fellow trail mates. Another good way to help out is to show up, ready to work, on a Saturday morning with a few riding buddies at your favorite off-road domain. With a good attitude, thick gloves, and the local land manager's supervision, trail repair is fun and very rewarding. It's important, of course, that you arrange a trail-repair outing with the local land manager before you start pounding shovels into the dirt. They can lead you to the most needy sections of trail and instruct you on what repairs should be done and how best to accomplish the task. Perhaps the most effective means of trail maintenance, though, can be done by yourself and while you're riding. Read on.

On-the-Spot Quick Fix

Most of us, when we're riding, have at one time or another come upon muddy trails or fallen trees blocking our path. We notice that over time the mud gets deeper and the trail gets wider as people go through or around the obstacles. We worry that the problem will become so severe and repairs so difficult that the trail's access may be threatened. We also know that our ambition to do anything about it is greatest at that moment, not after a hot shower and a plate of spaghetti. Here are a few on-the-spot quick fixes you can do that will hopefully correct a problem before it gets out of hand and get you back on your bike within minutes.

Muddy trails. What do you do when trails develop huge mudholes destined for the EPA's Superfund status? Corduroy (not the pants) is the term for roads made of logs laid down crosswise. Use small- and medium-size sticks and lay them side by side across the trail until they cover the length of the muddy section (break the sticks to fit the width of the trail). Press them into the mud with your feet, then lay more on top if needed. Keep adding sticks until the trail is firm. Not only will you stay clean as you cross, but the sticks may soak up some of the water and help the puddle dry. This quick fix may last as long as one month before needing to be redone. And as time goes on, with new layers added to the trail, the soil will grow stronger, thicker, and more resistant to erosion. This whole process may take fewer than five minutes, and you can be on your way, knowing the trail behind you is in good repair.

Leaving the trail. What do you do to keep cyclists from cutting corners and leaving the designated trail? The solution is much simpler than you may think. (No, don't hire an off-road police force.) Notice where people are leaving the trail and throw a pile of thick branches or brush along the path, or place logs across the opening to block the way through. There are probably dozens of subtle tricks like these that will manipulate people into staying on the designated trail. If executed well, no one will even notice that the thick branches scattered along the ground in the woods weren't always there. And most folks would probably rather take a moment to hop a log in the trail than get tangled in a web of branches.

Mountain Biking Guidelines

If every mountain biker always yielded the right-of-way, stayed on the trail, avoided wet or muddy trails, never cut switchbacks, always rode in control, showed respect for other trail users, and carried out every last scrap of what was carried in (candy wrappers and bike-part debris included)—in short, if we all did the right things—we wouldn't need a list of rules governing our behavior.

The fact is, most mountain bikers are conscientious and are trying to do the right thing; however, thousands of miles of dirt trails have been closed due to the irresponsible habits of a few riders.

Here are some basic guidelines adapted from the International Mountain Bicycling Association Rules of the Trail. These guidelines can help prevent damage to land, water, plants, and wildlife; maintain trail access; and avoid conflicts with other backcountry visitors and trail users.

1. Only ride on trails that are open. Don't trespass on private land, and be sure to obtain any necessary permits. If you're not sure if a trail is closed or if you need a permit, don't hesitate to ask.

2. Keep your bicycle under control. Watch the condition of the trail at all times, and follow the appropriate speed regulations and recommendations.

3. Yield to others on the trail. Make your approach well known in advance, either with a friendly greeting or a bell. When approaching a corner, junction, or blind spot, expect to encounter other trail users. When passing others, show your respect by slowing to a walking pace.

4. Don't startle animals. Animals may be easily scared by sudden approaches or loud noises. For your safety—and the safety of others in the area as well as the animals themselves—give all wildlife a wide berth. When encountering horses, defer to the horseback riders' directions.

5. Zero impact. Be aware of the impact you're making on the trail beneath you. You should not ride under conditions where you will leave evidence of your passing, such as on certain soils after rain. If a ride features optional side hikes into wilderness areas, be a zero-impact hiker, too. Whether you're on bike or on foot, stick to existing trails, leave gates as you found them, and carry out everything you brought in.

6. Be prepared. Know the equipment you are using, the area where you'll be riding, and your cycling abilities and limitations. Avoid unnecessary breakdowns by keeping your equipment in good shape. When you head out, bring spare parts and supplies for weather changes. Be sure to wear appropriate safety gear, including a helmet, and learn how to be self-sufficient.

The Necessities of Cycling

When discussing the most important items to have on a bike ride, cyclists generally agree on the following four items:

Helmet. The reasons to wear a helmet should be obvious. Helmets are discussed in more detail in the "Be Safe—Wear Your Armor" section.

Water. Without it, cyclists may face dehydration, which may result in dizziness and fatigue. On a warm day, cyclists should drink at least one full bottle during every hour of riding. Remember, it's always good to drink before you feel thirsty—otherwise, it may be too late.

Cycling shorts. These are necessary if you plan to ride your bike more than 20 to 30 minutes. Padded cycling shorts may be the only thing preventing your derriere from serious saddle soreness by ride's end. There are two types of cycling shorts you can buy. Touring shorts are good for people who don't want to look like they're wearing anatomically correct cellophane. These look like regular athletic shorts with pockets, but they have built-in padding in the crotch area for protection from chafing and saddle sores. The more popular, traditional cycling shorts are made of skintight material, also with a padded crotch. Whichever style you find most comfortable, cycling shorts are a necessity for long rides.

Food. This essential item will keep you rolling. Cycling burns up a lot of calories and is among the few sports in which no one is safe from the "Bonk." Bonking feels like it sounds. Without food in your system, your blood sugar level collapses, and there is no longer any energy in your body. This instantly results in total fatigue and light-headedness. So when you're filling your water bottle, remember to bring along some food. Fruit, energy bars, or some other forms of high-energy food are highly recommended. Candy bars are not, however, because they will deliver a sudden burst of high energy, then let you down soon after, causing you to feel worse than before. Energy bars are available at most bike stores and are similar to candy bars, but they provide complex carbohydrate energy and high nutrition rather than fast-burning simple sugars.

Be Prepared or Die

Do you remember the Boy Scout motto? Always be prepared. The following is a list of essential equipment that will keep you from walking out a long trail, being stranded in the woods, or even losing your life.

- Spare tube
- Tire irons
- Patch kit
- Pump
- Money: Spare change for emergency calls.
- Spoke wrench
- Spare spokes: To fit your wheel. Tape these to the chain stay.
- Chain tool
- Allen keys: Bring appropriate sizes to fit your bike.
- Compass/GPS
- Duct tape
- First-aid kit: See First-Aid Kit section.

- Rain gear: For quick changes in weather.
- Matches
- Guidebook: In case all else fails and you must start a fire to survive, this guidebook will serve as excellent fire starter!
- Food and water
- Jacket

To carry these items, you will need a backpack. There are currently many streamlined backpacks with hydration systems on the market that you can choose from. If you're carrying lots of equipment, you may want to consider a set of panniers. These are much larger and mount on either side of each wheel on a rack.

Be Safe—Wear Your Armor

It's crucial to discuss the clothing you must wear to be safe, practical, and—if you prefer—stylish. The following is a list of items that will save you from disaster, outfit you comfortably, and most important, keep you looking cool.

Helmet. A helmet is an absolute necessity because it protects your head from complete annihilation. It is the only thing that will not disintegrate into a million pieces after a wicked crash on a descent you shouldn't have been on in the first place. A helmet with a solid exterior shell will also protect your head from sharp or protruding objects. Of course, with a hard-shelled helmet, you can paste several stickers of your favorite bicycle manufacturers all over the outer shell, giving companies even more free advertising for your dollar.

Shorts. Padded cycle shorts provide cushioning between your body and the bicycle seat. Cycle shorts also wick moisture away from your body and prevent chafing. Form-fitting shorts are made from synthetic material and have smooth seams to avoid chafing. If you don't feel comfortable wearing form-fitting shorts, baggy-style padded shorts with pockets are available.

Gloves. You may find well-padded cycling gloves invaluable when traveling over rocky trails and gravelly roads for hours on end. When you fall off your bike and land on your palms, gloves are your best friend. Long-fingered gloves may also be useful, as branches, trees, assorted hard objects, and, occasionally, small animals will reach out and whack your knuckles. Insulated gloves are essential for winter riding.

Glasses. Sunglasses protect your eyes from harmful ultraviolet rays, invisible branches, creepy bugs, dirt, and may prevent you from being caught sneaking glances at riders of the opposite sex also wearing skintight, revealing Lycra.

Shoes. Mountain bike shoes are constructed with stiff soles in order to transfer more of the power from a pedal stroke to the drive train and to provide a solid platform to stand on, thereby decreasing fatigue in your feet. You can use virtually any good, light, outdoor hiking footwear, but specific mountain bike shoes (especially those with inset cleats) are best. They are lighter, breathe better, and are constructed to work with your pedal strokes instead of the natural walking cadence.

First-Aid Kit

- Band–Aids
- mole skin
- various sterile gauze and dressings
- white surgical tape
- an Ace bandage
- an antihistamine
- aspirin
- Betadine solution
- a first-aid book
- Tums
- tweezers
- scissors
- antibacterial wipes
- triple-antibiotic ointment
- plastic gloves
- sterile cotton tip applicators
- syrup of ipecac (to induce vomiting)
- thermometer
- wire splint

To Have or Not to Have—Other Very Useful Items

There is no shortage of items for you and your bike to make riding better, safer, and easier. We have rummaged through the unending lists and separated the gadgets from the good stuff, coming up with what we believe are items certain to make mountain bike riding easier and more enjoyable.

Tires. Buying a good pair of knobby tires is the quickest way to enhance the off-road handling capabilities of a bike. There are many types of mountain bike tires on the market. Some are made exclusively for very rugged off-road terrain. These big-knobbed, soft rubber tires virtually stick to the ground with magnetlike traction, but they tend to deteriorate quickly on pavement. There are other tires made exclusively for the road. These are called "slicks" and have no tread at all. For the average cyclist, though, a good tire somewhere in the middle of these two extremes should do the trick. Realize, however, that you get what you pay for. Do not skimp and buy cheap tires. As your primary point of contact with the trail, tires may be the most important piece of equipment on a bike. With inexpensive rubber, the tire's beads may unravel or chunks of tread actually rip off the tire. If you're lucky, all you'll suffer is a long walk back to the car. If you're unlucky, your tire could blow out in the middle of a rowdy downhill, causing a wicked crash.

Clipless pedals. Clipless pedals, like ski bindings, attach your shoe directly to the pedal. They allow you to exert pressure on the pedals during the down- and up-strokes. They also help you to maneuver the bike while in the air or climbing various obstacles. Toe clips may be less expensive, but they are also heavier and harder to use. Clipless pedals and toe clips take a little getting used to, but they're definitely worth the trouble.

Bar ends. These clamp-on additions to your original straight bar will provide more leverage, an excellent grip for climbing, and a more natural position for your hands. Be aware, however, of the bar end's propensity for hooking trees on fast descents, sending you, the cyclist, airborne. Opinions are divided on the general usefulness of bar ends these days and, over the last few years, bar ends have fallen out of favor with manufacturers and riders alike.

Back pack. These bags are ideal for carrying keys, extra food and water, guidebooks, foul-weather clothing, tools, spare tubes, and a cellular phone, in case you need to call for help.

Suspension forks. For off-roaders who want nothing to impede their speed on the trails, investing in a pair of suspension forks is a good idea. Like tires, there are plenty of brands to choose from, and they all do the same thing—absorb the brutal beatings of a rough trail. The cost of these forks, however, is sometimes more brutal than the trail itself.

Bike computers. These are fun gadgets to own and are much less expensive than in years past. They have such features as trip distance, speedometer, odometer, time of day, altitude, alarm, average speed, maximum speed, heart rate, global satellite positioning, etc. Bike computers will come in handy when following these maps or to know just how far you've ridden in the wrong direction.

Hydration pack. This is quickly becoming an essential item for cyclists pedaling for more than a few hours, especially in hot, dry conditions. The most popular brand is, of course, the Camelback, and these water packs can carry in their bladder bags as much as 100 ounces of water. These packs strap on your back with a handy hose running over your shoulder so you can be drinking water while still holding onto the bars with both hands on a rocky descent. These packs are a great way to carry a lot of extra liquid on hot rides in the middle of nowhere, as well as keys, a camera, extra food, guidebooks, tools, spare tubes, and a cellular phone, in case you need to call for help.

Types of Off-Road Terrain

Before roughing it off-road, we may first have to ride the pavement to get to our destination. Please don't be dismayed. Some of the country's best rides are on the road. Once we get past these smooth-surfaced pathways, though, adventures in dirt await us.

Rails-to-Trails. Abandoned rail lines are converted into usable public resources for exercising, commuting, or just enjoying nature. Old rails and ties are torn up and a trail, paved or unpaved, is laid along the existing corridor. This completes the cycle from ancient Indian trading routes to railroad corridors and back again to hiking and cycling trails.

Unpaved roads are typically found in rural areas and are most often public roads. Be careful when exploring, though, not to ride on someone's unpaved private drive.

Forest roads. These dirt and gravel roads are used primarily as access to forestland and are generally kept in good condition. They are almost always open to public use.

Singletrack can be the most fun on a mountain bike. These trails, with only one track to follow, are often narrow, challenging pathways. Remember to make sure these trails are open before zipping into the woods. (At the time of this printing, all trails and roads in this guidebook were open to mountain bikes.)

Open land. Unless there is a marked trail through a field or open space, you should not plan to ride here. Once one person cuts his or her wheels through a field or meadow, many more are sure to follow, causing irreparable damage to the landscape.

Techniques to Sharpen Your Skills

Many of us see ourselves as pure athletes—blessed with power, strength, and endless endurance. However, it may be those with finesse, balance, agility, and grace who get around most quickly on a mountain bike. Although power, strength, and endurance do have their places in mountain biking, these elements don't necessarily form the complete framework for a champion mountain biker.

The bike should become an extension of your body. Slight shifts in your hips or knees can have remarkable results. Experienced bike handlers seem to flash down technical descents, dashing over obstacles in a smooth and graceful effort as if pirouetting in *Swan Lake*. Here are some tips and techniques to help you connect with your bike and float gracefully over the dirt.

Braking. Using your brakes requires using your head, especially when descending. This doesn't mean using your head as a stopping block, but rather to think intelligently. Use your best judgment in terms of how much or how little to squeeze those brake levers.

The more weight a tire is carrying, the more braking power it has. When you're going downhill, your front wheel carries more weight than the rear. Braking gently with the front brake will help keep you in control without going into a skid. Be careful, though, not to overdo it with the front brakes and accidentally toss yourself over the handlebars. And don't neglect your rear brake! When descending, shift your weight back over the rear wheel, thus increasing your rear braking power as well. This will balance the power of both brakes and give you maximum control.

Good riders learn just how much of their weight to shift over each wheel and how to apply just enough braking power to each brake, so not to "endo" over the handlebars or skid down a trail.

Going Uphill—Climbing Those Treacherous Hills

Shift into a low gear. Before shifting, be sure to ease up on your pedaling so there is not too much pressure on the chain. With that in mind, it's important to shift before you find yourself on a steep slope, where it may too late. Find the best gear for you that matches the terrain and steepness of each climb.

Stay seated. Standing out of the saddle is often helpful when climbing steep hills on a bike, but you may find that on dirt, standing may cause your rear tire to lose its grip and spin out. Climbing is not possible without traction. As you improve, you will likely learn the subtle tricks that make out-of-saddle climbing possible. Until then, have a seat.

Lean forward. On very steep hills, the front end may feel unweighted and suddenly pop up. Slide forward on the saddle and lean over the handlebars. Think about putting your chin down near your stem. This will add more weight to the front wheel and should keep you grounded. It's all about using the weight of your head to your advantage. Most people don't realize how heavy their noggin is.

Relax. As with downhilling, relaxation is a big key to your success when climbing steep, rocky climbs. Smooth pedaling translates into good traction. Tense bodies don't balance well at low speeds. Instead of fixating grimly on the front wheel, look up at the terrain above, and pick a good line.

Keep pedaling. On rocky climbs, be sure to keep the pressure on, and don't let up on those pedals! You'll be surprised at what your bike will just roll over as long as you keep the engine revved up.

Going Downhill—The Real Reason We Get Up in the Morning

Relax. Stay loose on the bike, and don't lock your elbows or clench your grip. Your elbows need to bend with the bumps and absorb the shock, while your hands should have a firm but controlled grip on the bars to keep things steady. Breathing slowly, deeply, and deliberately will help you relax while flying down bumpy singletrack. Maintaining a death-grip on the brakes will be unhelpful. Fear and tension will make you wreck every time.

Use your eyes. Keep your head up and scan the trail as far forward as possible. Choose a line well in advance. *You* decide what line to take—don't let the trail decide for you. Keep the surprises to a minimum. If you have to react quickly to an obstacle, then you've already made a mistake.

Rise above the saddle. When racing down bumpy, technical descents, you should not be sitting on the saddle, but hovering just over it, allowing your bent legs and arms, instead of your rear, to absorb the rocky trail. Think jockey.

Remember your pedals. Be mindful of where your pedals are in relation to upcoming obstacles. Clipping a rock will lead directly to unpleasantness. Most of the time, you'll want to keep your pedals parallel to the ground.

Stay focused. Many descents require your utmost concentration and focus just to reach the bottom. You must notice every groove, every root, every rock, every hole, every bump. You, the bike, and the trail should all become one as you seek singletrack nirvana on your way down the mountain. But if your thoughts wander, however, then so may your bike, and you may instead become one with the trees!

Last-Minute Check

Before a ride, it's a good idea to give your bike a once-over to make sure everything is in working order. Begin by checking the air pressure in your tires before each ride to make sure they are properly inflated. Mountain bikes require about 45 to 55 pounds per square inch of air pressure. If your tires are underinflated, there is greater likelihood that the tubes may get pinched on a rock, causing the tire to flat.

Looking over your bike to make sure everything is secure and in its place is the next step. Go through the following checklist before each ride.

- **Pinch the tires to feel for proper inflation.** They should give just a little on the sides but feel very hard on the treads. If you have a pressure gauge, use that.
- **Check your brakes.** Squeeze the rear brake and roll your bike forward. The rear tire should skid. Next, squeeze the front brake and roll your bike forward. The rear wheel should lift into the air. If this doesn't happen, then your brakes are too loose. Make sure the brake levers don't touch the handlebars when squeezed with full force.
- **Check all quick releases on your bike.** Make sure they are all securely tightened.
- **Lube up.** If your chain squeaks, apply some lubricant.
- **Check your nuts and bolts.** Check the handlebars, saddle, cranks, and pedals to make sure that each is tight and securely fastened to your bike.
- **Check your wheels.** Spin each wheel to see that they spin through the frame and between brake pads freely.
- **Have you got everything?** Make sure you have your spare tube, tire irons, patch kit, frame pump, tools, food, water, foul-weather gear, and guidebook.

Need more info on mountain biking? Consider reading *Basic Essentials Mountain Biking.* You'll discover such things as choosing and maintaining a mountain bike; useful bike-handling techniques; preparing for long rides; overcoming obstacles such as rocks, logs, and water; and even preparing for competition.

Repair and Maintenance

Fixing a Flat

TOOLS YOU WILL NEED

- Two tire irons
- Pump (either a floor pump or a frame pump)
- No screwdrivers!!! (This can puncture the tube.)

REMOVING THE WHEEL

The front wheel is easy. Simply disconnect the brake shoes, open the quick release mechanism or undo the bolts with the proper sized wrench, then remove the wheel from the bike.

The rear wheel is a little more tricky. Before you loosen the wheel from the frame, shift the chain into the smallest gear on the freewheel (the cluster of gears in the back). Once you've done this, removing and installing the wheel, like the front, is much easier.

REMOVING THE TIRE

Step one: Insert a tire iron under the bead of the tire and pry the tire over the lip of the rim. Be careful not to pinch the tube when you do this.

Step two: Hold the first tire iron in place. With the second tire iron, repeat step one, 3 or 4 inches down the rim. Alternate tire irons, pulling the bead of the tire over the rim, section by section, until one side of the tire bead is completely off the rim.

Step three: Remove the rest of the tire and tube from the rim. This can be done by hand. It's easiest to remove the valve stem last. Once the tire is off the rim, pull the tube out of the tire.

CLEAN AND SAFETY CHECK

Step four: Using a rag, wipe the inside of the tire to clean out any dirt, sand, glass, thorns, etc. These may cause the tube to puncture. The inside of a tire should feel smooth. Any pricks or bumps could mean that you have found the culprit responsible for your flat tire.

Step five: Wipe the rim clean, then check the rim strip, making sure it covers the spoke nipples properly on the inside of the rim. If a spoke is poking through the rim strip, it could cause a puncture.

Step six: At this point, you can do one of two things: replace the punctured tube with a new one, or patch the hole. It's easiest to just replace the tube with a new tube when you're out on the trails. Roll up the old tube and take it home to repair later that night in front of the TV. Directions on patching a tube are usually included with the patch kit itself.

INSTALLING THE TIRE AND TUBE

(This can be done entirely by hand.)

Step seven: Inflate the new or repaired tube with enough air to give it shape, then tuck it back into the tire.

Step eight: To put the tire and tube back on the rim, begin by putting the valve in the valve hole. The valve must be straight. Then use your hands to push the beaded edge of the tire onto the rim all the way around so that one side of your tire is on the rim.

Step nine: Let most of the air out of the tube to allow room for the rest of the tire.

Step ten: Beginning opposite the valve, use your thumbs to push the other side of the tire onto the rim. Be careful not to pinch the tube in between the tire and the rim. The last few inches may be difficult, and you may need the tire iron to pry the tire onto the rim. If so, just be careful not to puncture the tube.

BEFORE INFLATING COMPLETELY

Step eleven: Check to make sure the tire is seated properly and that the tube is not caught between the tire and the rim. Do this by adding about five to ten pounds of air, and watch closely that the tube does not bulge out of the tire.

Step twelve: Once you're sure the tire and tube are properly seated, put the wheel back on the bike, then fill the tire with air. It's easier squeezing the wheel through the brake shoes if the tire is still flat. Place the wheel back in the dropout and tighten the quick release lever. Reconnect the brake shoes. When installing the rear wheel, place the chain back onto the smallest cog (farthest gear on the right), and pull the derailleur out of the way. Your wheel should slide right on.

Step thirteen: Now fill the tire with the proper amount of air, and check constantly to make sure the tube doesn't bulge from the rim. If the tube does appear to bulge out, release all the air as quickly as possible, or you could be in for a big bang.

Lubrication Prevents Deterioration

Lubrication is crucial to maintaining your bike. Dry spots will be eliminated. Creaks, squeaks, grinding, and binding will be gone. The chain will run quietly, and the gears will shift smoothly. The brakes will grip quicker, and your bike may last longer with fewer repairs. Need I say more? Well, yes. Without knowing where to put the lubrication, what good is it?

THINGS YOU WILL NEED

- One can of bicycle lubricant, found at any bike store
- A clean rag (to wipe excess lubricant away)

WHAT GETS LUBRICATED

- Front derailleur
- Rear derailleur
- Shift levers
- Front brake
- Rear brake
- Both brake levers
- Chain

WHERE TO LUBRICATE

To make it easy, simply spray a little lubricant on all the pivot points of your bike. If you're using a squeeze bottle, use just a drop or two. Put a few drops on each point wherever metal moves against metal, for instance, at the center of the brake calipers. Then let the lube sink in.

Once you have applied the lubricant to the derailleurs, shift the gears a few times, working the derailleurs back and forth. This allows the lubricant to work itself into the tiny cracks and spaces it must occupy to do its job. Work the brakes a few times as well.

LUBING THE CHAIN

Lubricating the chain should be done after the chain has been wiped clean of most road grime. Do this by spinning the pedals counterclockwise while gripping the chain with a clean rag. As you add the lubricant, be sure to get some in between each link. With an aerosol spray, just spray the chain while pedaling backwards (counterclockwise) until the chain is fully lubricated. Let the lubricant soak in for a few seconds before wiping the excess away. Chains will collect dirt much faster if they're loaded with too much lubrication.

Appendix A: Contacts

Beaverdam
Beaverdam State Recreation Area
(919) 676–1027

Bicycle Post
The Bicycle Post
(919) 756–3301, (919) 757–3616

Blue Clay
New Hanover County Parks and
Recreation
(910) 343–3680

Cane Creek
Union County Parks and Recreation
(704) 843–3919

Country Park
Country Park
(336) 545–5342

Governor's Creek, Devil's Ridge
Fit To Be Tried
(919) 776–2453

Hobby Park
Paul's Schwinn
(336) 777–1002

Hog Run
Harris Lake County Park
(919) 387–4342

Kitsuma
Epic Cycles
(828) 669–5969

Lake Crabtree
Lake Crabtree County Park
(919) 460–3390

Lake Fontana
Fontana Village
(800) 849–2258

Lake Johnson
Raleigh Parks and Recreation
(919) 831–6675

Pisgah, Asheville area
Pisgah District Ranger
(336) 877–3265

Pisgah, Boone area
Grandfather Ranger District
(704) 652–2144

San-Lee Park
San-Lee Park Office
(919) 776–6221

South Mountain
South Mountain State Park
(828) 433–4772

Umstead Park
Umstead State Park
(919) 787–3033

UNC Outdoor Education
Carolina Adventures
(919) 962–4179

UNCW
Chain Reaction
(910) 256–0828

Uwharrie—Supertree and Keyauwee
USDA Forest Service District Office
(910) 576–6391

Watershed Trails
Bur-Mill Park
(336) 545–5300

Appendix B: Ride Index

Technical Playgrounds

Epic Rides
(all day—maybe all night, too)

Appendix C: Other Places to Ride

In the course of writing this book and balancing life with a new family, I've finally had to admit that I'll never get to ride all of the cool places that are available across North Carolina. As I get a chance to nab the better ones, I'll be sure to include them in future revisions. If you can't find a particular trail, check out one of the major mountain biking Web sites, as many of them have trail guides included. Here are a few spots that I know of and either haven't had time to ride yet or couldn't feature in the book for various reasons.

Alexander Mountain Bike Park: Located on the north side of Asheville, this reclaimed landfill is a good template for similar developments. Six miles of relatively mild (compared with what's available nearby in Pisgah, at least) singletrack, with a dual slalom course. Site is host to several local races.

Beech Mountain Ski Resort: Excellent downhills and some challenging, rocky singletrack. Pay for a lift ticket and a map to ride all day. Hosts several races throughout the year. Located near Banner Elk. Fee for lift ticket and trail map.

Biltmore Estate: Bike rides at the estate are available only through prior arrangements. Wide-open parklike setting, with easy trails and fantastic views of the Biltmore House. Call for tour schedule.

Dupont State Forest: This beautiful piece of private/public land has recently been opened to mountain biking outside Hendersonville. This parcel is laced with old fire roads, doubletrack, and some singletrack, but it is known best for its rare eastern slickrock (actually granite, but still cool to ride) and its spectacular waterfalls.

New Light trails: These are probably the most popular trails in the Raleigh area, and Sig Hutchinson and the North Raleigh Mountain Bike Association spent a lot of blood, sweat, and tears finally getting them in on wildlife resources land. More than 15 miles of prime singletrack, including a bevy of bridges, teeter-totters, and other craziness for the young and/or foolhardy. These trails weren't included in the book only because they have limited access (Sunday riding only during hunting season, September 1 to May 15), and because logging and other developments could soon bring about their demise. Excellent trails; ride them while they're there. Located thirty minutes north of Raleigh; check www.trianglemtb.com for directions and maps.

Sugar Mountain Ski Resort: Another opportunity to take the easy way to the top, then zoom downhill all day. Mostly wide-open downhill runs. Located near Banner Elk. Fee for lift ticket and trail map.

Bandit trails: Many bandit trails are open on a don't ask/don't tell basis. No one will chase you off for riding, but they won't give actual permission to ride either, for liability reasons. Seems like every town has some of these sweet pieces of singletrack, hidden away like some crazy aunt that no one wants to talk about. These trails often provide superb riding but don't really help our cause. Ride them and take care of them. Just don't forget to push land managers for full and legal access.

Glossary

Baby heads: Small, loose, round boulders.

Bail: Attempting to abandon your bike in the middle of a dicey move. Often a precursor to a crash.

Berm: Dirt mounded along the outside edge of a curve, which lets you carry a lot of speed through it without sliding out.

Biff: Crash; see also *bust, dump, powder, splatter, stack,* or *wrestle the dirt monkeys.*

Big ring: The largest chainring up front for going really fast. Though this one doesn't see much use on most trails, it does work well as a crampon when you're riding those really big logs.

Bomb: To ride a downhill with as little brake and as much abandon as possible.

Bonk: When you don't eat enough, and your brain and body run out of fuel.

Buff: Smooth, polished track that allows you to just cruise along.

Bullhorn: To snag a tree or vine with your bar-ends. Usually results in an immediate dismount.

Bunny hop: Bouncing the bike off the ground, often using some small root or rise as a launching ramp. With speed, you can sail a long distance like this and take certain trail elements completely out of play. Required technical move for *clearing* some sections.

Chicken heads: Fist-sized, sharp-edged rocks.

Clean: To conquer a tough section or a big move without crashing, stopping, or putting down a foot. The opposite of *dab.*

Clip/Unclip: Becoming attached or unattached to your pedals.

Contour: As a noun, a horizontal line that runs at the same elevation across the landscape. As a verb, to follow a slope's edge with little up or down.

Dab: To put a foot down in the middle of a move. As in, *I dabbed on those roots and busted my head. I'm going back to try again.*

Dialed: A rider with incredible technical skills, who seems to harmonize with his or her bike on a soul level.

Dicey: Trail section that requires very fine technical skills. Failure here usually results in some serious pain.

Ding: To hurt yourself or (gasp!) your bike.

Dive: To run brakes-free through a section. See *bomb.*

Doubletrack: An old road or path that's left two distinct tracks to choose from. Can vary from soft grassy tracks to crumbling, near-vertical jeep roads. For purposes of this book, any trail that offers you multiple lines or tracks to ride.

Dragonsteeth: Water bar made from sharp, flat stones stuck edge-first into the ground. Fall on one, and you'll understand the name.

Endo: A crash in which you fly over the handlebars. Also known as doing a face-plant or stacking.

Faceplant: An endo that requires you to use your face as landing gear.

Fall line: The direction in which the ground slopes away. *Contouring* generally calls for you to ride across the fall line.

Granny: As in Granny gear. Your smallest (and most powerful) chainring up front. Necessary for climbing the steepest slopes.

Grinder: Long, unending climb.

Hammer: To ride a trail wide open, cranking up the climbs and bombing the downhills.

Hammerhead: He or she who likes to hammer.

Lariat: A loop with a tail on it.

Line: The clear track through an otherwise gnarly section. Often switches back and forth, or even ends suddenly, in more serious technical terrain.

Portage: Carrying your bike. Extended portages are called *hike-a-bike* sections. No fun.

Pusher: Just like the name implies: a hill you can't ride.

Rhodo: Rhododendron, as in a rhodo tunnel.

Roller coaster: A steep, sweeping series of curves, often running down the length of a ravine or gully.

Root drop: An erosion gully caused by water running over the lip of some trail-crossing root. The holes on the backs of these buggers are often quite deep, so best to slalom around or hop over them when possible.

Root lace: A living carpet of roots, lacing back and forth over an area, that love nothing better than to deflect or grab hold of a front wheel and bring a once-proud rider crashing to the ground.

Saddle: Long dip between two high points, usually on a ridgeline. Also, another name for your bike seat.

Singletrack: What we live for: a narrow ribbon of dirt, not much wider than your tires, that slips and dances through the woods. Good singletrack brings you as close to flying as you can get without wings.

Sketchy: Treacherous trail section, often filled with loose rocks, that threatens to chew you up and spit you out.

Superman: Landing with both arms stretched out in front of you. Good way to break both wrists, unless you are indeed the Man of Steel.

Surf: When the front wheel bobbles riding through deep sand or gravel.

Switchback: A sharp turn in the trail, generally with a steep incline either up or down. Uphill, they're as mean as they come: slow-motion, anaerobic charges that can challenge you a dozen times over. Downhill, they test your balance and courage in the face of an imminent faceplant.

Swoopy: A trail that swings back and forth, with nice rounded corners and maybe some small berms set up so you can just lean and carve through them without any brakes.

Taco: To bend a wheel into a decidedly curved shape that rolls very poorly. Extremely tuned trailside wrenches can repair this problem with a single whack on the properly sized oak tree.

Tombstone: Large, flat-faced rock sticking up out of the ground. Hitting one of these head-on can earn you one with your name carved in it. Avoid or hop at all cost.

Trail toll: Some form of bloody sacrifice, as demanded by the trail gods.

Trail surface: The type of trail surface you're riding on.

Water bar: Any construction for diverting water from the trail to limit erosion. May be a smooth, angled mound of dirt like a big speedbump, a 6- to 8-inch log laid secured across the trail, or even a row of planted rocks. Old water bars often sport significant drops off their back sides. Most provide opportunities for some serious air time. The log varieties often offer some serious faceplant potential as well.

Waterdog: Rider known for the ability to ride his or her bike across watery stretches that normally require a pontoon boat. Accomplished waterdogs earn the title of River MacDaddy.

Whoop-dee-doos: Large dirt humps, sort of like giant water bars, generally placed to keep motorized traffic off a trail. They're usually big and nasty, and they like to travel in packs.

About the Author

Timm Muth is a writer, adventurer, mountain biking addict, perpetual martial arts student, tiger handler, and sometimes engineer. He lives with a family of mountain biking fools.